Cenote of Sacrifice

Maya Treasures from the Sacred Well at Chichén Itzá

An exhibition organized by the Science Museum of Minnesota
in cooperation with the Peabody Museum of Archaeology and Ethnology,
Harvard University, under the Collection-Sharing Program of the Peabody Museum

An exhibition organized by the Science Museum of Minnesota
in cooperation with the Peabody Museum of Archaeology and Ethnology,
Harvard University, under the Collection-Sharing Program of the Peabody Museum

Cenote of Sacrifice
Maya Treasures from the Sacred Well at Chichén Itzá

Edited by Clemency Chase Coggins and Orrin C. Shane III

Catalogue by Clemency Chase Coggins
With contributions by Gordon R. Willey and Linnea H. Wren
Forewords by C. C. Lamberg-Karlovsky and Wendell A. Mordy
Photographs by Hillel Burger

University of Texas Press
Austin

LIBRARY OF CONGRESS
CATALOGING IN PUBLICATION DATA

Main entry under title:

Cenote of sacrifice.

Catalogue of an exhibition organized by the
Science Museum of Minnesota in cooperation
with the Peabody Museum of Archaeology and
Ethnology, Harvard University.
    Bibliography: p.
    Includes index.
    1. Chichén Itzá (Mexico)—Exhibitions.
2. Mayas—Antiquities—Exhibitions.
3. Indians of Mexico—Yucatán—Antiquities—Exhibitions.   4. Peabody Museum of
Archaeology and Ethnology—Exhibitions.
I. Coggins, Clemency.   II. Shane, Orrin C.,
1939–   .   III. Science Museum of Minnesota.   IV. Peabody Museum of Archaeology
and Ethnology.
F1435.1.C5C46 1984   972'.01   84-10458
ISBN 0-292-71097-6
ISBN 0-292-71098-4 (pbk.)

*Figures 6, 7, 10, 12, 13, and 14 are reprinted
from S. K. Lothrop 1952 and Figures 8, 9, 11,
and 15 from T. Proskouriakoff 1974, all by
permission of the Peabody Museum, Harvard
University.*

Frontispiece.
Chichén Itzá: the Castillo as seen from
the entrance to the Temple of the Warriors.
Photograph by Jeffrey Jay Foxx.

The Collection-Sharing Program of the
Peabody Museum is a unique loan program for developing collaborative exhibitions. Since the Peabody Museum's
facilities do not permit the full in-house
exhibition of its vast archaeological and
ethnographic collections, this program
enables audiences nationwide to enjoy
them. The Peabody Museum Collection-
Sharing Program has been generously
supported by the National Endowment
for the Humanities.

Contents

Figures

Foreword

C. C. LAMBERG-KARLOVSKY
Director, Peabody Museum of Archaeology and Ethnology, Harvard University

The site of Chichén Itzá was first described by that extraordinary chronicler Bishop Diego de Landa in the late sixteenth century. In his *Relación de las cosas de Yucatán* Bishop Landa described the ruins of Chichén Itzá and published one of the first plans of an American ruin. Since that time Chichén Itzá has been one of the most renowned sites of the Maya civilization. It was the dredging of the Sacred Well at Chichén Itzá, however, that placed this site within a special category of Maya communities. From 1904 to 1911 Edward H. Thompson recovered almost thirty thousand ceremonially broken artifacts from this sacred repository. Thompson, an early explorer-archaeologist of Yucatán, began to publish his Maya discoveries in the *Memoirs of the Peabody Museum* as early as 1897. The extraordinary objects recovered from the Cenote at Chichén Itzá document almost eight centuries of political, economic, social, and religious change in Maya civilization. The Maya archaeologist Alfred M. Tozzer, distinguished curator of Maya archaeology at the Peabody Museum, observed decades ago, "There is perhaps no other single collection in New World archaeology that has afforded so comprehensive a view of the aesthetic life of an ancient people" (Tozzer 1957:196). This statement remains true to this day!

The collection recovered from the Cenote was given to the Peabody Museum in the early years of this century; however most of the collection has remained unexhibited for over seventy years.

The Peabody Museum is extremely grateful to the National Endowment for the Humanities for its support in making this exhibit available in museums throughout the country. The exhibit *Cenote of Sacrifice: Maya Treasures from the Sacred Well at Chichén Itzá* is the sixth major exhibition of artifacts from the Peabody Museum to be exhibited in museums around the nation through our Collection-Sharing Program. Funded by the National Endowment for the Humanities, this program has pioneered the accessibility of the rich collections of this museum to a far wider public.

The Peabody Museum is most grateful to Lea McChesney, Director of our Collection-Sharing Program, and to Clemency Coggins for the production of the accompanying collection. To the above, and to all who have contributed to the success of this exhibit, the Peabody is deeply appreciative. The Peabody Museum has for over a hundred years been committed to the view that a deepening appreciation and understanding of our past secures a richer present and a more secure future.

Foreword

WENDELL ALLEN MORDY
President, The Science Museum of Minnesota

The Yucatán peninsula is a low, flat limestone shelf jutting northward from the mountainous spine of the continent and separating the Gulf of Mexico from the Caribbean Sea. Its climate is semitropical, with alternating wet and dry seasons producing hot, humid, rainy summers and the pleasant dry winters that have made modern Yucatán a mecca for tourists from the northern latitudes. Northern Yucatán has few rivers or lakes, and during the dry season fresh water can be obtained only from wells or from the numerous natural water-filled limestone sink-holes called *cenotes* which dot the landscape. *Cenote* is the hispanicized form of the Maya name for these vital natural sources of water.

In this environment the ancient northern lowland Maya developed one of the world's great civilizations, wherein cenotes played a vital role as a major source of fresh water. Maya towns and cities were built around these natural wells, and one cenote, within the great "Maya-Toltec" city of Chichén Itzá, became the most sacred shrine of the peoples of Yucatán. Offerings made to the Sacred Cenote, later called by early Spanish chroniclers the "Cenote of Sacrifice" because of the human sacrificial rites conducted there, are the subject of this book.

Chichén Itzá was founded by people who were culturally northern Maya. Later the city was controlled by Mexicanized Maya or perhaps people who came to Yucatán from Central Mexico. Many of the offerings made to the Sacred Cenote were manufactured in other parts of lower Central America and Mesoamerica and brought to Chichén Itzá along commercial trade networks linking distant regions. Gold artifacts from Panama and Costa Rica, jade and obsidian from the highlands of Guatemala and Mexico, copper and marble from Mexico are among the treasures offered to the Cenote, making it a repository of objects representing many artistic traditions.

We are indebted to many who made the exhibition *Cenote of Sacrifice: Maya Treasures from the Sacred Well at Chichén Itzá* possible. The idea was first suggested to me by Louis Casagrande, Science Museum of Minnesota Curator of Ethnology, as a Peabody Museum Collection-Sharing project. Orrin C. Shane III, SMM Curator of Anthropology for Archaeology, developed the conceptual design of the exhibition in collaboration with Peabody Museum staff and has guided the project as SMM exhibit Curator-in-Charge and coeditor of this volume. Terry Sateren, Head of SMM's Exhibits Division, John Polenek (design), and Mark Odegard (graphics) are responsible for the artistic design and installation of the exhibition.

The exhibition and this catalogue could not have come about without financial support through grants for planning and implementation from the National Endowment for the Humanities and the Dayton Hudson Foundation.

Acknowledgments

Any major interpretive exhibition is a cooperative endeavor involving specialists from widely divergent fields. This is especially true for *Cenote of Sacrifice* both because of the diverse artifacts and materials in the Cenote collection and because the exhibition involved close collaboration between two museums. In this collaborative Collection-Sharing project the Peabody Museum was responsible for the conservation of the exhibit collection and the preparation of entries and photographs for the catalogue, while the Science Museum of Minnesota designed the exhibition, constructed the casework, and prepared the graphics and interpretive copy.

We wish to acknowledge with special thanks the consultants to the exhibition, Linnea H. Wren, Associate Professor of Art History, Gustavus Adolphus College, and Gordon R. Willey, Bowditch Professor of Mesoamerican Archaeology, Peabody Museum of Archaeology and Ethnology, Harvard University. These scholars prepared essays for this catalogue and also gave valuable advice on interpretations of Chichén Itzá and the Cenote collection. Dr. Wren also prepared the introductory audio-visual presentation for the exhibition. We wish also to thank Jeffrey Jay Foxx, who assisted in the preparation of photographs for the exhibition and the catalogue. Mr. Foxx also aided in the selection of images for the audio-visual introduction to the exhibition.

We are especially grateful to the Instituto Nacional de Antropología e Historia of Mexico, and to Edward Kurjak and Pedro Schmidt, who gave freely of their time and expertise during a visit to Chichén Itzá by the exhibit design team. Our thanks are also due to Guillermo Schmidhuber de la Mora, Director of the Centro Cultural Alfa, Monterrey, Mexico, for his aid in securing casts of Pre-Columbian sculpture for the exhibition, and to Mario Cirett Avila for providing casts of sculpture from Chichén Itzá.

For the catalogue entries the author is especially grateful to Restaurador Agustín Espinoza Chávez, Director de la Dirección de Restauración del Instituto Nacional de Antropología e Historia, for permission to study some of the unpublished organic materials found in the Sacred Cenote by the Mexican expeditions of the 1960s. In addition, the author is deeply appreciative of the kindness of Elizabeth K. Easby for her thoughtful comments on the jade entries.

This exhibition would not, however, have been possible without the vision and dedication of the Collection-Sharing staff of the Peabody Museum, beginning with the early organizing efforts of former Director Fran Silverman and continuing for the past year and a half under the direction of Lea McChesney and of her assistant Germaine Juneau. This work has been generously assisted by the staff of the Peabody Museum Photo Archives, Daniel

Jones, Melissa Banta, and Linton Watts, and ultimately made possible through the attentions of Peabody Museum conservators Greta Hansen, Marilyn Lenz, and Nicole Sears, as well as members of the Fogg Museum Conservation Laboratory, especially Arthur H. Beale and Marjorie B. Cohn. All have worked to clean and consolidate these fragile objects so they may travel and be exhibited widely. Conservation work and the Collection-Sharing Program at the Peabody Museum have been generously supported by the National Endowment for the Humanities.

Cenote of Sacrifice is one of the most ambitious projects undertaken by the Science Museum of Minnesota, and many staff members throughout the museum have contributed significantly to the organization of the exhibition. Although we lack the space to acknowledge each contribution individually, we extend our sincere gratitude to all who have given of their time and energy to make this exhibition and its catalogue possible. We are especially indebted to Terry Sateren, Head of the Exhibits Division, who directed the design and installation of the exhibition. John Polenek designed the exhibit hall, cases, and artifact mounts, while Mark Odegard and Chris Burda designed and prepared the interpretive graphics for both the exhibition and the catalogue. David Evans had overall responsibility for electronics, audio-visual equipment and computer programming, and Paul Mauer supervised the construction crew. Eileen Flory, Director of Education, and James Erickson, Educational Specialist in Anthropology, directed interpretive programs, and Sondra Quinn, Director of Special Projects, coordinated interpretive programs, operations, and opening events.

Special thanks are due Louis Casagrande, Head, Department of Anthropology, for initiating the exhibit concept, and for his guidance, support, and encouragement. Finally, Joel Orlen, Vice-President, and Wendell A. Mordy, President, provided direction, momentum, and inspiration over the three and one-half years that *Cenote of Sacrifice* was being developed.

The exhibition and the catalogue could not have come about without the financial support for planning and implementation from the National Endowment for the Humanities and from the Dayton Hudson Foundation, with funds provided by B. Dalton, Bookseller, and Target Stores.

CLEMENCY CHASE COGGINS
ORRIN C. SHANE III

Chichén Itzá and Maya Archaeology

GORDON R. WILLEY

The great ruin of Chichén Itzá, in northern Yucatán, is one of the most impressive and among the better known of Maya archaeological sites. Its majestic stone pyramids, temples, and palaces tower above the jungle-covered plain to excite the wonder and imagination of tourists today as they did for the Spaniards who first saw it in the sixteenth century. Like many other Maya ruins, it was found in an abandoned state. What was its history or prehistory, and what do we know of the ancient Maya past in general? How does Chichén Itzá, which is celebrated by this present exhibit, fit into that past?

Systematic archaeological research in the Maya area of southern Mexico and Central America is a little over one hundred years old. A great deal has been discovered and studied through surveys and excavations; much more remains to be done; but the outlines of a story are beginning to emerge. We know that there were Maya farmers living in small villages in these tropical lowlands as far back as 2000 B.C. From these communities we can trace the gradual rise toward a more complex type of society, toward what may be called civilization. By about 300 B.C., or what archaeologists recognize as the beginning of the Late Preclassic Period, paramount centers or towns had appeared. These, presumably, exercised political and religious sovereignty over other towns, villages, and regions. Monumental architecture, the characteristic pyramids, platforms, and temples, marked these centers or politico-religious "capitals." Evidences of social differentiation had begun to appear in public art, in varied treatment of burials, and in the distribution of luxury goods. From this Late Preclassic point in time the trajectory of development, while not always steady, was generally upward. The trajectory can be followed in continued architectural elaboration in the centers or cities, in the sculptural arts, in ceramics and other crafts, and, especially, in the intellectual pursuits of calendrics, astronomy, and hieroglyphic writing. Indeed, the first appearance of hieroglyphic texts carved on stone monuments is taken as the hallmark of the beginning of the Classic Period of Maya civilization (ca. A.D. 250). These hieroglyphic texts have provided fascinating insights into the nature of royal dynasties, wars, conquests, and marriages and deaths among the elite. This Maya Classic Period civilization flourished from about A.D. 250 until 800. Then, during the ninth century, a rapid decline set in throughout the Maya cities of the southern Maya lowlands. The causes for this decline, which was marked by a cessation in major architectural construction and in the carving of hieroglyphic texts, have been the source of much speculation, and they are not really known. One fact that has emerged, however, is that the northern Maya lowlands, including Yucatán, did not suffer the decline; instead, the cities there thrived as never before and many new ones sprang up in the centuries immediately after A.D. 800. This was

Figure 1. Chichén Itzá: serpent columns at the entrance to the Temple of the Warriors. Photograph by Jeffrey Jay Foxx.

especially true of the so-called Puuc sites of the northeastern part of the Yucatán Peninsula. It is at this point that Chichén Itzá comes into the story.

Chichén Itzá is located some distance to the east of the main cluster of the great Puuc sites—Uxmal, Kabáh, Labná, Sayil—but it nevertheless has clear Puuc architectural affinities. A series of buildings at the site—the Monjas, the Akab Dzib, the Iglesia, and some others—are definitely Puuc-like in form and decoration. These stand in contrast, however, to other Chichén structures—the Great Ball Court, the Temple of the Warriors, and the Castillo, to name only three—which are in what is best described as a Mexicanized or Toltec-Maya style. For a long time this was interpreted as, in effect, two cities, or at least one city with two separate and major building phases, the earlier Puuc Maya and the later Toltec-Maya. The first phase was believed to have been contemporaneous with Uxmal and the other Puuc sites alluded to with all of these subsumed in a Late Classic–Terminal Classic Period, dating prior to A.D. 1000; the second phase, the Toltec-Maya phase, then pertained to the Early Postclassic Period (A.D. 1000–1250). From a larger regional perspective, this interpretation was extended to mean that a conquest of the Puuc Maya by Toltec or Toltec-inspired peoples had occurred at about A.D. 1000. The conquerors settled at Chichén, rebuilt it, and rapidly brought about the decline and abandonment of the other Puuc centers of the peninsula. Recently, however, this traditional archaeological interpretation has been questioned, and some archaeologists feel that Chichén Itzá and the major Puuc sites were partially or even wholly contemporaneous. This questioning would not deny the Toltec influences at Chichén Itzá, or even its conquest by Toltec or Toltec-affiliated warriors; however, it would lead to another interpretation, one which would view the Terminal Classic and Early Postclassic periods as a gradual cultural continuum rather than as discrete periods separated by a widespread Mexican or Toltec conquest of northern Yucatán.

Whatever the events of the Terminal Classic–Early Postclassic era, there is general agreement among archaeologists that Chichén was abandoned as a major city at about A.D. 1250, or the beginning of the Late Postclassic Period. From early historic and legendary accounts, we learn that the site continued to be used, however, as a place of pilgrimage and sacrifice for the Maya of northern Yucatán. The main Cenote, the awesome natural well in the limestone whose water surface is some eighty feet below the surrounding ground level, was featured in these sacrifices. According to these accounts, both people and goods were thrown into the murky depths of the Cenote. The Cenote was explored by divers and archeologists many years ago, and evidences of these sacrificial practices have been attested to by finds of human skeletal material and artifacts brought up from the depths of the well. These are discussed and described by Clemency Coggins, who has prepared this catalogue, and they compose the theme of this exhibition. They offer a unique insight into ancient Maya society and culture.

With reference to the archaeological history of Chichén Itzá, as recounted here, the objects from the great Cenote indicate that the custom of such sacrifices was an old one. Precious goods, including jades and goldwork, as well as wooden objects and pottery, were thrown into the well throughout the active life of the city, beginning back as early as A.D. 700 and continuing up until A.D. 1250. Then, as has been noted, sacrificial rites continued to be consummated there during the Postclassic Period and up until the entry of the Spanish into Yucatán.

RELATED READINGS

General Books on the Maya

Hammond, Norman. *Ancient Maya Civilization.* New Brunswick, N.J.: Rutgers University Press, 1982.

Henderson, John S. *The World of the Ancient Maya.* Ithaca, N.Y.: Cornell University Press, 1981.

On Chichén Itzá and the Cenote of Sacrifice

Ruppert, Karl. *Chichen Itza: Architectural Notes and Plans.* Carnegie Institution of Washington, Publication 595. Washington, D.C., 1952.

Tozzer, Alfred M. *Chichen Itza and Its Cenote of Sacrifice: A Comparative Study of Contemporaneous Maya and Toltec.* Memoirs of the Peabody Museum, Harvard University, vols. 11 and 12. Cambridge, Mass., 1957.

Chichén Itzá:
The Site and Its People

LINNEA H. WREN

Chichén Itzá is an impressive archaeological site located in the northern Maya lowlands of the Yucatán Peninsula. As mapped by Karl Ruppert (1952), Chichén Itzá includes hundreds of structures within an area of about five square kilometers. Loosely grouped around open plazas, the monumental structures are placed upon a series of artificial raised terraces constructed along a north-south axis and connected by a system of raised causeways, called *sacbes*. The largest terrace, the North Terrace, is surrounded by a low wall with several entrances. It is linked by a *sacbe* to the Cenote of Sacrifice, a focus of religious and ritual activity at Chichén Itzá.

The principal building materials in the architecture at Chichén Itzá are locally quarried limestone and burnt lime mortar. The substructures, i.e., the terraces, platforms, and pyramids on which the buildings rest, are solid masses constructed of rough stone and mortar. The superstructures, i.e., the buildings which contain interior spaces, consist of heavy load-bearing walls supporting narrow corbel vaults. Both walls and vaults are constructed with a thick core of mortar and rough stone faced with finely cut veneer masonry.

Wood was another building material used at Chichén Itzá, and it has provided a source of evidence about the dating of the structures. Although their reliability is influenced by many factors, Carbon 14 dates have been obtained from samples of the wood from the architectural members and have yielded a series of dates ranging from 600 A.D. ±70 to 810 A.D. ±200 (Andrews V 1977). At Chichén Itzá, as in other areas of Mesoamerica, wooden beams were used to reinforce the vaults and wooden lintels were used to span doorways. At Chichén Itzá, however, wooden lintels were also employed in an architecturally innovative manner not found elsewhere in Mesoamerica. Rows of columns spanned by wooden lintels were substituted for walls as the primary supports for vaults. As a result, the builders of Chichén Itzá achieved the largest vaulted interior spaces known in Mesoamerica.

The monumental structures at Chichén Itzá are varied in plan and function. The Castillo, the tallest pyramid-temple complex at the site, may have been used for religious ceremonies. Enclosing an earlier pyramid and temple within it, the outer pyramid of the Castillo rises in nine stages. Each of the four staircases has ninety-one steps. It has been suggested (Cirerol Sansores 1940) that the number of steps plus the final platform refers to the 365-day solar year, while the raised geometric pattern that ornaments the terraces refers to the fifty-two-year Maya calendrical cycle. The dramatic effect created by the setting sun on the equinoxes highlighting the serpent body as it descends the balustrade of the north staircase has been noted (Rivard 1970).

The Temple of the Warriors, constructed above the earlier, partially dismantled Temple of the Chac Mool, may also have been used for religious rituals. A colonnaded hall, the Northwest Colonnade, formed an enclosed anterior space in front of the western façade of the Temple of the Warriors. The two structures were connected by a staircase rising through the roof vaults of the colonnade to the entrance of the double-chambered temple above. At the eastern end of the interior chamber a low stone table supported by nineteen Atlantean figures with upraised arms has been identified as an altar (Morris, Charlot, and Morris 1931).

The Caracol seems to have been built as an astronomical observatory. Located in the southern section of the site, it is raised on a substructure formed by ascending platforms. The superstructure, which is circular in plan, consists of a lower storey with two concentric chambers and two sets of four doorways and an upper storey with radial shafts emerging from its center. The platforms, doorways, and shafts appear to have been aligned in accordance with the cycles of the Sun, the stars, and the planet Venus (Ruppert 1935; Aveni et al. 1975).

The Great Ball Court is the largest and most elaborate of the many ball courts found at the site. The I-shaped playing field, oriented approximately north and south, is over 167 meters long and 70 meters wide at the ends. Four temples, the Lower Temple of the Jaguars, the Upper Temple of the Jaguars, the North Temple, and the South Temple, are associated with the ball court (fig. 16). Five small shrines are located above the east and west platforms. The ball game required great skill and stamina from the players, who attempted to drive a rubber ball through the pair of rings mounted on the vertical walls. Although the meaning of the ball game is the subject of debate, the game's importance as a ceremonial activity in Mesoamerica is evident from the frequent and widespread occurrence of ball courts.

Other types of buildings designed for ceremonial purposes were also constructed at Chichén Itzá. Sweat houses, such as the structures in the Court of the Thousand Columns and near the Caracol, were built for purification rites. Dance platforms, such as the Venus Platform and the Platform of the Eagles, were probably used for the re-enactment of sacred dramas.

Administrative and commercial needs were also served by monumental structures. It has recently been suggested that buildings with entrances framed by massive serpent columns, such as the Castillo and the Temple of the Warriors, were intended primarily as governmental council chambers, rather than as temples (Kubler 1982). The Court of the Thousand Columns, with its many small constructions suggesting booths and stalls, could well have been used as a marketplace.

Residential architecture can also be found at Chichén Itzá. It is possible that the long, low buildings, such as the Temple of the Three Lintels and the Akab Dzib, and palace-like structures such as the Monjas were used to house the elite. Although the Mercado, with its outer colonnade and inner patio, has been likened to a tribunal (Ruppert 1943, p. 230), the possibility has recently been raised that it might have served a residential function (Freidel 1981; Chase and Chase 1982). However, the majority of the residences at Chichén Itzá consisted not of vaulted structures at the center of the site but of small thatched buildings located in areas surrounding the main plazas. The modern-day Maya of Yucatán build round-ended houses with stone foundations, wattle and daub, dry masonry or wicker walls, and thatched roofs. Both in their design and in their construction these houses are almost identical to the small residential structures excavated at Dzibilchaltún (Kurjack and Garza T. 1981) and those illustrated in the painting and sculpture of Chichén Itzá.

The emergence of Chichén Itzá as an important site in the northern Maya lowlands was in part the result of the ability of the inhabitants to exploit a wide range of ecological resources. The Yucatán Peninsula is a vast limestone shelf that divides the Gulf of Mexico from the Caribbean Sea. Chichén Itzá is located approximately sixty miles south of the northern shore and almost equidistant between the eastern and western coastlines. A flat, low plain surrounds the site and extends across the central and eastern regions of the northern part of the peninsula.

Both the marine resources of the nearby sea and the agricultural resources of the surrounding land were available to the peoples of Chichén Itzá. The shallow coastal waters teemed with life. Fish and shellfish were abundant and were easily harvested with nets, wicker baskets, and hooks and lines. Shells, used for personal adornment and for ritual objects, were a valued elite commodity throughout Mesoamerica. Salt, an essential element in the local diet and an important item of trade, was easily obtained by evaporation from shallow saline pools.

Although marine resources were important, the basic subsistence needs of the inhabitants of the northern Maya lowlands were met by agriculture. Corn, beans, and squash formed the basis of the diet. Fruits and vegetables, including tomatoes and chile peppers, were also cultivated to supplement the basic foodstuffs. Wild fruits and berries were gathered from the dry scrub forest that surrounded the cultivated areas. In times of famine, the people relied increasingly upon foods like *ramón* fruit, which could be boiled and eaten or ground to make a kind of bread, and *jicama* tubers, which could be eaten raw (Marcus 1982). In addition, cotton and cacao were grown for local use and long distance trade.

The discovery of sophisticated techniques of intensive agriculture, including raised fields, terracing, and irrigation systems, in other areas of Mesoamerica has led to the search for evidence of similar practices in the northern lowlands. Canal systems have been identified along lowland areas in the Tabasco Gulf plain, in Veracruz, and also around the site of Edzna in Campeche (Matheny 1978). However, no conclusive evidence of similar hydraulic systems related to agricultural activities has yet been found at Chichén Itzá. It is possible that the inhabitants of the ancient site, like the Maya of nearby present-day communities, relied primarily on slash-and-burn techniques of agriculture (Roys 1943).

Because rain seeps rapidly through the limestone to the water table below, there are few rivers or lakes in the northern Yucatán peninsula. For potable water, the Pre-Columbian peoples of this region relied on a number of sources, including caves, artificial wells, reservoirs called *chultunes*, and natural wells called *cenotes*. For agricultural purposes, they depended on the rains. In most years, the rains begin in late May or early June and end in late October or early November, but in prehispanic times drought was frequent. When the rains failed, the crops withered in the intense heat and, according to native accounts, misery settled over the parched land (Roys, ed. 1967, p. 104).

The life-sustaining power of water was symbolized for the Maya of the northern lowlands by the god Chac, and for the peoples of central Mexico by the god Tlaloc. The fierce visage of Chac is represented by the long-nosed masks which appear with slightly varied details in the mosaic panels that decorate the exteriors of such monumental buildings as the Temple of the Three Lintels, the Temple of the Warriors, the Monjas, and the Castillo. The features of Tlaloc are depicted by the raised faces with ringed eyes and fanged mouths that adorn the ceramic censers found in the cave of Balankanche near Chichén Itzá (Andrews IV 1970). Different aspects of the rain god and his powers were also suggested by the plants and animals that thrived in aquatic environments. Waterlilies, snakes, frogs, turtles, fish, and herons are depicted in the sculpture of Chichén Itzá. Monolithic sculptures of frogs are located at the rim of the Cenote of Sacrifice, and small gold images of frogs were recovered from the bottom of the well. Other aquatic plants and animals are encountered in isolation or in combination with each other and with deity masks, as in the lower panels of the pillars of the Lower Temple of the Jaguars. Among the twentieth-century Maya, many of these same plants and animals are still held in high esteem. The eyes of the tortoise are said to weep in the heat of the Sun and to draw the rains, and the croaking of the frogs is said to signal the onset of the rains (Redfield and Villa Rojas 1962).

The nature of the prehispanic religion of Mesoamerica may never be fully known. The Spanish friars condemned the Mesoamerican gods as heathen idols and, in their attempt to abolish the worship of native deities, they emptied the shrines and temples, burned the religious texts called *codices*, and persecuted priests, nobles, and peasants who continued to practice traditional rituals such as those that were conducted at the rim of the Cenote of Sacrifice. Many sources of information have been irretrievably lost. However, some understanding of the ancient Maya system of beliefs can be reconstructed from existing sources. These include ethnographic studies of present-day communities, such as that of Chan Kom (Redfield and Villa Rojas 1962), in which traditional beliefs and customs survive; post-Conquest descriptions written by Spanish observers, such as the *Relación de las cosas de Yucatán* by Bishop Landa (Tozzer, ed. 1941); pre-Conquest codices which escaped destruction, such as the Dresden Codex (J. E. S. Thompson 1972); and the art and iconography of pre-Columbian sites, such as Chichén Itzá.

Many of the important religious and cosmological concepts of the Pre-Columbian peoples of Mesoamerica are reflected in the art of Chichén Itzá. According to a widely held belief, the cosmos was divided into three realms—the sky, the earth, and the underworld. The sky was regarded as a realm of light, warmth, and vitality. Existing in a celestial sphere, the stars and planets were addressed as deities capable of bestowing or withholding the beneficence of the natural sphere. Mesoamerican astronomers calculated the lengths of the solar, lunar, and Venus cycles with a high degree of accuracy and incorporated units of time based on these cycles into their solar and sacred calendars.

A number of different motifs in the art of Chichén Itzá can be interpreted as representations of the Sun God. The circular designs with projecting solar rays in the reliefs of the Lower Temple of the Jaguars and the pillars of the Northwest Colonnade have been identified as Sun Discs (Tozzer 1957, p. 119) and the male figures surrounded by the discs as Sun Gods (Morris, Charlot, and Morris 1931, p. 273). The reclining figures with the ringed eyes and beaded hair carved on the frieze of the Temple of the Warriors have been interpreted as representations of the rising Sun (J. E. S. Thompson 1943). The crouching figures carved on the Venus Platform, the Northwest Colonnade, and the Temple of the Warriors that combine features of men, jaguars, serpents, and birds have been identified by Eduard Seler (1902–1923, p. 367) as symbols of the planet Venus and by Alfred M. Tozzer (1957, p. 120) as representations of the Earth Monster at the entrance to the underworld.

The underworld was considered a dark, cold region of death and destruction. Deities of death are suggested in the art of Chichén Itzá by the images of male and female figures with skeletal features carved in low relief at the entrance of the Lower Temple of the Jaguars. Armed figures with their arms, legs, and spinal columns stripped of flesh are represented on the balustrades of the skull rack, or Tzompantli. A low, T-shaped platform, located near the Great Ball Court, the Tzompantli is carved with rows of human skulls.

The Earth was imagined as a great disc floating in a vast sea. Stationed at the cardinal points were the sky-bearers or Bacabs. At Chichén Itzá, the male figures with wrinkled faces, toothless gums, and upraised arms, such as those found on the jambs of the Lower Temple of the Jaguars and the pillars of the Temple of the Chac Mool, represent these Bacabs (J. E. S. Thompson 1970a). Trees depicted on the balustrades of the north and south staircases of the Great Ball Court suggest the great flowering tree which was believed to grow at the center of the Earth. With its roots extending into the underworld and its branches reaching upward into the heavens, the cosmic tree united the different levels of the universe in a primordial symbol of life and fertility.

In Mesoamerican thought, deities were often considered not so much as distinct personages but rather as metaphors for the spiritual energy that activated the universe. To the peoples of this region, the cosmos was much more than a mere backdrop for humanity. It was an immensely vital realm in which everything was alive and intimately connected. The sacred quality that pervaded the universe was manifested in a multiplicity of ways, in men of extraordinary character, in natural phenomena of striking power, and in places of unusual configuration, such as the Cenote of Sacrifice at Chichén Itzá (Townsend 1979). In the art of Chichén Itzá, the supernatural presence that filled the natural realm was revealed by one of the most important iconographical motifs, the feathered serpent. Depicted on a monumental scale on the columns, balustrades, and moldings of many architectural structures at the site, the feathered serpent is also represented in the reliefs and murals. This motif incorporates both naturalistic features such as serpent fangs, tongues, and rattles and non-naturalistic elements such as the feathered body.

Called Kukulcan by the Maya peoples of Yucatán and Quetzalcoatl by the Mexican peoples of the central plateau, the feathered serpent suggests both the fertility of the Earth and the heat and light of the sky. According to written sources from Central Mexico, Quetzalcoatl was identified with the Morning Star, Venus, and with the god of the wind, Ehecatl. He was also honored as the patron deity of the arts and as a legendary ruler of Tula. According to written sources from the northern Maya lowlands, Kukulcan, in addition to being venerated as a god, was described as a foreign captain who arrived with a people called the Itzá and as a ruler who established his seat of power at Chichén Itzá.

Written sources dating from the post-Conquest period contain many references to Chichén Itzá. These sources include Spanish documents such as *Relación de las cosas de Yucatán*, a lengthy manuscript written by Bishop Diego de Landa in 1566 (Tozzer, ed. 1941) and *Relaciones de Yucatán*, a set of written responses to a questionnaire sent from Spain in 1577 by the Council of the Indies (Colección de documentos inéditos 1885–1900). Other sources include Maya documents written phonetically in Spanish characters. The most important of these are the Books of Chilam Balam of Chumayel (Roys, ed. 1967), of Maní (Craine and Reindorp, eds. 1979), and of Tizimín (Edmonson, trans. 1982). While providing a valuable basis of information for understanding the Maya of the pre-Conquest period, these sources cannot be read simply as historical narratives, particularly as they refer to the more distant past. In describing events such as those that occurred at Chichén Itzá, myth, legend, prophecy, and history have been interwoven so that the accounts of the past simultaneously reflect the requirements of the present.

However, a set of written sources from the pre-Conquest period of Yucatán has survived at Chichén Itzá. Using two different systems of writing, the inhabitants of Chichén Itzá recorded information in inscriptions. One system consisted of simple pictographic signs, usually placed near the heads of human figures. These signs, which are found in the Lower Temple of the Jaguars, the Temple of the Warriors, the Northwest Colonnade, and elsewhere, resemble glyphs found in systems of writing used in central Mexico and Oaxaca; their purpose may have been to indicate the personal names of the individuals represented (Tozzer 1957, p. 151; Morris, Charlot, and Morris

CENOTE OF SACRIFICE

Northwest Group

Sacred Way

Ball Court

Tzompantli

Platform of the Eagles

Venus Platform

Temple of the Warriors

Castillo

Group of the Thousand Columns

High Priest's Grave

House of the Deer

Causeway

Causeway

Red House

Caracol

Temple of the Wall Panels

Akab Dzib

Monjas

1931, pp. 311–313). Another system of writing consisted of more extended inscriptions formed with Maya hieroglyphs. These inscriptions can be found in many structures, including the Temple of the Three Lintels, the Monjas, and the Caracol. Twentieth-century efforts at the decipherment of the Maya inscriptions have revealed some of the themes that were important to the people of Chichén Itzá, the dates that were significant in the site's history, and the names of the personages who were prominent there.

On the basis of his study of the glyphs, Thomas S. Barthel (1955; 1964) has suggested the importance of fire symbolism and sacrificial rituals. The clustering of the majority of hieroglyphic dates into a single twenty-year period, corresponding to A.D. 866–886 in the Goodman-Martinez-Thompson correlation, has been noted by J. Eric S. Thompson (1937). The name of a ruler has been read phonetically as Kakupacal by David H. Kelley (1962). Referred to repeatedly in the inscriptions, Kakupacal also is described as a captain of the Itzás in a number of the *Relaciones de Yucatán* and in the Chilam Balam of Chumayel (Kelley 1968). Michel Davoust (1977) has suggested identifications of other glyphs which he argues represent the names, titles, and kinship ties of rulers and other important personages at Chichén Itzá.

Besides being studied through written sources, Chichén Itzá can also be studied through the visual images of its art. The sculptures and murals of the site depict many subjects, including the individuals who lived in Chichén Itzá and their deeds. Sculpture can be found on the exterior and interior surfaces of the structures. Human figures appear on the central panels of the columns of the Temple of the Chac Mool, the Temple of the Warriors, and the Northwest Colonnade, as well as on many other buildings. These figures, almost all of whom are male, have been identified as warriors, captives, elders, dignitaries, priests, sorcerers, and god-impersonators (Morris, Charlot, and Morris 1931, pp. 253–256, 304–309). Warriors, captives, and priests arranged in rows decorate the low benches in the Northwest Colonnade, the Mercado, and elsewhere. The walls and vault of the Lower Temple of the Jaguars are lined with bas-reliefs that depict five files of male figures arranged in procession and advancing toward a central axis (see fig. 5). The interior surfaces of the North Temple are covered with complex scenes that illustrate bloodletting rites, ceremonial dances, and rituals of death.

Murals executed in brilliant colors have survived at Chichén Itzá. Although now badly damaged, the interior walls of the Upper Temple of the Jaguars were painted with large frescoes (see figs. 17–20). The central fresco in the interior chamber represented two large male figures in ceremonial garb isolated against an empty background. Six more frescoes in the same chamber represented battle scenes involving armies and including village and siege scenes. Human sacrifice was also illustrated. Murals discovered during the excavation of the Temple of the Warriors depicted a wide array of subjects, including battles, sacrifices, and processions. Among these scenes is a village with yellow thatched huts on the banks of a river. In addition to the warriors who are being transported along the river in canoes, fifteen villagers, both men and women, are represented engaged in everyday occupations such as grinding corn, cooking, and carrying burdens.

Besides being varied in imagery, the art of Chichén Itzá is eclectic both in style and in iconography. Similarities in visual motifs and stylistic qualities exist between Chichén Itzá and sites in many regions of Mexico and Central America, including Central Mexico, Veracruz, Oaxaca, the Huasteca, and the Pacific coast of Guatemala, as well as in the southern Maya lowlands. At the time of the Spanish Conquest, an extensive trade network linked the northern Yucatán peninsula to Honduras and Tabasco. During the Terminal Clas-

Figure 2. Plan of Chichén Itzá. After Morris, Charlot, and Morris 1931, pl. 2.

sic and Early Postclassic periods, Chichén Itzá was in all probability the nexus of an ever wider-reaching trade network extending as far north as the central Mexican plateau and as far south as Costa Rica and Panama. Commercial contacts may have contributed to Chichén's dramatic rise and to the exchange of cultural influences between Chichén and its mercantile partners.

However, so strong are the artistic ties between Chichén Itzá and two specific areas of Mesoamerica, the Maya region of the Puuc in the northwestern part of the Yucatán Peninsula and the Toltec site of Tula in Central Mexico, that most scholars have concluded that Chichén Itzá was occupied by two peoples, the native Maya of Yucatán and the foreign Toltec of Mexico. The traditional reconstruction of the history of the site has divided its occupation into two successive periods: a "Chichén-Maya" period that began between A.D. 600 and 750 and ended in approximately A.D. 950, and a "Chichén-Toltec" period that began in approximately A.D. 950 and ended around A.D. 1250 (Tozzer 1957). According to this view, the Chichén-Maya period is seen as contemporaneous with the flourishing of the Puuc sites to the West. Because of the similarity in style with the architecture of the Puuc area, structures such as the Temple of the Three Lintels, the Akab Dzib, and the Monjas have been assigned to this period. The Chichén-Toltec period is believed to have followed the abandonment of the Puuc sites. Structures such as the Castillo, the Temple of the Warriors, and the Great Ball Court have been attributed to this period. It is argued that, during this period, Chichén Itzá was a political and artistic dependency of the central Mexican site of Tula, while the end of the Chichén-Toltec period is considered coeval with the emergence of the site of Mayapán as a political force.

This traditional reconstruction of the history of Chichén Itzá has recently been challenged from many different directions. Because the shallowness of the soil prevents the recovery of clear stratigraphic sequences for the site, it has not been possible to determine the absolute chronological placement of the structures through archaeological excavation. However, a number of different dates have been proposed both for the architectural structures and for the periods of occupation. Lee A. Parsons (1969, pp. 198–199) has dated the Castillo and other structures traditionally considered Chichén-Toltec to A.D. 650–750 on the basis of comparisons with sculptures at the site of Bilbao in Guatemala. Marvin Cohodas (1978a; 1978b) has suggested dates ranging from A.D. 600–900 for the Great Ball Court and other Chichén-Toltec structures on the basis of similarities between the ball game cult at Chichén Itzá and in other regions of Mesoamerica in the Middle Classic Period (A.D. 400–700). Comparisons between ceramic and architectural evidence at the site of Dzibilchaltún in the northwestern region of the Yucatán Peninsula and at sites in the southern Maya lowlands have suggested to E. Wyllys Andrews V (1978) that the Puuc style associated with the Chichén-Maya period emerged around A.D. 800, although an earlier date is not precluded, especially if serious consideration is given to an earlier cluster of radiocarbon dates from Chichén Itzá.

The sharp division of the history of Chichén Itzá into two periods has also been questioned. J. E. S. Thompson (1970b) has suggested that Mexican influences were brought to the site by two migrations, the first by Mexicanized Putún Maya originally from Tabasco and the second by Toltec from Central Mexico. Because Mexican motifs are depicted in a Maya style on the gold discs from the Cenote of Sacrifice, Samuel K. Lothrop (1952) argued that the Chichén-Maya and Chichén-Toltec occupations may have been partly contemporaneous. Tatiana Proskouriakoff (1970) noted the presence of Mexican traits in Puuc art and in Chichén-Maya art and the continuation of Maya traits in Chichén-Toltec art. She therefore proposed that small bands of Toltec may have entered the northern Maya lowlands prior to their emergence as the dominant group at Chichén Itzá and that these Toltec bands may have formed political and military alliances with Maya groups in order to acquire control of Chichén Itzá.

Recent investigations of the parallels in costume and weaponry between the figures in the sculpture of Chichén Itzá and that of other Maya sites, particularly those located in the northwestern region of the Yucatán Peninsula, support Proskouriakoff's interpretation (Wren 1982a; 1982b). The depiction in the Northwest Colonnade of bound Toltec prisoners wearing costumes that share many attributes with depictions of warriors at the Central Mexican site of Tula, in addition to the depiction of Maya prisoners, demonstrates that political status was not dependent solely on ethnic identity. During the Chichén-Toltec period, power and prestige were evidently shared and defeat and humiliation experienced by Toltecs and Maya alike (Wren n.d.).

In addition, the relationship of Chichén Itzá to sites in neighboring Maya areas has been re-evaluated. Joseph W. Ball (1977) and E. Wyllys Andrews V (1977) have argued that ceramic evidence from the northern Maya lowlands suggests that the Chichén-Toltec occupation of Chichén Itzá preceded the abandonment of the Puuc centers. According to the partial overlap reconstruction proposed by Ball (1977, p. 33), a Maya group from the northwestern, or Puuc, region or from the southwestern, or Río Bec and Chenes, region of the Yucatán Peninsula may have entered the northern plains and established Chichén Itzá as a major economic and political center. The growing prominence of Chichén Itzá, in Ball's view, contributed to the increasing instability of the Puuc region and to the eventual eclipse of the Puuc sites. Ball has also tentatively suggested a second possible reconstruction involving a total overlap (1977, pp. 33–34), which he thinks is less plausible. This would view the occupation of the Puuc sites and of Mayapán and related sites in northeastern Quintana Roo as overlapping. Rather than being considered as a separate temporal phase in northern Maya lowland chronology occurring after the abandonment of the Puuc sites and before the emergence of Mayapán, the Chichén-Toltec occupation of Chichén Itzá would be identified as a distinctive culture system that was confined to a small geographical area and was contemporaneous with the occupation of other major sites in the Yucatán Peninsula.

Finally, the relationship of Chichén Itzá to the distant city of Tula has been re-examined. Noting that the artistic style referred to as Toltec is much richer and more varied at Chichén Itzá than it is at Tula and that the formative stages of this style seem to appear only at Chichén Itzá, George Kubler (1961) has argued that it is most reasonable to consider Chichén Itzá as the place of origin of the style. He has suggested that the Chichén-Toltec style arose from a fusion of concepts alien to the northern Maya lowlands with the artistic and expressive skills developed by local Maya craftsmen. In Kubler's view the concrete stylistic influences were then transmitted to Tula by the Toltec rather than being imposed on Chichén Itzá from Tula.

Although the history of the site will always be a matter of debate and speculation, the grandeur of Chichén Itzá and its ruins is beyond doubt. The grandeur, which survived even after the economic and political power of the site had waned, was once expressed by Edward Herbert Thompson, the American investigator who recovered the treasures of the Cenote of Sacrifice:

Pen cannot describe or brush portray the strange feelings produced by the beating of the tropic sun against the ash-colored walls of those venerable structures. Old and cold, furrowed by time, and haggard, imposing and impressive, they rear their rugged masses above the surrounding level and are above description. (E. H. Thompson 1932, p. 193).

GULF OF MEXICO

CARIBBEAN SEA

2 •   1 •   •18
         23 •   •17   •20
         19 •
                •21

4 •   •3

         •24   22 •
   •7
6 •   8 •   •9
   •5   16 •
         10 •
              11 •
         •12   14 •
              •15
         •13

PACIFIC OCEAN

1. El Tajín
2. Tula
3. Cholula
4. Xochicalco
5. Monte Albán
6. San Lorenzo
7. La Venta
8. Palenque
9. Piedras Negras
10. Yaxchilán
11. Seibal
12. Nebaj
13. Bilbao
14. Quiriguá
15. Copán
16. Tikal
17. Chichén Itzá
18. Dzibilchaltún
19. Uxmal
20. Cobá
21. Tulum
22. Santa Rita
23. Mayapán
24. Xicalango

Usumacinta R.
Grijalva R.
Chixoy R.
Pasión R.
Hondo R.
Motagua R.

BORUCA
REGION

CHIRIQUÍ
REGION

DIQUÍS
REGION

VERAGUAS
REGION

Figure 3. Map of Mesoamerica and lower Central America showing sites and regions discussed in the Catalogue.

Introduction

The Cenote of Sacrifice Catalogue

CLEMENCY CHASE COGGINS

"At four o'clock we left Pisté, and very soon we saw rising high above the plain the Castillo of Chichen. In half an hour we were among the ruins of this ancient city, with all the great buildings in full view, casting prodigious shadows over the plain." Thus John Lloyd Stephens described his arrival, in 1842, at Chichén Itzá, Yucatán. This visit concluded:

. . . setting out from the Castillo, at some distance we ascended a wooded elevation, which seemed an artificial causeway leading to the cenote.* The cenote was the largest and wildest we had seen; in the midst of a thick forest, an immense circular hole, with cragged perpendicular sides, trees growing out of them and overhanging the brink, and still as if the genius of silence reigned within. A hawk was sailing around it, looking down into the water, but without flapping its wings. The water was of a greenish hue. A mysterious influence seemed to pervade it, in unison with the historical account that the well of Chichen was a place of pilgrimage, and that human victims were thrown into it in sacrifice. In one place on the very brink, were the remains of a stone structure, probably connected with ancient superstitious rites; perhaps the place from which victims were thrown into the dark well beneath. (Stephens 1843, p. 182)

Stephens' account, published in New York in 1843 with Frederick Catherwood's magnificent illustrations, introduced the general public to Maya civilization. In 1864 the Abbé Brasseur de Bourbourg translated the work of the sixteenth-century bishop Diego de Landa who, in his report to the Spanish Crown, had described the great cenote at Chichén Itzá as a sacred place where in addition to "throwing men alive . . . They also threw . . . a great many other things. Like precious stones and things which they prized. And so if this country possessed gold, it would be this well that would have the greater part of it, so great was the devotion which the Indians showed for it" (Tozzer, ed. 1941, pp. 180, 182).

On March 5, 1904, Edward H. Thompson lowered a steel bucket into the Sacred Cenote at Chichén Itzá to find out if the Bishop de Landa was right. On April 12, after more than a month of inconclusive results, Thompson dredged up a wooden object which he described as having "the lower end, or butt . . . beautifully carved into the figure of a personage richly dressed and ornamented. The face is covered with a mask of beaten gold" (cat. no. 123). Although the bishop had no way of knowing if the ancient Maya had ever had any gold (and really they did not), he had been right about gold in the Sacred Cenote of Chichén Itzá.

---

*Cenote is the Spanish equivalent of the Yucatec Maya word ts'onot, which refers to a natural well or limestone sinkhole.

COCLÉ REGION

DARIEN REGION

Early Archaeological Work at Chichén Itzá

Since Stephens' trip a number of other travelers had visited the site, including Augustus and Alice Dixon Le Plongeon, who spent three months there at the end of 1875. Among other explorations they excavated two of the platforms in the great plaza in front of the Castillo. In the one faced with reliefs of jaguars and eagles they found a reclining stone figure (the first known of its type) which they fancifully named Chac Mool (Great Jaguar Paw) after the presumed name of a person depicted in the nearby Upper Temple of the Jaguars, whom they believed the reclining figure represented. In association with this sculpture they found a large round limestone cache vessel containing, among other things, what Le Plongeon believed to be the heart of the dead king Chac Mool, and at least seventeen beautifully worked jasper and chalcedony projectile points (cat. nos. 11, 105, 106).

In 1882 Désiré Charnay had also visited Chichén Itzá and tried, unsuccessfully, to dredge the Cenote. Although this effort failed, his visit was of particular historical interest because he was the first to note the resemblances between the architecture and sculpture of Chichén and the remote Central Mexican site of Tula, which he had also visited (1887, pp. 341ff.). In 1889 Alfred P. Maudslay spent six months at the site, mapping, drawing, photographing, and describing the ruins for publication in London in his monumental volumes on twelve Maya sites. Shortly afterward, Teobert Maler, who had explored Maya sites for the Peabody Museum at Harvard, excavated in several structures at Chichén, publishing this work in *Globus*, a German news magazine (1895).

This travel and exploration was largely generated by the romantic and neoclassical interests of the nineteenth-century public, and interest in Central America and Mexico was stimulated by Stephens' volumes in particular. In 1879 the young Edward H. Thompson of Worcester, Massachusetts, was inspired to write "Atlantis Not a Myth" for the *Popular Science Monthly*. This article came to the attention of Stephen S. Salisbury, a member of the American Antiquarian Society of Worcester, patron of that city, and sponsor of Le Plongeon's work. Six years later, when the society's arrangement with Le Plongeon was terminated, Salisbury called upon Thompson, as a native of Worcester and an aspiring antiquarian, to continue these pursuits in Yucatán. He arranged to have Thompson made American consul in Mérida, and in 1885, with his wife and baby daughter, Edward H. Thompson embarked on an adventure that was to occupy some forty years of his life. Shortly after he began work in Yucatán, Charles P. Bowditch of the Peabody Museum at Harvard, another member of the American Antiquarian Society, joined Salisbury as Thompson's sponsor. In the early years Thompson worked at the sites of Labná, Chacmultún, and in the Cave of Loltún, and accounts of these explorations were published by the Peabody Museum (1897a; 1897b; 1904). He made casts of the façades of structures at Labná and Uxmal for the 1893 Columbian Exposition (a world's fair) in Chicago, and thus came to the attention of Allison V. Armour, who became a new sponsor and helped Thompson buy the hacienda of Chichén Itzá and its ruins in 1894.

Edward H. Thompson's Work in the Sacred Cenote

Ten years later, under the joint patronage of Salisbury and Bowditch, Thompson rigged up a dredge with a steel "orange-peel" bucket that was operated on a boom from a derrick on the south shore of the Cenote, using five hundred ards of steel cable and rope. At first, the bucket brought up only decayed leaves, branches, and tree trunks with the creamy yellowish ooze, or "muck" as Thompson called it, that covered the rocky bottom of the Cenote to a depth of about twelve feet. Five days after dredging began in March 1904, a few bones and small shells came up, and the next day several pieces of pottery.

Thompson had established what he called "the fertile zone," a wedge-shaped area that fanned out from the shrine on the south side of the Cenote, from which he postulated sacrifices had been made. The extent of the zone had been determined by tossing logs of approximately human weight into the Cenote. Although Thompson made a rough sketch of this fertile zone, and began by recording "stations" within it, this system was soon abandoned, and no records of the relative locations of dredging were kept. In fact it proved impossible to establish any kind of stratigraphic or contextual control. Recurrent problems were the tendency of the muck and stone and branches surrounding any particular dredged pit to fall back in as soon as the operation was stopped, and of lightweight objects to move around a great deal. It should be noted here that the divers of the Mexican operations of the 1960s had many of these same problems, even though they worked under the water; they did, however, manage to establish stratigraphy in a limited area below the southern structure (Piña Chan 1970).

Thompson dredged in the Cenote between 1904 and 1907, usually from spring until fall. In 1909, after taking deep sea diving lessons in Boston Harbor, Thompson hired a Greek sponge diver and together they descended into the Cenote in diving suits. With this cumbersome equipment they found small heavy objects between the stones on the bottom, but there was essentially no visibility, and the shifting stones and trees proved hazardous. This method lasted but a season, and it is not clear if Thompson ever used the dredge again.

Publication of Thompson's Work on the Sacred Cenote

After the Mexican Revolution Thompson's land was occupied by squatters, and the hacienda, with its "museum" full of records, photographs, and copper bells, copal, and bones from the Cenote, was burned down in 1920. In 1923 the Carnegie Institution of Washington established an archaeological research center at Chichén Itzá, and Thompson's role steadily diminished. In 1926 his friend and great admirer, T. A. Willard, published a romantic account of Thompson and his life in Yucatán, culminating with the story of the dredging of the Cenote. This highly colorful volume included exaggerated descriptions of the perfect condition and great monetary value of the Cenote finds; these provoked a Mexican embargo on the Chichén plantation and claims for over a million pesos in compensation for the objects removed from the Cenote. The claims were finally settled by the Mexican Supreme Court in favor of Thompson's heirs in 1944, nine years after his death.

Not until the suit was settled could the Peabody Museum publish the collections. In 1952 Samuel K. Lothrop published *Metals from the Cenote of Sacrifice*, and in 1957 Alfred M. Tozzer's two-volume *Chichen Itza and Its Cenote of Sacrifice* appeared. Two years later, in 1959, the Peabody Museum presented Mexico with a representative collection of ninety-two gold and copper artifacts from the Cenote, in exchange for a study collection of ancient Mexican ceramics.

In 1974 the Peabody Museum published *Jades from the Cenote of Sacrifice* by Tatiana Proskouriakoff. Two years later the museum presented Mexico with 246 worked jade objects in exchange for a Spanish Colonial study collection, with the understanding that the jades would be exhibited in Yucatán.

Among the unpublished collections, the human bones from the Cenote were briefly described by Earnest A. Hooton in 1940, in a volume dedicated to Alfred M. Tozzer, and some work had been done on the faunal remains by Glover Allen shortly after the collections arrived in the Peabody Museum (Cole, Glover, and Barbour 1906). But it was the human bones that had long attracted interest. Popular accounts had described the sacrificial victims as virgins. Hooton protested that he could not determine this point, but his analysis of the bones of forty-two individuals indicated that more than half were younger than twenty and fourteen were younger than twelve years old. Bones from the 1967 Mexican excavation are reported to have included many of children (Ediger 1971, p. 141). This accords with evidence for the sacrifice of boys in Colonial Yucatán (Tozzer 1957, pp. 212, 213), although there is also the often-repeated description of a ceremony in which young women were thrown or pushed into the Cenote to procure a prophecy from the rain deity presumed to live there (Tozzer, ed. 1941, p. 223). Sacrificing or offering human beings was evidently a Late Postclassic and Colonial practice. Whether it was associated with the Early Phase offering of broken jade and crushed gold, or with the Late Phase offering of copper bells and copal-filled tripod dishes, we do not know.

All of the other artifacts from the Cenote—the textiles, basketry, wood, pottery, stone, bone, shell, copal, rubber, and other vegetal materials—are currently being prepared for publication by several authors. They will constitute the final Peabody Memoir on the Cenote of Sacrifice (Coggins, ed. n.d.).

Offerings to the Sacred Cenote

The Cenote of Sacrifice lived up to its reputation as a repository of human sacrifice and precious goods, but it is in the preservation of perishable objects that it is most remarkable. After jade, the largest category of Cenote finds in the Peabody Museum consists of textiles, of which over seven hundred small fragments have survived (Tozzer 1957, p. 198; J. M. Lothrop n.d.). Although the raising, spinning, weaving, and export of cotton was, with salt production, one of the principal industries of Yucatán, the bits of fabric in the Cenote are the only direct evidence of this occupation, and indeed they have been among the few extant ancient Mesoamerican textiles (King 1979). The Peabody Museum collection is, however, small compared to the great number and variety of textiles brought up by the two more recent Mexican expeditions; these are now under study in Mexico (García L. 1981).

Wooden objects constitute another very small class of ancient artifacts, since the climate quickly rots and insects devour them. Immersed in the water of the Cenote, however, these organic materials were deprived of the oxygen which would lead to their decay. Most of the once-waterlogged wood is in good condition today because the Maya coated wooden artifacts with a resinous preservative and because Thompson kept them moist until, at the museum, the water was replaced by alcohol, then by xylol, and finally by paraffin (Willoughby 1908). Unlike the other categories of artifacts, the wooden ones represent a great variety of objects: scepters, idols, weapons, tools, and items of personal adornment.

Copal and rubber are also little known from excavations, although they were both burned for ceremonial purposes everywhere, and probably throughout the millennia of ancient Mesoamerican history. From the Cenote we find that these saps, the blood of trees, were shaped into balls and effigy forms, painted blue, and studded with rubber, jade, and shells before being offered to the Cenote.

The jade, gold, and copper from the Cenote are well known, and of extraordinary interest because these raw materials and much of their workmanship was foreign to Yucatán. Jade, still relatively plentiful at the end of the Classic Period, was worked with drills and with saws which, since metal tools were lacking, drew their effectiveness from stone abrasives. The gold was hammered or cast in the lower Central American regions of its origin. Similarly, copper was probably hammered and cast far from Chichén Itzá, in Central Mexico, Oaxaca, the Guatemalan highlands, or Honduras. These exotic riches testify to widespread contact with Chichén Itzá, and to the singular fame of the Sacred Cenote.

Pottery, stone, bone, and shell are commonly found in excavating Mesoamerican sites, so while their presence in such a ritual context is not surprising, it is particularly useful here for dating the phases of ceremonial use of the Cenote. The absolute dates (in our time reckoning) of these centuries of use are not clear, although the almost eight centuries between about A.D. 800 and the Spanish Conquest encompassed it, with a century or more of inactivity between about A.D. 1150 and 1250.

Exhibition of Objects from the Sacred Cenote

This exhibition is the first time all of the different kinds of offerings to the Sacred Cenote have ever been displayed together, and the first time many have been published. To exhibit such a selection some chronological order should, ideally, be made from these objects, but they came from a single vast archaeological context which provided Thompson no clue to sequence of deposition or other relative placement. It is, however, clear they were not all thrown in at the same time. They vary tremendously in style of decoration and manufacture, as well as in material and in function. By comparing these attributes to those of published objects that were excavated from datable archaeological contexts, it has been possible to postulate a sequence of ceremonial deposition for the Cenote. Reasons for assigning each object to a specific phase of Cenote ritual are explained in the catalogue entries.

Theoretically every offering made to the Cenote might have been cast in at any time after it was made, although it is most likely to have been used relatively close to its date of manufacture. A good example of this principle is found in the carved jades which came from the western Maya lowlands. It is most economical to assume that these many foreign objects, which were broken in their ritual consignment to the Cenote, were taken to Chichén Itzá during the Terminal Classic Period when they were carved rather than that they were all heirlooms, or much later looted from tombs. There is, however, an extraordinary exception to this rule in other jades that were found in the Cenote. These are unbroken jades of Late Preclassic and Early Classic date that were associated with offertory copal of later Postclassic times and had apparently been taken from tombs or caches that were over a millennium old, for offering to the Cenote at a time when jade was very scarce.

Chronology of Sacred Cenote Ritual

There were two phases of Cenote ritual: roughly A.D. 800–1150 and 1250–1539 (see chronological chart, fig. 21). The Early Phase probably began late in the eighth century A.D., at the same time that dates written in the Maya Long Count were being carved on the stone lintels of Chichén Itzá. This Early Phase has been divided into two parts. The first part lasted until about A.D. 900 and marked the beginning of a kind of Cenote ritual that included objects resembling others found cached contemporaneously at the Puuc site of Uxmal, and included offerings exemplified by the numerous imported objects that depict and symbolize the victorious role at Chichén Itzá of the Central Mexicans usually called "Toltec." These "Toltec" are shown with a subordinate Maya elite in the reliefs and paintings of the Great Ball Court complex at Chichén Itzá a century or more before their namesake city of Tula, Hidalgo, had become a great capital. These warriors may have been among the founders of Tula, but in the first part of the Early Phase of Cenote ritual they were apparently occupied in founding a capital at Chichén Itzá, and in consecrating its Sacred Cenote for their purposes.

In the second part of the Early Phase, in the tenth and eleventh centuries A.D., Chichén Itzá had become much more genuinely Toltec, with a glorification of militarism evident in offerings to the Cenote, while evidence of Maya influence declined.

Throughout the Early Phase, the valuable imported objects were broken, crushed, and usually burned before they were cast in to the Cenote. The jades, which represented the personal wealth of Maya rulers to the southwest, may have been tribute sent or taken to the new, foreign-dominated capital, whereas the scenes of conquest and other items of "Toltec regalia" were perhaps the personal sacrifices of the victorious foreigners. The cast gold may have drawn its significance from its Mesoamerican rarity and the great distance it had come, thus exemplifying a kind of trading prowess that complemented the role of warrior. The only evidence for rain-making ceremonies at the Cenote is found at this time in numerous domestic jars and basins. Possibly popular rain-making activities coexisted with the more elite political and social ones, as in a cathedral, where the king may be crowned, yet the poor may light a candle.

The Early Phase was over in the twelfth century as Tula's role in Central Mexico came to an end. At this time Chichén Itzá was apparently abandoned by much of its resident population and it is difficult to identify objects that might have been offered to the Cenote for the next century or more. This hiatus would not be so long if a different correlation between the Maya and Christian calendars were in use by archaeologists—but in defense of these many apparently empty years, it might be said that a long period of time is necessary to account for the complete change in offerings that characterizes the Late Phase.

The Late Phase probably began in the second half of the thirteenth century, in conjunction with the founding of the new capital of Mayapán, to the southwest. Pilgrimages were made to Chichén Itzá, and objects were cast into the Sacred Cenote that were both poorer and more parochial than those of the Early Phase. Copal incense, often in tripod bowls, was among the most common late offerings. Unidentifiable wooden idols and some deity images were cast in (none suggesting supplication to Chac, the rain god). Imported copper bells are the main indication of wealth, after an unknown quantity of undatable jade beads that must belong to this period. Cotton textiles that attest to an important local industry may also be evidence of personal wealth, and finally a group of figural wooden scepters suggest that a kind of lineage ceremony was performed at the Cenote. This Late Phase may have continued well into the sixteenth century, although it is likely to have diminished with the fall of Mayapán, in A.D. 1450.

The Offering of Objects to the Sacred Cenote

Many of the objects thrown into the Cenote appear to have been damaged intentionally, or "killed," beforehand, especially in the Early Phase. Most of the jade was smashed or broken from the sequential effects of fire and cold water. Cast gold was crushed and melted; embossed sheet gold was cut, crumpled, and torn. Cast copper bells, mostly from the Late Phase, lost only their clappers. Wooden objects were usually broken or cut, sometimes both, although the wooden idols from the later period of use were intact when they were offered. Shattered jade and melted gold from the Early Phase, and burned rubber and copal from the Late, all suggest that fire was an important part of the Cenote ritual; perhaps some of this ceremony took place at night. However, we do not know at what hour, on what occasions, or in what seasons most of these activities occurred. Nor do we know what verb best describes the consignment of these objects to the Cenote. Were they thrown? dropped? or lowered? Did they just fall in? Presumably not. Some of the ceramic and perishable vessels once had cords attached to them. These may have been lowered, but on the whole it is reasonable to assume most of them were offerings, and that they were cast respectfully into the Cenote.

Yucatán has many cenotes in its karstic limestone terrain, and for the ancient people they were the most important source of water. The Sacred Cenote at Chichén Itzá is unusual, however, in offering no direct access to the water, while several others at the site did provide access. Vessels that were lowered into the Sacred Cenote may have been securing the kind of holy water necessary for many Maya rituals, rather than simply seeking water for consumption, since that was available nearby.

There is little or no evidence for a ceremony that involved consigning valuable objects to the Cenote before Terminal Classic times. Whether this cult of the Sacred Cenote was introduced and promoted by the foreigners depicted on the walls of Chichén Itzá, and whether it was preceded by or coexisted with an indigenous ritual of different character, we may never know, but it is clear that, once established as a sacred place, the Sacred Cenote at Chichén Itzá never entirely lost its religious aura, or its renown.

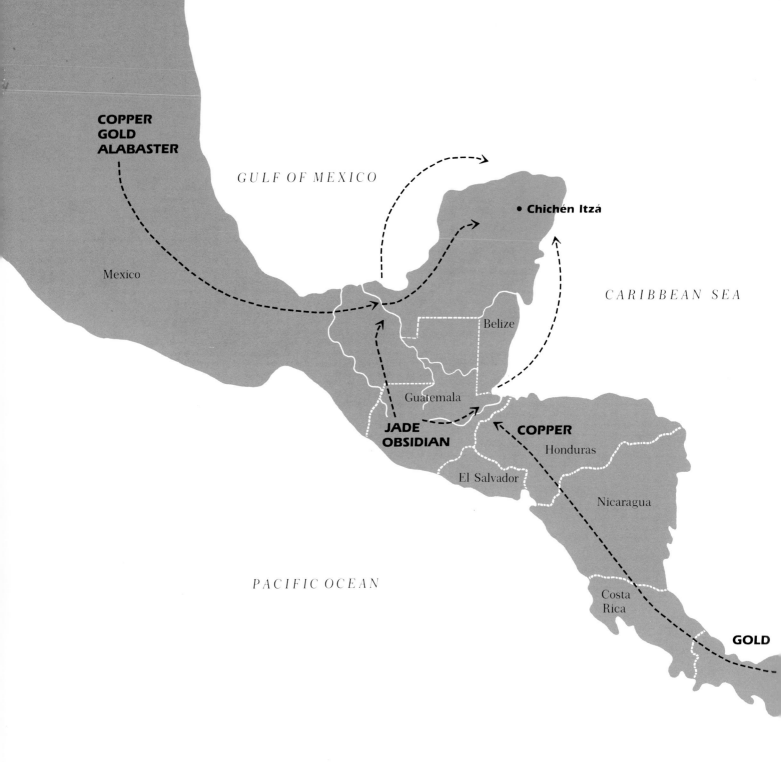

COPPER
GOLD
ALABASTER

GULF OF MEXICO

Mexico

• **Chichén Itzá**

CARIBBEAN SEA

Belize

Guatemala

JADE
OBSIDIAN

COPPER

Honduras

El Salvador

Nicaragua

PACIFIC OCEAN

Costa
Rica

GOLD

Figure 4. Map of Mesoamerica and lower Central America showing sources of materials found in the Cenote.

A Regional Ceremonial Assemblage

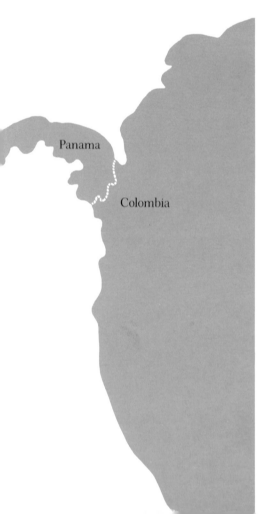

Two broad phases of Sacred Cenote ritual are postulated for Chichén Itzá: A.D. 800–1150 and A.D. 1250–1539. The first of these in all likelihood began before A.D. 800 and may possibly have continued for as long as four centuries, but activity had diminished significantly by A.D. 1100. This phase includes what are generally known as the Terminal Classic and the Early Postclassic periods, or in Yucatán as the Pure Florescent and the Modified Florescent periods. The second phase—of very different character—is Middle to Late Postclassic, or the Decadent Period (fig. 21).

In this preliminary section of the catalogue, elite ritual objects from the northwestern part of the Yucatán Peninsula are grouped in order to present a regional ceremonial assemblage. Eight of these objects actually came from the Sacred Cenote (see nos. 3, 5, 6, 7, 8, 10), but most of them are stylistically and functionally related to others found at the site of Uxmal. They date from the Terminal Classic, when Chichén Itzá and Uxmal were somehow inter-related and the Early Phase of Cenote ritual was at its height.

This grouping helps both to explain the ways in which the Sacred Cenote was part of contemporary ritual practice and, more strikingly in the next group, to show how at the same period of time offerings made to the Cenote differed from contemporary ritual practice elsewhere in involving both kinds and numbers of objects otherwise unknown locally.

NOTE ON CATALOGUE ENTRIES

At the beginning of each catalogue entry there are four lines of descriptive information:

1. Description/name of object.
2. Material(s) of which object is made. If more than one, they may be separated by a comma or by a semicolon. The semicolon implies a different, usually later component, as for instance red pigment, which is often added for the final ritual consignment of an object.
3. Steps in the working and later alteration of the object. These may be separated by commas or by semicolons, the latter indicating a different stage or process. The initial phases of sawing, grinding, polishing, etc., have been omitted for jade.
4. Museum accession and catalogue numbers followed by maximum dimensions. H. = height, W. = width, L. = length, Th. = thickness, D. = diameter.

At the bottom of the catalogue entry the first bibliographic citation is the primary one for the object. Later ones are organized chronologically (except for subsequent works by an author already cited).

1. Thin Slate Ware cylinder from Chichén Itzá

Fired cream/buff-slipped clay
Hand built; broken; partially restored
Peabody Museum 00-37-20/C2900,
H. 16.0 cm., Rim D. 15.0 cm.

Edward H. Thompson excavated this Thin Slate Ware vessel from a burial somewhere at Chichén Itzá early in this century. Relatively few burials are known from Chichén Itzá, however, since the ceremonial structures at the center of the site that were excavated and reconstructed by the Carnegie Institution were not used for funerary purposes, and there has been little further archaeological excavation.

Thin Slate Wares were among the most important elite ceramics in Yucatán between about A.D. 800 and 1000, and both plain and decorated vessels of the type were offered to the Cenote, although much more unslipped pottery was found there from this period (Brainerd 1958, p. 45). This suggests that activity at the Cenote was not exclusively ceremonial and elite at this time. Vertical crazing, from the firing of this vessel, and purplish dendritic markings from its interment are particularly noticeable on the creamy translucent slip characteristic of Slate Wares.

Terminal Classic (A.D. 800–900)

2. Carved tripod plate from near Uxmal

Fired buff-slipped clay
Hand built, carved, perforations in feet; broken; partially restored
Peabody Museum 25-41-20/C9869,
H. 11.0 cm., D. 29.2 cm.

Edward H. Thompson reports that this Puuc Slate Ware plate came from near Uxmal. It has hollow hemispherical rattle feet and two bands of carved (gouged-incised) decoration on the outside of the flaring wall. The lower band is a guilloche; the upper has seven remaining motifs—probably in formal imitation of a glyph band. These are: another guilloche, three cross-hatched cartouches, a crossed bands element, seven vertical bars or separators (two with a row of internal dots), one long panel with a horizontal row of dots in a rounded frame, a second elongated panel with a highly stylized bird, and a third with "comb" elements surmounted by a plant-like form. Among these the guilloches and the bird are common carved Slate Ware motifs.

Terminal Classic/Early Postclassic (A.D. 800–1000)
Brainerd 1958, fig. 57a

3. Pedestal vessel

Tecali (calcite)
Ground, polished; broken; partially restored
Peabody Museum 07-7-20/C4748,
H. 16.7 cm., Rim D. 16.6 cm.

A flaring pedestal base supports this marble-like tecali vessel instead of the three solid spherical feet found on the similar one dredged with it from the Cenote (no. 31), but both have everted rims, as do other flaring tecali cylinders in contemporary caches.

A larger tecali pedestal vessel excavated from a cache at Uxmal is unlike others at Uxmal, Chichén Itzá, or Xochicalco in having a scene carved in a panel on the side (Ruz Lhuillier 1954, p. 62, fig. 6, pl. 24). This scene depicts an enthroned Maya lord facing a subsidiary figure with glyphs above that identify each person. The carving is Late to Terminal Classic Maya in style, although the vessel was probably imported from Oaxaca, like the two from the Cenote.

Terminal Classic (A.D. 800–900)
Moholy-Nagy and Ladd n.d.

4. Rattle pedestal vessel from Uxmal

Fired cream/gray-slipped clay
Hand built, incisions, perforations in bottom; broken; restored
Peabody Museum 89-9-20/C2357,
H. 22.0 cm., Rim D. 13.7 cm.

This tall, subtly flaring Thin Slate Ware vessel came from a chultun (underground cistern) at the Palace of the Governors at Uxmal. Its elegant form is enhanced by a rattle base that sounds when it is shaken. The color, slightly everted rim, and flaring base recall one of the imported tecali vessels from the Cenote (no. 3), as well as a carved tecali pedestal vessel excavated from the Adoratorio at Uxmal very near the source of this one. The classic simplicity of Puuc Slate Ware is exemplified in this cylindrical form which, coupled with a monochrome aesthetic, may be traceable to south-central Mexico.

Terminal Classic (A.D. 800–900)
Brainerd 1958, fig. 50g

6. Bone with hieroglyphic inscription

Tapir scapula; red pigment
Carved; perforated; polished; broken
Peabody Museum 24-41-20/C10075,
L.9.8 cm., W. 5.9 cm.

This hieroglyphic inscription is carved on a flaring tapir scapula with a hole in its concave base which might have held the inscribed bone upright on a staff or headdress.

Before it was broken the carving probably consisted of a central scene or inscription surrounded on all four sides by a single band of hieroglyphs. Such an arrangement is found in the northern Maya lowlands, especially at Chichén Itzá (Bolles 1977, pp. 269–273). Almost all of the scene design and most of the glyphs are lost. The third glyph apparently records the name of a Maya lord. Stylistically, the glyphs are closest to a monument from Uxmal now in the Ermita, Mérida, and dating to the ninth century A.D. (Peter Mathews, Corpus of Maya Hieroglyphic Inscriptions Project, personal communication)

Terminal Classic (A.D. 800–900)
Moholy-Nagy and Ladd n.d.

5. Three stuccoed and painted sherds

Fired gray and cream-slipped clay; post-fire stucco, red, orange, blue, black pigments
Hand built; broken
Peabody Museum 07-7-20/C4756, C4758, C4933, Max. H. 7.2 cm., Th. 0.3–0.6 cm.

These Cenote rim sherds were part of two large, round-sided Thin Slate Ware bowls decorated with a thin layer of white stucco painted with polychrome figural designs and glyphic inscriptions.

The stucco of the single sherd once had an orange-painted background over white; a blue vertical panel was painted over a black-outlined glyph and black vertical bar just below, on the right. The joined sherds used the same colors in much the same way, but the glyphs and feathers were more lightly and cursively painted in black before red and blue paints were added. The remaining head glyph in this inscription was at the end of a horizontal line and at the beginning of a vertical one. It is painted in a glyphic style related to the Dresden Codex, an Early Postclassic ritual-astronomical Maya manuscript which is a copy of an earlier one. The copy was probably painted at Chichén Itzá (J. E. S. Thompson 1972, p. 16).

Edward H. Thompson sent the few decorated sherds he found to the Peabody Museum, while plain ones were bagged for study at the site. However the Mexicans have recently excavated many stuccoed and painted Thin Slate Ware sherds (Piña Chan 1968, photo 8; Ediger 1971, color photos 8–13) and two vessels that were almost complete. Many of their examples exhibit a lively and anecdotal figural style that may have been found on these as well. A stuccoed and painted Thin Slate Ware sherd excavated from the lower western temple of the Adivino pyramid at Uxmal resembles these in ceramic type and in glyphic style and is very likely contemporary (Ruz Lhuillier 1954, pl. 12).

Terminal Classic (A.D. 800–900)
Ball and Ladd n.d.

7. Picture plaque, carved on two sides

Jadeite; emerald to lighter green over mottled gray stone
Horizontally drilled; broken into fragments; reconstructed
Peabody Museum 10-71-20/C6669,
H. 17.8 cm., W. 10.6 cm., Th. 1.1 cm.

This Nebaj-type plaque from the Cenote (see also nos. 57, 58) was first carved somewhere in the southwestern Maya regions and brought, perhaps in tribute, to Chichén Itzá like most of the great quantity of jade offered to the Cenote. In working the stone the original vertical saw cut (made with abrasive-coated "string" or fiber) was left in order to conserve the finest jade for the hem, loincloth knot, bracelet, pectoral, earflare, and the lower jaw of the Long Nose Head headdress; a tubular drill was used at an angle for the "arc drilling" so characteristic of the Nebaj style, here delineating scrolls, ornaments, and the outlines of bodies.

A single allegorical mask serves as a frame on the figure's right, while below two heads suggest that captives are used for support—although that is a convention of monumental sculpture, not jade. On the back two unframed figures are carved in a different, northern Maya style that uses soft grooved outlines in a simplified rendering of two figures that face each other. The smaller figure, which may be a dwarf, wears a plain collar with two discs or balls at the center; this unusual device is worn by figures both at Uxmal, and at Chichén Itzá (Proskouriakoff 1970, p. 464), underscoring the Terminal Classic relationship between the sites that is also suggested by the similarity of objects that were offered to the Cenote and those that were cached at Uxmal. There is a hieroglyph in a square frame above the smaller figure which suggests a Terminal Classic date for the secondary carving. A matching plaque was found in the Cenote; it was carved from the same piece of jade and exhibits the same combination of southern and northern, early and late, front and back carving styles. It was presented to Mexico in 1976.

Late-Terminal Classic (A.D. 750–900)
Proskouriakoff 1974, pp. 175–176, pl. 72:1; Tozzer 1957, fig. 696.

8. Head pebble pendant

Jadeite; bright green splotches on white to gray
One horizontal, three edge perforations; broken; reconstructed
Peabody Museum 10-71-20/C6655,
H. 9.2 cm., W. 5.2 cm., Th. 1.4 cm.

Pebble carvings are made on slightly modified pieces of jade, often in the Terminal Classic "drooping mouth" style exemplified by this pendant from the Cenote. The style is the final development in the use of arc drilling, which can be seen on the earlier Nebaj-type plaques from the Cenote (nos. 7, 57). In this style almost every element of the design, like the three circles of the earflares and headdress, the scrolls, the features, and most characteristically the drooping mouth, are all made by the arcs of tubular drills of various sizes.

Examples of the style are known from Oaxaca, although it is likely they were carved in Maya regions. A dozen or so "drooping mouth" pendants came from the Cenote, and two were found in the cache at the foot of the stairway of the inner Castillo at Chichén Itzá (Marquina 1964, photo 428). As a group these jades provide evidence for the wide spread of southern Maya culture in Terminal Classic times, as can also be noted in the caching of such foreign jades at Uxmal as well as at Chichén Itzá (Ruz Lhuillier 1954, pls. 25, 26), and more broadly in the Mayoid monumental sculpture of Xochicalco, Morelos, and wall paintings of Cacaxtla, Tlaxcala, in Central Mexico.

Terminal Classic (A.D. 800–900)
Proskouriakoff 1974, pp. 97, 98, color pl. 1b, pl. 53b:2

9. Phallus effigy pendant

Shell (?); burned (?)
Carved; two perforations; broken
Peabody Museum 984-2-20/25614,
L. 2.2 cm., W. 0.7 cm.

Edward H. Thompson excavated this tiny
phallic amulet from a cremation burial in a
chultun near the House of the Phalli at
Chichén Itzá. The monumental sculpture
of this same group of buildings features
phallic motifs, whereas at the center of
Chichén Itzá a phallic monument is depicted only in the reliefs of the North
Temple of the Great Ball Court (Marquina
1964, photo 440). Freestanding stone phalli
and megaphallic figures are, however, more
common in the Puuc region to the southwest from which Terminal Classic Chichén
Itzá may have been founded (Willard 1941,
Ch. 14).

Terminal Classic–Early Postclassic (A.D.
800–1000)

10. Earflare (?) with figure

Wood; paraffin impregnated
Carved; flare broken off
Peabody Museum 10-71-20/C6710,
L. 3.5 cm., W. 1.2 cm.

Unlike three of these wooden objects from
the Cenote (no. 40), the figure on this flare
is not cut out or silhouetted and does not
represent a ball player. He wears only a
typical Maya loincloth, a conventional earflare, and a brimmed hat, in distinction to
the feathered headdresses and ball game
paraphernalia worn by the others. While
this one is narrower, it employs the same
framed, low relief carving as the others.

Most of eight more wooden ones, three
with figural designs, were found in the
Cenote at Chichén Itzá, and four with
nonfigural designs came from the Cenote
Xlacah at Dzibilchaltún (Taschek n.d.).
Shell, bone, ceramic, and copper earflares
are known from burials in Honduras, Guerrero, Veracruz, and the Maya regions, but
only one of these depicts a similarly upside-
down figure; this is a silhouetted limestone
example from a Late Classic burial in the
Maya highlands (Kidder 1942, p. 39a).

Terminal Classic (A.D. 800–900)
Coggins and Ladd n.d.

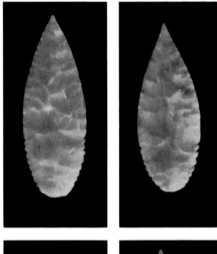

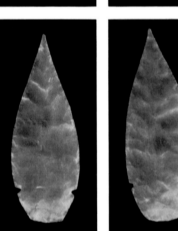

11. Four lanceolate projectile points

White chalcedony; red pigment; hafting
resin
Bifacially flaked
Notched, Peabody Museum
10-4-20/C5291, L. 7.6 cm., Th. 0.4 cm.;
83-42-20/30577, L. 7.4 cm., Th. 0.4 cm.
Serrated, Peabody Museum 10-4-20/C5291
(2), L. 6.7, 7.2 cm., Th. 0.4 cm.

Augustus Le Plongeon found a cylindrical
limestone cache bowl near the head of the
famous Chac Mool statue when he excavated it from the Platform of the Eagles in
the Great Plaza at Chichén Itzá in 1875.
This bowl contained what Le Plongeon believed to be the ashes of the heart of a ruler
named Chac Mool (Great Jaguar Paw),
some shells, and seventeen beautifully
worked projectile points. Thirteen of these,
gifts of Le Plongeon and of his patron,
Stephen Salisbury, are now in the Peabody
Museum. Ten of the points (including
seven in the Peabody Museum) are chalcedony like these, flaked to a delicate tapering form, with two notches or with ser-

rations near the bases of the points where
traces of dark resin remain. The resin suggests the points were once hafted, although
there is no other evidence of functional use.
Red pigment, apparently under the resin,
may indicate a ceremonial nature for the
hafting process itself. (See also nos. 105,
106.)

Serrated lanceolate flint points were included in the large cache excavated from
the Adoratorio in front of the Palace of the
Governors at Uxmal (Ruz Lhuillier 1954,
p. 63, pl. 28). This is a low, four-stairway
structure like the Platform of the Eagles,
but the Uxmal cache includes many Terminal Classic objects and is probably somewhat earlier than the Chichén offering.

Early Postclassic (A.D. 900–1100)
Salisbury 1877, p. 74, facing plate;
Proskouriakoff 1962b, fig. 53f.; Sheets,
Ladd, and Bathgate n.d.

12. Slate Ware tripod cylinder from Mérida

Fired brown-slipped clay
Hand built; rim incision; broken; partially restored
Peabody Museum 12-77-20/C6928,
H. 16.0 cm., Rim D. 12.0 cm.

Edward H. Thompson found this nubbin-footed Puuc Slate Ware cylinder in "a grave in an ancient mound at Tiho." Tiho was the original Maya name for Mérida, capital of Yucatán. The town was renamed "Mérida" because its "superb buildings" are said to have reminded the conquistadores of Roman ruins at Mérida, Spain (Tozzer, ed. 1941, p. 174, n. 909). The structures of ancient Tiho were transformed into the masonry of the modern city, unlike those of Chichén Itzá, far from the center of Colonial activity and power.

Terminal Classic–Early Postclassic (A.D. 800–1000)

13. Black-on-slate tripod plate

Fired buff/gray-slipped clay; post-fire burned organic paint
Hand built
Peabody Museum 24-42-20/C9727,
H. 7.2 cm., D. 26.7 cm.

With its "trickle" decoration, this Sacalum Black-on-slate tripod plate with slab feet is typical of ceremonial pottery of the Puuc region and as far north as Dzibilchaltún (Andrews and Andrews 1980, fig. 248b) between about A.D. 800 and 1000, but Edward H. Thompson no longer knew its provenience when he presented it to the Peabody Museum. Six splotches were placed around the rim of the plate and a goggle-eyed face, possibly Tlaloc, was cursively drawn in the center. This black paint was a runny organic substance that was charred in a final, post-fire phase of manufacture.

Terminal Classic–Early Postclassic (A.D. 800–1000)
Brainerd 1958, fig. 47c

The Early Phase of Sacred Cenote Ritual: Part I

This group of offerings to the Cenote reflects the initial, ninth-century period of foreign presence at Chichén Itzá, when at Uxmal and elsewhere in northern Yucatán objects like those in the first group (nos. 1–13) were being offered in caches and burials. Many of these offerings relate directly to the imagery of the reliefs and paintings in the structures of the Great Ball Court and particularly in the Upper Temple of the Jaguars, which was probably completed near A.D. 850. Victorious Central Mexican warriors, known as "Toltec," and a subordinated northern Maya elite are shown pictorially on these offerings, or represented by elements of their regalia.

At this time sheet gold and cast gold alloy figurines were imported to Chichén Itzá from lower Central America. Since gold played no known role in Maya culture, these exotic goods, previously unknown in Yucatán, must have been symbolically identified with the new foreign overlords whose militaristic expansion involved long distance trade. Carved Maya jades brought, or sent, to Chichén Itzá from the southern Maya lowlands were probably emblematic of western Maya allies, or subjects, of the new Toltec dominion. Although domestic pottery also found its way into the Cenote in this early phase, elite offerings, like the carved jade, were probably made (and broken) in homage and perhaps in fealty to the foreign warriors who cast in their own weapons and most precious trade goods.

Figure 5. Reliefs, center, west wall, Lower Temple of the Jaguars. From Maudslay 1889–1902, vol. 3, pls. 49, 50.

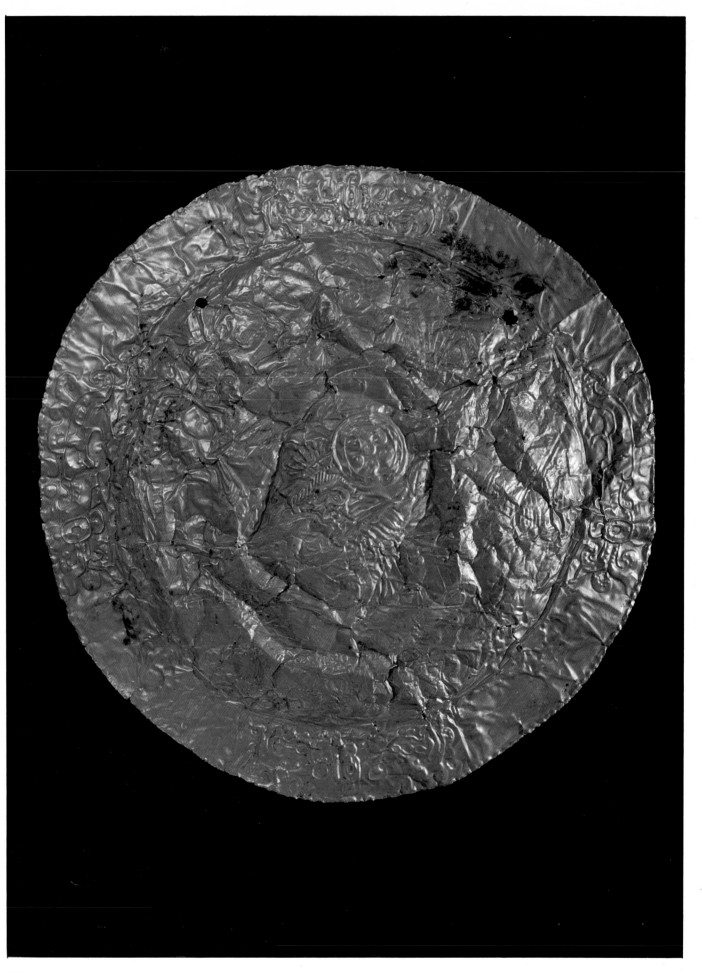

14. Disc F

Sheet gold; black coating
Hammered; cut, embossed, two
perforations; crumpled; partially reflattened
Peabody Museum 10-71-20/C10047,
D. 20.7 cm.

This scene might be the prelude to the
heart sacrifice on Disc H (no. 25); the
Toltec warrior and his assistant appear to be
the same people (figs. 6, 7). Here the warrior with a mustache and three nose beads
is dressed for battle. He wears the characteristic Toltec spangled headband with a
crest of feathers above and a diving bird at
the front, like figures in the reliefs in the
Lower Temple of the Jaguars (fig. 5) and
like the Atlantean column warriors at Tula;
also like the latter he wears a tied belt and
folded cloth ties at the calves (Acosta 1961).
However, this warrior differs from all of
them in carrying a round shield emblazoned with a heraldic device composed of
seven crescents framed by a chevron band.
Shields with crescents prominently adorned
the facades of the early temple beneath the
Castillo and of the Upper Temple of the Jaguars (Marquina 1964, pls. 263, 267). Such a
shield is also carried by a feathered serpent
captain depicted in the murals of the Upper
Temple of the Jaguars (fig. 19), and ten
sheet gold crescents were found in the
Cenote (no. 15). This warrior is about to
throw a spear with a spearthrower held in
his left hand and behind his back. This unusual position conforms to the menacing
left-handed position of the personified
planet Venus on pp. 46–50 of the Dresden
Codex (J. E. S. Thompson 1972); this may
be a typically Toltec identification with the
militant Venus, as in the cycle of wall paintings in the Upper Temple of the Jaguars
(figs. 17–20). In this connection it is interesting to note that the Yucatec Maya word
for "left-handed" (*ts'ik*) can mean both "valiant" and "sinister" (Barrera Vásquez 1980).
However, such left-handedness may simply
be a compositional device that places the
principal character on the dominant right
side of the scene, while displaying his
shield. The warrior on Disc F wears a single
large bell on his left calf and has a collar of
long beads with angled ends like spiral obsidian ones that were found in the Cenote
(no. 18). Behind him an attendant holds a
fur-covered spearthrower, or atlatl, in his
right hand and two darts or spears in his
left. He wears a headband decorated with
perforated discs and a feather cape like the
similarly placed figure on Disc H.

The two defeated Maya await their fate.
Fallen and wounded, the centrally placed
one tries to pull a spear from his back with
his right hand while holding his own bro-

Figure 6. Gold Disc F. From S. K. Lothrop 1952, fig. 34.

ken spear in the left. He and his companion
wear Maya nose bars and have feathered
back shields, as does the Maya victim on
Disc L (no. 98). The standing Maya holds a
spear, apparently of Mexican type, turned
backward under his right arm in a gesture
of submission, while returning it to the man
who has just hurled it at him.

In the sky above, a coiling, open-jawed
Cloud Serpent (with scrolls on its body)
monitors the scene as on Disc H, but without a sky warrior. Below there is a Maya
device signifying the underworld, and four
Maya emblems frame the scene. At the two
sides of this small cosmos there are profile,
lower-jawless serpentine heads; at the top
and bottom twin skeletal Long Nose Heads
face away from each other, sharing a single
earflare.

In view of the tutelary Cloud Serpent and
the facial hair, this disc may exalt the exploits of the same mustached Toltec who is
depicted on Disc H. The Cloud Serpent
might possibly be emblematic of a warrior
from the Central Mexican site of Xochi-

calco, where such serpents are of prime
symbolic importance (Marquina 1964,
pls. 40–43), or this might even portray the
mythical Mixcoatl (Cloud Serpent), of
Xochicalco ancestry, who as father of
Quetzalcoatl (Feathered Serpent) was described in Toltec history as co-conqueror of
Maya lands (Kelley 1983, pp. 168–171).

This disc is, however, Maya in world view
and execution. From its convex form it is
clear that some of these crushed discs were
not originally flat; all may have been
mounted on a wooden backing to protect
the thin embossed gold. They were probably worn as pectorals.

Terminal Classic (A.D. 800–900).
S. K. Lothrop 1952, figs. 10f, 34, pp. 49 ff.;
Tozzer 1930, fig. 7; 1957, figs. 529f, o, 681f;
Willard 1941, facing p. 56; Morley 1946,
fig. 57a; Haberland 1953; Marquina 1964,
fig. 33; Wardwell 1968, no. 122; Cohodas
1978a, fig. 104; Ruz Lhuillier 1979, p. 269;
Piña Chan 1980, fig. 90

15. Five crescents

Sheet gold
Hammered; cut
Peabody Museum 10-71-20/C7686A–E,
D. 3.6–3.7 cm., Th. 0.03 cm.

Crescents are shown as heraldic devices on shields at Chichén Itzá (see no. 14, figs. 6, 19) and on the skirt of a Maya (?) dignitary in the lowest register of the Lower Temple of the Jaguars (Tozzer 1957, fig. 622).

Edward H. Thompson found ten gold crescents in the Cenote (four of them were presented in 1959 to Mexico), and at least one more came from the 1967 Mexican expedition (Ediger 1971, color pl. 18).

Like the sheet gold rings (no. 38), these crescents were made uniformly thin, small accidental blobs of melted gold remain on the surface, and they were similarly cut out with a tool that left scratches paralleling the edges.

Terminal Classic–Early Postclassic (A.D. 800–1000)
S. K. Lothrop 1952, p. 67, fig. 51a

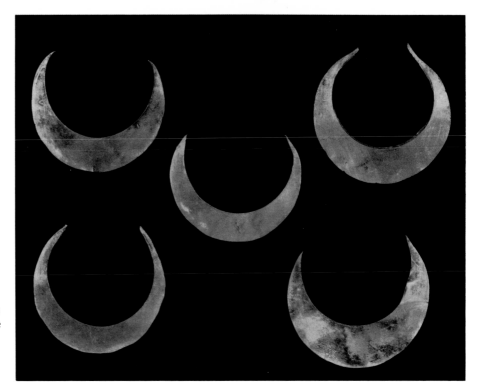

16. Three nose buttons

Jadeite
Small perforations
Peabody Museum 10-70-20/C6080,
H. 1.5 cm., D. 1.9 cm.; 10-71-20/C6424,
H. 1.5 cm., D. 1.0 cm.; 10-71-20/C6432,
H. 0.8 cm., D. 1.2 cm.

At Chichén Itzá nose buttons indicate a Toltec affiliation, in distinction to the more Maya nose bar, as can be seen on Discs F and H (nos. 14, 25). Emissaries from several highland Guatemalan groups that had emigrated to Tula traveled to Chichén Itzá to receive their royal insignia from Naxcit, ruler of that northern capital. This ceremony included bestowing titles and costumes and piercing their noses, probably for nose buttons (Recinos and Goetz, trans. 1953, p. 64). Nose piercing of the Mixtec noble Eight Deer is depicted in the Codex Nuttall as well (Nuttall, ed. 1902, p. 52).

Many of the nose buttons found in the Cenote came in pairs. They were worn one, or sometimes two or three, on a side, probably over the wing or through the side of the nose. The perforations served to hold them in place.

Jade nose buttons were often cut down from spherical and cylindrical beads.

Terminal Classic–Early Postclassic (A.D. 800–1100)
Proskouriakoff 1974, p. 29, pl. 28b

17. Carved nose button

Jadeite, bright to olive green
Four tiny perforations
Peabody Museum 10-71-20/C6641,
H. 1.6 cm., D. 2.1 cm.

This is one of a pair of nose beads carved with open-mouthed simian faces. The perforation through the monkey's mouth presumably secured it after the uncarved side was inserted through a slit in the side of the nose, as on the sacrificer on Disc H (no. 25), and the warrior on the door jamb of the Upper Temple of the Jaguars (fig. 19).

Terminal Classic–Early Postclassic (A.D. 800–1000)
Proskouriakoff 1974, p. 87, pl. 47a:IX

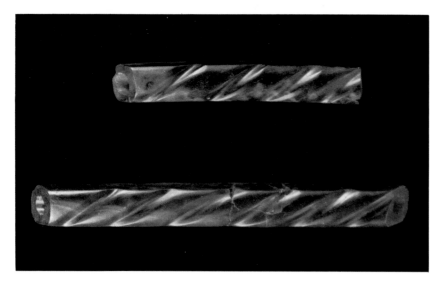

18. Two spiral tubular beads

Obsidian, gray, green; burned
Drilled, ground, polished; broken
Peabody Museum 07-7-20/C5034,
L. 9.4 cm., D. 1.0 cm., Hole D. 0.4 cm.;
10-70-20/C6037, D. 1.0 cm., Hole D.
0.4 cm.

The spiral obsidian beads from the Cenote
all have one or two beveled ends and at
least one flattened side in order to fit into
angular collar assemblages like the one
worn by the bearded warrior on gold Disc F
(no. 14, fig. 6).

Such specialized beads are known from
only four, widely separated sites, in Guerrero, Central Mexico, western Guatemala
(Woodbury and Trik 1953, p. 241), and
Chichén Itzá, where five complete gray
beads and forty-eight fragments of gray and
green beads were found in the Cenote. Yet
they are all alike in form and craftsman-
ship, and all were associated with Early
Postclassic objects. It is likely that they
were made in Central Mexico, since they
are so much alike and include both gray
and green obsidian—the latter believed to
come from Pachuca, Hidalgo.

The Chichén Itzá beads were burned and
most were broken before they were thrown
into the Cenote. The green obsidian bead is
warped (?) and broken from burning and
has red iron oxide splotches caused by the
heat.

The beads may have been made from
cores left by hollow drills. The cores would
have been drilled longitudinally, then the
tubular beads cut to size and the spiral
grooves ground, perhaps with abrasive-
coated string.

Early Postclassic (A.D. 800–1000)
Proskouriakoff 1962b, fig. 53j; Moholy-Nagy
and Ladd, n.d.

19. Bell with neck

Tumbaga
Cast; crushed
Peabody Museum 10-71-20/C7664,
H. 3.5 cm.

The bells that were thrown into the Cenote
in the Early Phase were probably worn
by the Toltec warrior elite (as on Disc F,
no. 14), and some of the earliest ones, perhaps before cast copper was available in
Mesoamerica, were imported from lower
Central America where metal casting was
more advanced. Jar-shaped bells like this,
with tubular necks (possibly to insert a
handle, or to affix to a headdress) are
characteristic of the Cocle region of Panama,
but many have been found near Guapiles in
the Atlantic watershed of Costa Rica—the
most likely source for this one. The perforation of the neck is not a Cocle feature and
suggests the kind of adaptation, or local
modification of a foreign prototype, that can
be seen in the "Darien" pendant, which also
came from Costa Rica (no. 48).

The metal postulated to have been imported to Chichén Itzá from the south in
the Early Phase is most, if not all, made of
tumbaga, a copper/gold alloy, and was cast
by the lost-wax process (see no. 44).

Terminal Classic (A.D. 800–900)
S. K. Lothrop 1952, pp. 104, 105, figs. 108,
109

20. Atlatl (dart-thrower)

Wood; dark coating; paraffin impregnated
Carved; broken, cracked
Peabody Museum 10-71-20/C6736,
L. 53.5 cm., W. 3.7 cm.

Although they were called *hul che* in
Yucatec Maya, the Nahuatl word *atlatl* is
generally used to describe a dart-thrower. It
was the characteristic weapon and insignia
of the Toltec and of warriors from Central
Mexico who came both before and after
them. However, the Toltec had a unique
multiple weapon assemblage which they
are shown carrying on the walls and columns of Chichén Itzá and Tula (figs. 5,
6, 19; Tozzer 1957, pp. 158–161,
figs. 534–575).

The Toltec weapon assemblage consisted
of a fur-covered atlatl held in the right
hand, with a sheaf of darts (no. 21) and a
fending stick (no. 24) held in the left.

The Toltec apparently threw their
weapons into the Cenote, where Edward H.
Thompson found parts of this characteristic
assemblage, including nine functional atlatls. This one is the most complete; only
the finger holes were broken off and the
shaft partially broken, probably in the offering ritual. It is well-made, sturdy, and
weighted toward the hook end. There is no
indication, however, of how the lobed fur
pieces, which usually covered the shaft
from finger holes to hook, might have
been attached; nor indeed what their purpose was.

Tlaloc, the Mexican rain and storm god,
used the atlatl to hurl serpentine lightning
bolts, and the Sun and Venus to send dangerous rays upon the earth. The weapon
represented masculinity, military prowess,
and an association with celestial deities.
These were attitudes and prerogatives
claimed by the intrusive Toltec, who associated themselves with Venus, with the Sun
and its messenger eagles, and with the
plumed celestial serpent, all of which could
descend dangerously or hurl perilous rays
toward the earth.

An early date is postulated for these
weapons in the Cenote because there is no
evidence that the ritual concerns of the militaristic Toltec played any role in Cenote
ceremony after about A.D. 1150, when the
northern Toltec capital at Tula had declined.

Terminal Classic–Early Postclassic (A.D.
800–1150)
Coggins and Ladd n.d.; Willard 1926,
facing p. 125

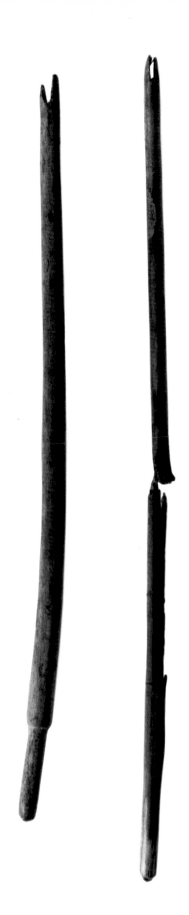

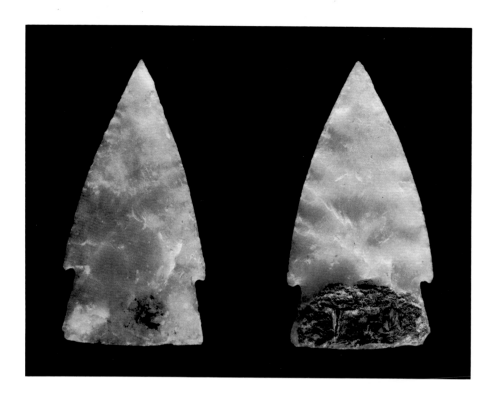

21. Two foreshafts

Wood; dark coating; copal; paraffin
impregnated
Carved; fire hardened; cut, broken
Peabody Museum 10-71-20/C6748,
L. 40.5 cm.; 10-71-20/C6749 (2),
Est. L. 45.0 cm.

Projectile points would have been hafted in
the notches of these foreshafts, secured by
resin and with fiber for which evidence remains in parallel lines below the notches.
The proximal ends of the foreshafts, which
were fire hardened, fit into hollow cane
shafts that were directly propelled by an
atlatl. Edward H. Thompson reported that
some darts were recovered with fine white
stone points still in place (see no. 22).
  These foreshafts are of two different
types; one sturdy and broken only at the
notch, which still held a point when found,
the other lightweight and cut, with splin-
tered ends that had been thrust into copal
before being offered. The two pieces of
lighter-weight shaft may not belong together, but others in the collection suggest
this relationship. They are probably of later
date than the heavier one and might even
be arrow shafts.
  Foreshafts are not depicted with extension shafts as part of the Toltec weapon
assemblage, but the fine chalcedony points
(no. 22) with which some were associated
are Early Postclassic in date.

Postclassic (A.D. 900–1539)
Coggins and Ladd n.d.

22. Two corner-notched projectile points

White chalcedony; hafting resin
Bifacially flaked
Peabody Museum 10-56-20/C5932,
19-37-20/C9253, both L. 5.4 cm., W.
2.9 cm., Th. 0.3 cm.

Twenty-nine whole and three fragments of
fine white chalcedony projectile points were
dredged from the Cenote by Edward H.
Thompson. Eighteen of these retain hafting
resin and red pigment, including one that
was still in the notch of a wooden foreshaft
(see no. 21). It is likely these unburned
points were for use with an atlatl, or dart-
thrower, and that they were all hafted when
they were thrown into the Cenote—perhaps
as part of the offering of the characteristic
Toltec weapon assemblage of atlatl, darts,
and fending stick (see figs. 5–7, 19)—all of
which are represented in the Cenote collection (see nos. 20, 21, 24). The fine, identical
workmanship in this group of points suggests specialized manufacture, and the
presence of examples in a cache at Mata-
capán, Veracruz (Valenzuela 1945, fig. 38)
indicates more than local use and an Early
Postclassic date.

Early Postclassic (A.D. 800–1100)
Sheets, Ladd, and Bathgate n.d.; Kidder
1947, p. 9, fig. 3d; S. K. Lothrop 1952, p. 42,
fig. 27; Tozzer 1957, fig. 504; Proskouriakoff
1962b, fig. 53f; Piña Chan 1980, fig. 108

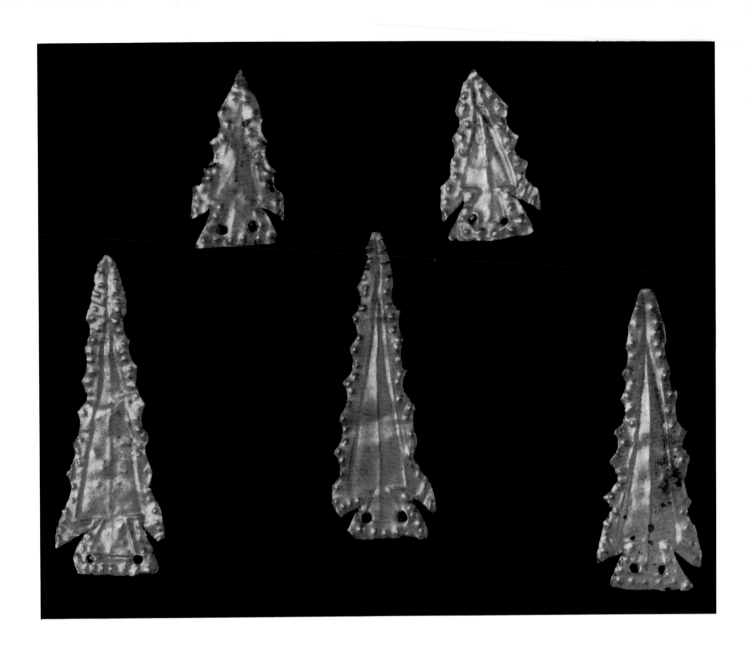

23. Five effigy projectile points

Sheet gold
Hammered; cut, embossed, perforated
Peabody Museum 10-71-20/C7674A,
L. 4.2 cm.; 10-71-20/C7674B, L. 4.0 cm.;
10-71-20/C7674C, L. 4.0 cm.;
10-71-20/C7674D, L. 2.4 cm.;
10-71-20/C7674E, L. 2.2 cm.

Thirteen gold, corner-notched projectile points, six long and seven short, came from the Cenote (three were presented to Mexico in 1959). The edges of the points were cut with a wavy outline, and dots were embossed along the edges to suggest flaked stone. These very thin metal effigies may have been part of necklaces or, more likely, were sewn on a backing where they would have hung with points down.

Terminal Classic–Early Postclassic (A.D. 800–1100)
S. K. Lothrop 1952, p. 67, fig. 51c

24. Five fragments of two fending sticks

Wood; yellow paint (?); dark coating; paraffin impregnated
Carved, grooved; cut, broken; warped; partially restored
Peabody Museum 10-71-20/C6743 (5), Est. L. 47.0 cm., Th. 1.5 cm.

Edward H. Thompson and others noticed that these flat, curved and pointed, striated objects from the Cenote resembled those carried by Toltec warriors (figs. 17–20). But there has been little agreement as to their purpose. They are an integral part of the characteristic Toltec weapon assemblage, carried in the left hand, with the darts, and they replace shields. Usually these weapons are called "fending sticks," suggesting that they may have intercepted darts and spears. But it seems likely that they were parrying sticks as well, and they may also have been thrown, as similar ones have been reported used to kill small game (Heizer 1942, p. 50). The Toltec were above all fearsome warriors, and they had the best weaponry their technology and training could provide. These indispensable sticks must have been very effective.

Excavation in the U.S. Southwest has found that such objects are associated there with atlatls, as they are in the portraiture of the reliefs at Chichén Itzá. However, they disappear with the introduction of the bow and arrow, which in Yucatán apparently occurred in Middle Postclassic times, after the decline of the Toltec and of Chichén Itzá (Proskouriakoff 1962b, p. 360). There are cut fragments of six to eight fending sticks in the Peabody Museum Cenote collection. None is intact. They are all flat and slightly curved, with longitudinal grooves on both sides. These are constant identifying traits everywhere they are found, although the number of grooves varies, from three to four in the Southwest to as many as twelve on the Cenote examples. The purpose of the grooves is unknown. Possibly they made the wood more flexible, without weakening it.

The two narrow end pieces here belong to one stick and the three wider ones to another, if indeed three different sticks are not represented. These pieces appear to have been painted or stained yellow; fending sticks are often shown as yellow on the painted columns of the Temple of the Warriors complex (Morris, Charlot, and Morris 1931).

Terminal Classic—Early Postclassic (A.D. 800–1100)
Coggins and Ladd n.d.; Tozzer 1957, pp. 160–161

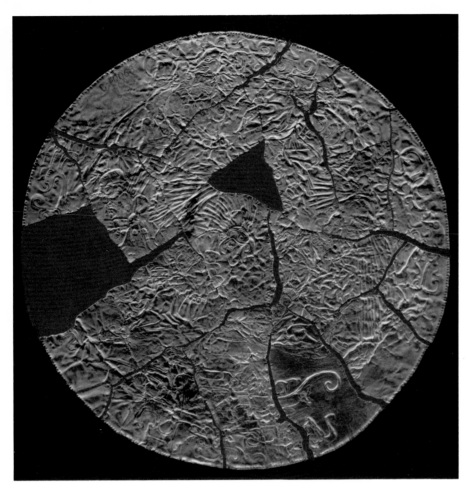

25. Disc H

Sheet gold
Hammered, cut; embossed,
two perforations; torn, crumpled;
partially reflattened
Peabody Museum 10-71-20/C10068,
D. 22.6 cm.

This heart sacrifice of a Maya captive by a Toltec wearing an eagle headdress takes place in a Maya world as defined by four bordering skeletal heads entwined with waterlilies (fig. 7)—an act symbolic of the raptorial power of the intrusive northern Toltec at Maya Chichén Itzá. Within the scene the earth is similarly designated as Maya by a long-snouted head with crossed bands in its eye. These motifs are worked in the sinuous calligraphic style of the vocabulary of Maya allegorical form.

In the sky a Cloud Serpent (outlined by shell/scrolls) disgorges an armed figure which descends upon the scene. This celestial warrior wears Toltec regalia, including the characteristic pectoral (a stylized butterfly). He carries a fur-covered atlatl in his right hand and wears ruffs on the extended right arm. In his left hand he holds darts beneath the feather shoulder cape worn only over the left arm by warriors portrayed in the Lower and Upper Temples of the Jaguars (figs. 5, 19), and by the Atlanteans at Tula. His squared hat, with rows of decorative elements, is among the most characteristic parts of this uniform; other portrayals show this to be a headband tied at the back, probably sewn with plaques or spangles (Acosta 1961). Various elements of the uniform are also worn by the dominant protagonists below.

The eagle sacrificer himself signifies the descending bird of prey as he grasps the freshly extracted heart of his victim in his right hand, with a sacrificial knife in his left (see no. 26). Although left-handedness is unusual in portraits, two other sacrificers at Chichén Itzá also hold the knife in their left hand (Tozzer 1957, figs. 392, 395); it may have been an aspect of the ritual. Within the eagle helmet the sacrificer's features are not Maya; he has an aquiline nose with nose beads and a mustache like the left-handed warrior on Disc F (no. 14; fig. 6), and like the man on Disc F he has a tutelary Cloud Serpent. He wears four bells at his calf, like numerous gold and copper bells actually thrown into the Cenote.

On the left an attendant holds the eagle man's atlatl and spears and a bunched cloth with flower-like pendants. On the right a feather-caped attendant wearing a spangled headband holds the next sacrificial victim, who looks apprehensive. Four assistants,

Figure 7. Gold Disc H. From S. K. Lothrop 1952, fig. 1.

called Chacs by the Maya, splay the victim over the sacrificial stone—one at each corner of the person, corresponding to each corner of the Maya cosmos. These figures also wear the spangled headbands, flexible back discs, and leg ruffs of the Toltec. One of them looks at you—the witness.

Stylistically the Maya scrolls and masks resemble Terminal Classic southern lowland sculpture, as on Stela 10 at Seibal (A.D. 850), while the theme of a cloud warrior is found at Ucanal and elsewhere contemporaneously (Proskouriakoff 1950, figs. 76a, 77). Some evidence for the interconnectedness of Mesoamerican culture in the Terminal Classic Period and for the eclectic nature of the art is incorporated on this disc in the portrayal of heart sacrifice with an eagle officiant, a ritual that is implied in the reliefs of the South Ball Court at El Tajín, Veracruz, and in the Cloud Serpent, since Cloud Serpents dominate the extant sculptural program at Xochicalco, Morelos (Marquina 1964, pls. 41–43, photos 192–195). If the mustached, left-handed eagle warrior with a tutelary Cloud Serpent is the same person shown, victorious and taking a Maya captive, on Disc F, then this disc may record a specific event in the early history of the conquest of Chichén Itzá.

Terminal Classic (A.D. 800–900)
S. K. Lothrop 1952, pp. 52–55, figs. 1, 10-l; Tozzer 1957, figs. 254, 388a, 393, 529j, k, l, n, p; Covarrubias 1957, fig. 124; Haberland 1953; Marquina 1964, fig. 32; Furst 1964, no. 5; Emmerich 1965, figs. 150, 151; Wardwell 1968, no. 121; Cohodas 1978a, fig. 104; Ruz Lhuillier 1979, p. 270

26. Sacrificial knife

Blade: chert; hafting resin; red pigment; copal
Bifacially flaked; edge wear; broken across; repaired
Handle: wood; dark coating; paraffin impregnated
Carved; split in drying
Peabody Museum 10-71-20/C6755, Total L. 34.5 cm., Est. Biface L. 19.0 cm., W. 7.1 cm.

Two intertwined rattlesnakes form the handle of this knife. The open jaws of one hold the blade while the rattles of the second rest on top of its head. The serpents have reticulated skins and are feathered only around the eye sockets. They most nearly resemble the descending and ascending rattlesnakes of the balustrades of the Caracol at Chichén Itzá (Tozzer 1957, fig. 120). Descending deity figures are found on the handles of later Mixtec knives, perhaps connoting the divine function of knives used for heart sacrifice. In Yucatec Maya such knives are called *u kab ku* "hand or arm of the god" (Tozzer 1957, p. 216).

Nicks along the edges of the blade are probably from sacrificial use (see no. 25) rather than from being thrown into the Cenote because they are covered with traces of copal and red pigment. Snapping off the blade may have been part of its terminal ritual. Edward H. Thompson found the working end of the blade in the first season and the handle in the next, with the proximal end firmly secured by hafting resin, as it still is. This is the only knife Thompson mentioned in his letters to the museum, and its handle was not covered with gold, contrary to a published account (Willard 1926, p. 136). Gold-covered knife handles are, however, reported among the finds of the 1967 Mexican expedition (Piña Chan 1970, p. 51). Thompson described the wooden bodies of the serpents as "quetzal green," the eyes as red with blue pupils, the nostrils and interior of the mouth as red and the teeth as white.

All of the wood from the Cenote is covered to some degree with a black coating. This is most likely a resinous preservative used on wood to protect it from moisture and insect damage, as is the indigenous practice in humid zones today, and may be why so much wood was preserved in the Cenote.

Terminal Classic–Early Postclassic (A.D. 800–1100)
Coggins and Ladd n.d.; Willard 1926, facing p. 140; Follett 1932, fig. 34; Pijoán 1964, fig. 811; Easby and Scott 1970, no. 256; Piña Chan 1980, fig. 108

27. Four pear-shaped bells

Copper
Cast
Peabody Museum 07-7-20/C4947 (analysis no. 61), D. 1.1 cm.; 07-7-20/C4873, D. 1.8 cm.; 07-7-20/C4876 (analysis no. 57), D. 1.8 cm.; 10-70-20/C6004, D. 2.4 cm.

Pear-shaped bells are apparently worn below the knee by the sacrificer on Disc H (fig. 7), while the warrior on Disc F (fig. 6) wears a single large spherical one. These depicted bells, from Terminal Classic–Early Postclassic times, when copper bells are rare archaeologically, may actually have been cast gold or *tumbaga* imported from Costa Rica (see no. 19), and earlier than the copper ones.

Bells of this pear shape are S. K. Lothrop's style D. They vary in having single or double strand suspension loops, with or without a platform, and the bell may or may not have a wire bordering the mouth. The copper of the smallest bell includes tin, antimony, bismuth, lead, silver, gold, iron, and arsenic. Such a complex composition may reflect reworking by an itinerant metalsmith of previously cast, or miscast, metal from many sources, rather than the signature of a specific ore (Bray 1977, p. 393).

The pear-shaped copper bell with a platform, double loop, and wire border (07-7-20/C4876) has the impression of a fine textile on one side.

Postclassic (A.D. 900–1539)
S. K. Lothrop 1952, pp. 88–90, figs. 80–83, table 27; Willard 1926, facing p. 140; Pendergast 1962, p. 527, fig. 5; Spear 1978, fig. 255; Piña Chan 1980, fig. 111

28. Picture plaque

Jadeite, emerald green, mottled with white and black; black coating
Broken; reconstructed
Peabody Museum 10-71-20/C6666, H. 9.3 cm., W. 12.8 cm., Th. 0.5 cm.

Carved in a soft grooved style with little relief that is otherwise unknown, this plaque is extraordinarily thin and has a fine biconical horizontal bore, with three perforations along the top and seventeen spaced around the back edge of the other three sides, so that the plaque could have been invisibly attached to a backing. Although technically unusual, this plaque is recognizably Mexican in motif. A celestial warrior is depicted riding upon a serpent studded with *chalchihuitls* (perforated discs signifying preciousness) and with a feather tail. The warrior wears a star skirt, holds a dart in his left hand and hurls a second dart with the atlatl in his right hand; these weapons may symbolize the dangerous rays that emanate from Venus as Morning Star. Such warriors are depicted in the monumental art of Chichén Itzá and of Tula, where they denote the association between military prowess and celestial bodies which the northerners brought to Chichén and made explicit in their imagery (Tozzer 1957, p. 162). Star warriors riding serpent "boats" like this are shown attacking a town in the murals of the Upper Temple of the Jaguars (fig. 18). At the top of the headdress a glyphic form is used; this may be the bar that indicates "five" in Zapotec inscriptions, as on two carved beads which are also from the Cenote (Proskouriakoff 1974, fig. 15). The presence of this glyphic element suggests a relationship with Oaxaca that may also be noted in the similarity of cached objects in the two places (See nos. 7, 8, 57, 58, 60), and in the architectural style of the Castillo (Kubler 1961, p. 55). A black coating once covered this plaque, as it does other jade and gold pieces from the Cenote; this may be soot from burning copal.

Terminal Classic (A.D. 800–900)
Proskouriakoff 1974, p. 192, color pl. 2a, pl. 78a; 1978, p. 62; Tozzer 1957, fig. 131; Covarrubias 1957, fig. 118; Rands 1965, fig. 45

29. Annular picture plaque

Jadeite, speckled bright green to white/
gray; black discoloration
Two suspension holes, two small
perforations; burned, shattered;
reconstructed
Peabody Museum 10-71-20/C6677,
H. 10.5 cm., W. 12.3 cm., Th. 0.3–1.2 cm.

There were three of these rings in the collection (one was presented to Mexico in
1976). Each has a discontinuous framed
pictorial field, with a plain area at the top
serving to separate two elevated seated figures who look down upon a captive/victim.
The figure on the right, seated directly on a
dais, is dressed as a Mexican warrior. He
has a headband with four feathers above, a
"butterfly" pectoral on his chest, and a
fending stick in his left hand (see no. 24).
On the left, another Mexican is recognizable by his arm and leg ruffs and fending
stick. He points to the bound captive, who
looks up in response. The captive is a man
of some importance who still wears his jade
and feather backdress. The other two rings
show sacrificial victims in this location, so it
is likely this man is intended for sacrifice.
The jade worn by such important victims
may well have ended up in the Cenote,
whether or not the body did.

The low, smoothly rounded relief of this
carving probably represents a style found at
Chichén Itzá, where Mexican influences
led to the replacement of scrolls by frets and
of long graceful feathers by stubbier ones.

Terminal Classic (A.D. 800–900)
Proskouriakoff 1974, p. 88, color pl. 2b,
pl. 48a:2; Tozzer 1957, fig. 547; Kelemen
1969, pl. 244b; Rands 1965, fig. 24

30. Carved plaque

Jadeite, bright, speckled green, gray, black
Horizontal bore
Peabody Museum 10-71-20/C6665,
H. 7.0 cm., W. 7.9 cm., Th. 0.8 cm.

A great bird, possibly a Toltec eagle, with a
double-drilled, feathered eye and a curved
beak, dominates this plaque. From the open
beak emerges a Maya head delineated in a
bold northern Maya style that combines
Early Classic nose and mouth conventions
(see no. 172) with the Terminal Classic
double-drilled bird eye and the use of arc
drilling. Poor quality stone may have been
cut from the irregular, unsmoothed notch
below the beak.

Terminal Classic–Early Postclassic (A.D.
800–1000)
Proskouriakoff 1974, p. 158, pl. 64b:1;
Tozzer 1957, p. 162, fig. 589

31. Tripod vessel

Tecali (calcite); traces of cinnabar red, black, gray, blue-green pigments on stucco; paraffin fill
Ground, polished; broken; partially restored twice
Peabody Museum 07-7-20/C4749,
H. 18.9 cm., Rim D. 19.4 cm.

Remarkable for its translucency, tecali is a calcitic stone from the mountains of Puebla and northern Oaxaca, most widely used in Postclassic times.

This vessel from the Cenote resembles one excavated from a cache that preceded the construction of the Pyramid of the Plumed Serpent at Xochicalco, Morelos, in its material, in its form, and in having had a polychrome painted panel on one side, although the Xochicalco vessel depicts a diving bird (Sáenz 1963, pl. 3). Painted directly on the stone, this scene had a wide blue-green framing border, with a narrower cinnabar red band outside, and the background may also have been red. The remaining figural design, on the lower right, is painted in a black line so fine that it might have been accomplished with a single hair. Most of a reddish-brown-skinned figure is visible sitting, or crouching, with his left knee up. He wears a yellow necklace, cuff, and upper armband, ruffs at his knee and ankle, and a flexible back disc. This lower right location, the figure's position, and his Toltec ruffs and back disc resemble the nearer right-hand "Chac," or sacrificial assistant, in the scene of human sacrifice on Disc H (no. 25). This may have been another such depiction, although the blue/gray corporeal form in front of this figure, toward which he reaches with his cuffed right arm, is not quite identifiable.

A carved panel-decorated tecali pedestal vessel and five undecorated tecali tripod vessels were excavated from a rich cache in the Adoratorio in front of the Palace of the Governor at Uxmal (Ruz Lhuillier 1954, p. 62); as at Xochicalco, these represent a facet of the contemporary caching activities postulated for Terminal Classic Chichén Itzá.

Terminal Classic (A.D. 800–900)
Moholy-Nagy and Ladd n.d.

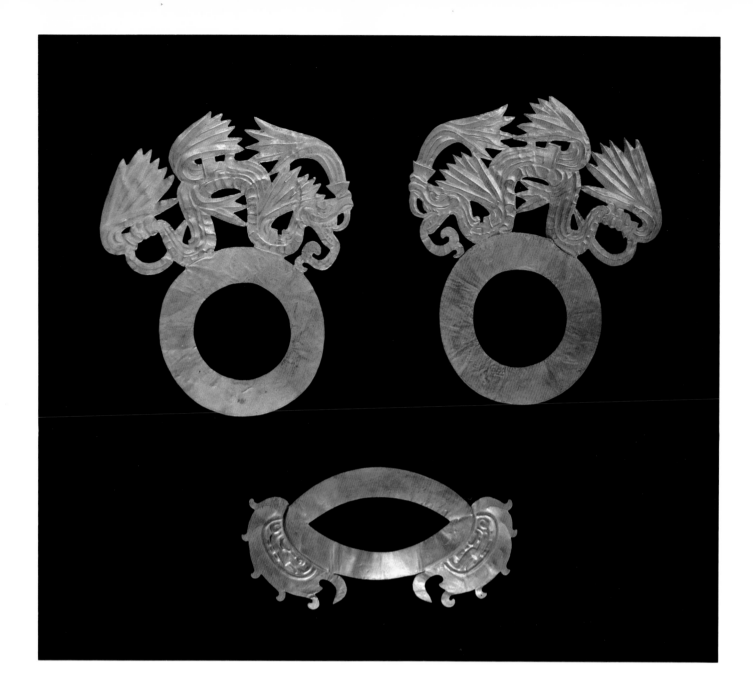

32. Three face ornaments

Sheet gold; traces of dark resinous material, red pigment
Hammered; cut, embossed; one serpent broken from ring
Eyepieces: Peabody Museum
10-71-20/C7679, H. 16.0 cm.
Mouthpiece: Peabody Museum
10-71-20/C7678, W. 14.8 cm.

Flamboyant feathered rattlesnakes with long venom-injecting fangs and forked tongues decorate these eyepieces with Central Mexican sky imagery, while the mouthpiece below has two cartouches that refer to the underworld by depicting profile

serpentine heads that lack lower jaws. As on Discs F and H (nos. 14, 25), underworld, or locational, imagery is Maya while celestial references are Mexican; feathered serpents were the principal emblem of the intrusive Toltec warrior elite, which came from Central Mexico.

These three elements may actually have been worn by the individual represented wearing such objects in the Lower and Upper Temples of the Jaguars at Chichén Itzá (figs. 5, 17). These figures are located on the east/west axis of each temple, surrounded by flames, within the protective coils of a feathered serpent, and they wear plain gold (?) discs on the head and chest (see no. 33).

While the sheet gold from which these ornaments were made was imported from

lower Central America, the design was surely embossed and the striking feather tracery cut out at Chichén Itzá. Vestiges of the offering ceremony, or of the original function of these mask elements, remain in traces of a dark resinous material and of bright red pigment on the back of the eyepieces.

Terminal Classic (A.D. 800–900)
S. K. Lothrop 1952, pp. 68–72, figs. 54, 55; Willard 1941, facing p. 56; Morley 1946, pl. 94c; Tozzer 1957, p. 114, figs. 213, 216; Covarrubias 1957, fig. 123; Emmerich 1965, fig. 153; Kelemen 1969, 2:281, pl. 234b; Coggins 1974, no. 209; Cohodas 1978a, fig. 100

33. Plain disc

Sheet gold; black coating
Hammered, cut; embossed; two
perforations; crumpled, folded, burned;
reflattened
Peabody Museum 10-71-20/C10051, D. 12.3
cm.

Three such discs are worn by the iconic
figure emanating flames in the reliefs of the
Lower Temple of the Jaguars (fig. 5) and
two by his counterpart in the Upper Temple
of the Jaguars (fig. 19); both also wear
mouth and eyepieces like the gold set found
in the Cenote (no. 32).

This plain disc has a border marked by an
embossed groove and two roughly gouged
suspension holes. Before it was offered to
the Cenote it was crumpled, then folded in
half toward the back, over a square of cloth
that protected the surface from a black,
smoky (?) deposit; finally the folded disc
was folded again in the opposite direction,
bringing the front surfaces together. Flow
patterns are evident in the sooty (?) and
iridescent coating on both sides.

Four gold discs from the Cenote were
analyzed; they contained 2–3 percent silver
and no copper. Samuel K. Lothrop believes
they came, as blanks, from the north coast
of Veraguas, Panama, where Columbus saw
such discs worn. Abundant evidence for an
active trade between Yucatán and the Caribbean coast of lower Central America is
present in the large collection of cast gold
and *tumbaga* found in the Cenote and included in this exhibition. The lowland Maya
were never goldsmiths, although they did
emboss and cut imported sheet gold.

Terminal Classic–Early Postclassic (A.D.
800–1100)
S. K. Lothrop 1952, pp. 28, 29, fig. 9b,
table 18

34. Two-sided god mask

Jadeite, opaque light green
Open-work; remains of ten perforations;
broken; partially reconstructed
Peabody Museum 10-71-20/C6683,
H. 9.1 cm., W. 4.6 cm., Th. 0.3 cm.

This thin, delicately carved jade device is
one of many shattered ones in the collection, of which three have been partially
reconstructed. Five of these clearly depict a
Long Nose Head, four with the scroll eye
indicative of underworld affiliation; three
still with crossed band medallions, two with
beards, and all with the raised fillet border
that signifies a Maya allegorical form. Such
two-faced objects were usually worn projecting from a headdress where they could
be seen from both sides (E. Easby 1964,
fig. 1a, b), and small beads were attached
at the perforations—as can be seen on
Maya lowland sculpture from early-eighth-
century portraits at Palenque to mid-ninth-
century ones at Seibal (Schele 1974, fig. 10;
Proskouriakoff 1950, fig. 77). The god mask
worn by the Mayoid captain in the Upper
Temple of the Jaguars at Chichén Itzá is
probably contemporary with the Seibal
monuments (fig. 19).

This Long Nose Head is "the Jester God,"
a personification of dynastic legitimacy and
an important element of Maya ruler por-

traiture in Late Classic times. However, the
figure that leans from the forehead cartouche, elbows resting on the upturned
snout of the Long Nose Head, is not found
on the Jester Gods on monuments. The figure has heavy, non-Maya features like those
on late Seibal stelae, and in its grim expres-
sion it resembles Escuintla sculpture (see
no. 39); his spangled headband suggests
the costume of Toltec warriors on the jambs
of the Upper Temple of the Jaguars (fig. 19)
and in the conquest and sacrificial scenes
on the gold discs from the Cenote (nos. 14,
25). Two-sided jade carvings are rare, as is
open-work like this which was achieved by
a combination of drilling and cord-sawing.

Terminal Classic (A.D. 750–900)
Proskouriakoff 1974, p. 157, color pl. 1d,
pl. 63b:5; E. Easby 1964, pp. 66, 71, fig. 6d;
Rands 1965, fig. 28

35. Two-sided god mask, fragment

Jadeite, pale gray-green, bright green
Horizontal bore; broken; partially reconstructed
Peabody Museum 63-32-20/21995,
H. 5.9 cm., W. 4.1 cm., Th. 0.7 cm.

This head emerges from the front of the "jester cap" of a Long Nose Head plaque, or "Jester God," like no. 34. But this two-faced device is much thicker, and the head has a frontal plane as well as the two sides, which differ from each other in detail; one has a standard double-drilled earflare, while the other ear is conventionalized like those of the figure in no. 34. At the center of the forehead there is a tassel, or hair brought forward through a flare, as is common on jade plaques (see nos. 51, 62).

Terminal Classic (A.D. 750–900)
Proskouriakoff 1974, p. 157, color pl. 1f, pl. 63a

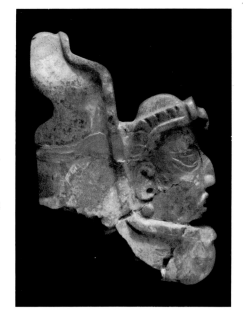

36. Hat/bowl

Sheet gold
Hammered, cut, thirty perforations
Peabody Museum 10-71-20/C10073,
Depth 8.0–9.0 cm., D. 28.2 cm.

Samuel K. Lothrop suggests that this extraordinary bowl-like object was the golden cap of an idol which might also have worn the gold mouth and eyepieces (no. 32), although no such hat is represented at Chichén Itzá, or elsewhere. It is probably too fragile to have been a functional bowl, and there is no indication of wear on the bottom. A shallow groove below the rim holes on the interior suggests the sharp edge of a circular band, or framework that could have supported the weight of the flexible metal if it was a cap; it weighs seventeen ounces (482.0 grams).

The holes (twenty-five small ones at the rim, plus two medium and three large in the wall) were all pierced from the outside, suggesting that the exterior was more visible. Small hammer marks can be seen on both surfaces.

Terminal Classic–Early Postclassic (A.D. 800–1000)
S. K. Lothrop 1952, pp. 67–69, fig. 54, table 36

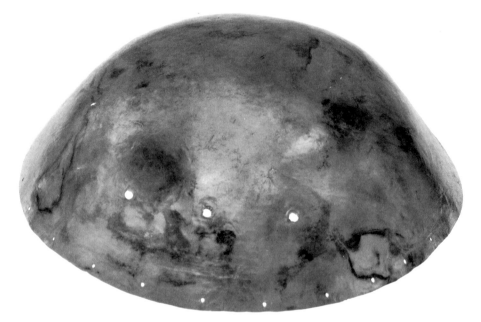

37. Effigy shell pendant

Gold
Hammered, cut, perforated
Peabody Museum 10-71-20/C7677,
H. 10.2 cm., W. 12.5 cm.

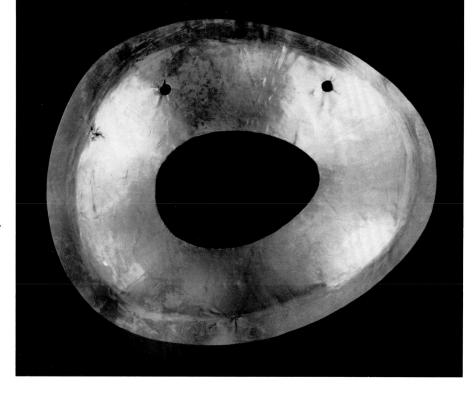

Inappropriately called "horse collars" (for
their shape) these pendants are, with the
exception of this one, all made from shell,
and sometimes from the limpet-like gastro-
pod *Patella mexicana* (Ekholm 1961). A
small natural shell one was also found in
the Sacred Cenote (Moholy-Nagy and Ladd
n.d.). Such pendants are known archaeologically in both Maya and Mexican regions,
from Early to Terminal Classic in date, and
the Nahuatl word *oyoualli* most commonly
describes them (Tozzer 1957, p. 108).

In the sculpture of Chichén Itzá these
ovate pectorals are worn by the Bacabs, or
sky-bearers, mythological beings who are
figured on the capitals, and sometimes the
basal panels, of 200 of the 694 carved columns at the site (Tozzer 1957, table 11).

Perhaps this golden pectoral was actually
worn by the Bacab impersonator who is
shown life-size wearing one over his giant
turtle carapace on the columns of the
Lower Temple of the Jaguars (Tozzer 1957,
fig. 614).

Terminal Classic (A.D. 800–900)
S. K. Lothrop 1952, p. 72, fig. 56; Tozzer
1957, p. 146, figs. 180, 261–266, 614

38. Three rings

Sheet gold
Hammered; cut
Peabody Museum 10-71-20/C7685,
D. 2.6–2.8 cm., Th. 0.03 cm.

Forty-four flat gold rings were found by Edward H. Thompson in the Cenote (nine of
these were presented to Mexico in 1959),
and at least sixteen more were brought out
by the 1967 Mexican expedition (Ediger
1971, color pl. 18). These rings are the same
on both sides; they have no holes for attach-
ment, and there is no evidence of adhesives,
or other indication of how they were used.
They may have been sewn to clothing, ceremonial shields, or other regalia. Signs of
wear are limited to scratches associated
with their manufacture.

Terminal Classic–Early Postclassic
(A.D. 800–1100)
S. K. Lothrop 1952, pp. 66, 67, fig. 51

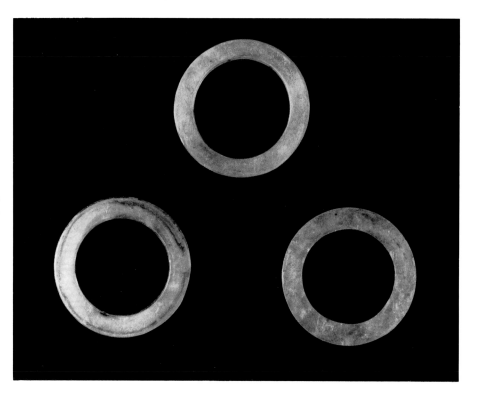

39. Picture plaque

Jadeite, speckled bright green to white
Horizontal bore, fourteen small perforations
at sides and bottom; burned, shattered;
reconstructed
Peabody Museum 10-71-20/C7410,
L. 13.7 cm., W. 11.4 cm., Th. 0.7 cm.

This picture plaque is carved in the
Escuintla style, found in monumental
sculpture at Bilbao on the Pacific slopes of
Guatemala. The stiff figure is arranged so
that his limbs are all clearly visible, with
feet turned on edge so as to display the toes.
He grasps the trunk of a cacao tree. Cacao
is an important theme in the art of this
region, as the crop was essential to its econ-
omy. Behind the figure, a column of five
circles suggests a day sign "5 trefoil/reptile
eye"; the latter is a name for the glyph
shown both at the top of the column and on
the front of the figure's headdress. These
probably refer to his name, which was derived from the day of his birth. The trefoil/
reptile-eye glyph occurs at Bilbao, where an
entire stela is dedicated to its repetition
(Parsons 1969, pl. 38a). In addition to these
prominent iconographic elements, the stern
face with beetling brow, outlined eye, down-
turned mouth, and low-hanging ear disc are
all characteristic of this style, and the oversized crab upon which the figure stands is
an element on Monument 18 from Bilbao,
not depicted elsewhere.

   Like Chichén Itzá, Bilbao had strong ties
with Central Mexico and Veracruz in Terminal Classic times, and similarly depicted
sacrifice and ball players in its monumental
sculpture.

Terminal Classic (A.D. 750–900)
Proskouriakoff 1974, p. 192, pl. 78b; Parsons
1969, pl. 61f

40. Three silhouette figure earflares (?)

Wood; red pigment; paraffin impregnated
Carved, perforations; broken
Peabody Museum 10-71-20/C6706,
L. 4.0 cm.; 10-71-20/C6708, L. 3.3 cm.;
10-71-20/C6709, L. 3.6 cm.; Flare D. (all three) 1.9 cm.

The purpose of these objects is not clearly understood. They resemble earflares but are seldom found in true pairs; nor are objects of this shape represented as worn in Meso-american art, which includes abundant and

detailed representations of costume. They are unlikely to be labrets, or lip plugs, since the flares are sometimes open into what would be the inside of the mouth. The form of the flares, with a small perforation below the rim, is, however, like that of many jade earflares (see no. 64). If the flares were worn through the earlobe, allowing a weight to be hung from the small hole, then the carved "foot" would face forward, but the figures would appear upright only if they stood up in front of the ear—an unlikely position.

However they were worn, these cut-out figures represent ball players like those depicted in the ball court reliefs at Chichén Itzá (Tozzer 1957, fig. 474). They wear the same protective flounced sleeves, woven slippers (worn on only one foot by most ball players), and heavy belts with *palmas* (palmate stones that project upward from the belt). If these ball players with their Mayoid profiles were worn upside down, then they may have been members of the losing team. At least one of them appears to have his arms tied behind, like a captive/sacrificial victim.

These are among the oldest wooden objects from the Cenote.

Terminal Classic (A.D. 800–900)
Coggins and Ladd n.d.

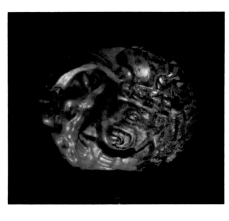

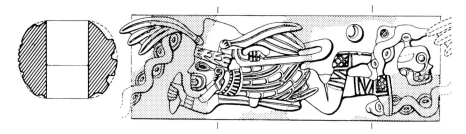

Figure 8a. Jade spherical bead. From T. Proskouriakoff 1974, pl. 43:8.

41. Carved spherical bead

Jadeite, gray, black, bright green spots
Wide vertical bore; burned, broken; reconstructed
Peabody Museum 10-71-20/C6351,
H. 2.7 cm., D. 3.5 cm., Hole D. 1.6 cm.

Like most of the twenty reconstructed spherical beads from the Cenote, this one is worked in sharp-edged high relief (fig. 8a). Here a figure is depicted in a horizontal (flying?) position, with kicking legs, that is also found on reliefs from the Burned Palace at Tula, in Central Mexico (Acosta 1957, pls. 2–5, 33, 34). The Tula figures carry a variety of weapons and are associated with

feathered serpents, as on several of these beads (nos. 42, 43). This figure wears a feathered cape and headband like those worn by the Toltec assistant on the gold disc with the sacrificial scene (no. 25). He carries a sacrificial knife in his right hand, and what resembles a sling in his left, although slings were not Mesoamerican weapons and this may be a folded cloth like the one held by the assistant on the left side of the sacrificial scene. Above the figure's feet a small raised circle with an inscribed crescent may be the Zapotec numeral "one," identifying the birth-date name of the figure, or it could be the date of the scene, or conceivably a new moon. On the opposite side of the bead a serpentine form intertwines with lenticu-

lar elements that may be eyes. This is the same motif that encircles the stone rings of the Great Ball Court at Chichén Itzá, and like the rings, which have skulls depicted on rubber balls in the reliefs immediately below, this bead shows a skull within the serpentine coils (Marquina 1964, photo 431). Thus the bead refers to several pictorial themes of the Great Ball Court: a figure holding an unhafted knife, intertwined serpents, and skulls—as well as suggesting some of the sacrificial symbolism shown on the gold discs.

Terminal Classic (A.D. 800–900)
Proskouriakoff 1974, pp. 83, 209, 210,
pl. 43:8

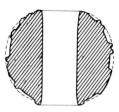

Figure 8b. Jade spherical bead. From T. Proskouriakoff 1974, pl. 43:9.

42. Carved spherical bead

Jadeite, dark green to black
Wide vertical bore; burned, broken;
reconstructed
Peabody Museum 10-71-20/C6344,
H. 3.2 cm., D. 3.7 cm., Hole D. 1.3 cm.

Two serpents with feathered tails and open jaws confront each other on this jade bead which, like no. 41, has a very wide perforation (fig. 8b), but this one is carved in a lower, softer relief, with finer incised detail. The smaller serpent here emerges from a conch shell, or wears one for identification. There is a flame, or a feather, above its eyebrow, and it has a curled nose, and molars and fangs like the facing serpent. A tongue hangs from the lower jaw of the smaller, while a bearded head with a nose bar emerges from the open jaws of the larger serpent. Bearded men are often identified as Quetzalcoatl, leader and deity of the Toltec, but nose bars are generally Maya, so the cultural identity of this individual is unclear. However, on the body of the large serpent there is a trident element that resembles the Zapotec glyph D, perhaps associating these beads with a Oaxacan elite.

Terminal Classic (A.D. 800–900)
Proskouriakoff 1974, p. 83, pl. 43:9, fig. 15;
Tozzer 1957, fig. 125; Easby and Scott 1970,
no. 257.

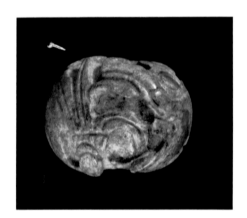

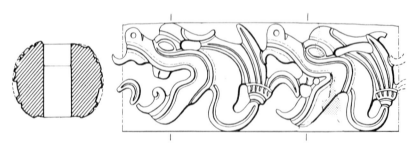

Figure 8c. Jade spherical bead. From T. Proskouriakoff 1974, pl. 42:4.

43. Carved spherical bead

Jadeite, light gray, green
Wide vertical bore; burned, broken;
reconstructed
Peabody Museum 10-71-20/C6346,
H. 2.5 cm., D. 3.3 cm., Hole D. 1.0 cm.

Small patches of vivid green remain on this burned bead that displays two open-jawed serpents perpetually about to swallow one another (fig. 8c). Although all four have feathered tails, these serpents differ from the two on no. 42 in details of nose, eye form, and in the shape of the flame, feather, or horn that projects upward from the eyebrow.

Terminal Classic (A.D. 800–900)
Proskouriakoff 1974, p. 83, pl. 42:4; Tozzer
1957, fig. 124

44. Two figurine pendants

Tumbaga; black coating
Cast; burned, crushed
Peabody Museum 10-71-20/C7707A,
Analysis no. 1261, H. 10.0 cm.

One of the least-understood aspects of the Cenote ritual is exemplified by these figures. They came from lower Central America, and they do not represent or relate to any known component of Mesoamerican culture or religion. In fact the importation of this Panamanian style goldwork may be among the initial Mesoamerican appearances of gold, or the gold/copper alloy *tumbaga*, early in the ninth century, not long after the legs of a *tumbaga* figurine were cached beneath Stela H at Copán (Stromsvik 1941, p. 71, fig. 12b, c).

Jade was considered the most valuable and desirable object by all Mesoamerican peoples, and perhaps even more so in Post-classic times when it became rare. There can be no question that gold ever supplanted jade in desirability, especially since its symbolic meaning was so different. Jade signified green and watery and precious, whereas gold had solar significance and thus stood more for heat, brilliance, and strength, with warrior associations. One wonders if the metal figurines could have been meaningless exotic objects for elite consumption when they were first brought to Chichén Itzá. Could there have been an element of lower Central American religion in the subculture of long distance sea traders? Or did people from those regions travel, themselves, to visit the Cenote at Chichén Itzá? Who offered these figurines? And what did they mean to those who offered them?

Goldworking techniques apparently traveled northward, from Colombia to Panama, and then to Costa Rica, where some of the earliest gold found in burials was imported from farther south (Bray 1981, p. 154). It is most likely that the Panamanian Cocle style cast *tumbaga* figurines found in the Cenote, like these, were imported from the Caribbean coast of Costa Rica, where metal work from other regions has been found and local work imitates foreign styles.

The figurines were cast by the lost-wax technique, in which molten metal replaced a wax figurine modeled over a clay and charcoal core, all inside an outer mold with holes for pouring the metal in and the wax out. Ideally the interior core would have been removed through holes in the final casting, but both of these figures retain the core in their legs. Fourteen small, symmetrically placed holes indicate where pegs would have secured the outer core to the inner one. As part of the finishing, these holes were filled with metal plugs, two of which are still visible at the knees of the smaller figure; the other plugs must have popped out in the heat of the final offertory fire.

These figures stuck together and melted more than many others from the Cenote because they were made from a gold and copper alloy (with silver impurity) called *tumbaga*. The melting point of this alloy is lower than those of its constituent metals alone and so it was easier to work; another important asset of this alloy was that its surface could be treated with a depletion gilding technique that removed the surface copper, leaving only brilliant gold visible. Here the gold-rich surface has worn down, revealing the coppery metal beneath. Metallurgic testing of the smaller figure showed its composition to be 77.8 percent copper, 19.4 percent gold, and 2.8 percent silver.

Like figures from throughout the gold-working province that extended from Costa Rica to Colombia, the smaller of these two holds objects in either hand. It is naked except for a flat bead collar that extends only over the visible front half of the body. Double spirals at either side of the head tie this figure to a regional style that is well represented in the Cenote collection. The larger figure differs in having ankle and calf bands, and in carrying some larger object. Both have suspension loops cast on to the back.

Terminal Classic (A.D. 800–900)
S. K. Lothrop 1952, pp. 7, 95, 96, fig. 92, table 31

45. Two figurine pendants

Tumbaga; black coating
Cast; burned, crushed, broken
Peabody Museum 10-71-20/C7694,
H. 7.3 cm.; 10-71-20/C7695, H. 6.9 cm.

Like the joined figures (no. 44), these naked Coclé style figurines hold objects in either hand and have the characteristic half-collar and double ear scrolls. But here symmetrical feather panaches flanking a triangular headdress above a segmented headband are still intact; as are eyes and mouth that were made of flattened pellets, or "coffee beans," of wax before casting. Another important trait of this style is the contrast between rounded legs with swelling thighs and skinny arms below angular shoulders.

The smaller figure apparently has both male genitalia and breasts, and a flat pendant that hangs to the waist. Its head is less triangular in shape than the other, and it holds objects like handbells instead of the three-part gourd rattles held by the larger figure. These variations may indicate important iconographic differences, or only different goldsmiths. Since the outer mold must be destroyed to remove the casting, each figurine is necessarily different to some degree. The back of each of these figures was left partially open, but the cores were not entirely removed. The larger figure is made of very thin metal, and its "false filigree" scrolls are supported on the back by small metal straps; the stump of a pouring funnel remains on the bottom of the right foot.

Terminal Classic (A.D. 800–900)
S. K. Lothrop 1952, pp. 95, 96, fig. 89d, h;
Bray 1977, fig. 17 : 1

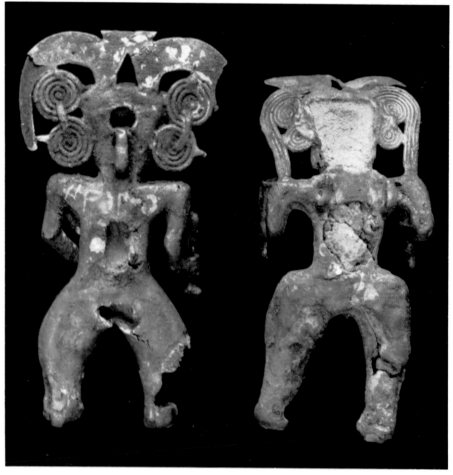

46. Figurine pendant

Tumbaga
Cast; burned, broken in half
Peabody Museum 10-71-20/C7708,
H. 4.7 cm.

Angular shoulders, thin arms, and a half-collar identify this fragmentary figurine as of Cocle style. It holds something to its mouth with the right hand while pressing an inverted jar to its chest with the left. The opening in this "jar" may, however, have been made to allow gases to escape, since castings were usually poured upside down in order to force the molten metal into the most complicated parts of the mold. An apparent navel is probably a peg hole that lost its finishing plug in the heat of the offertory ceremony (see no. 44).

The head of this large figure is unusually realistic, and true earspools of this type are an early Cocle trait. A second, smaller *tumbaga* figurine with such earspools also came from the Cenote (S. K. Lothrop 1952, fig. 89e), and two more were excavated in the Atlantic watershed region of Costa Rica (Balser 1966, fig. 3b, d). They represent an early period in Costa Rican goldworking when castings were imported from the south and often copied. These Cenote examples probably came from coastal Costa Rica and not from Cocle, Panama.

Terminal Classic (A.D. 800–900)
S. K. Lothrop 1952, p. 96, fig. 89c

47. Figurine pendant with bell

Tumbaga; black coating
Cast; burned, loop broken off
Peabody Museum 10-71-20/C7700,
H. 5.5 cm.

This Cocle style figure is unique in having a bell apparently cast onto its chest, as if hanging from the collar. The addition of a bell to the figure might have been expressly for export since, as noted for no. 44, gold figurine pendants were exotic to Meso-american culture. Bells, however, were early incorporated into the regalia of the Mexican warriors at Chichén Itzá (see nos. 14, 25), while not characteristic of Cocle.

Terminal Classic (A.D. 800–900)
S. K. Lothrop 1952, p. 96, fig. 89b

48. Figurine pendant

Tumbaga; black coating
Cast; burned, crushed, broken
Peabody Museum 10-73-20/C7725,
H. 9.8 cm., W. 7.0 cm.

This flat cast pectoral was made in "Darien" style. Most examples of such figurines come from the Sinú region of Colombia northeast of the Isthmus of Panama (Falchetti de Sáenz 1979), but, while flat, the Colombian ones all have a clear indication of separate legs and feet. This pendant has instead a flat expanding form like those on early "Veraguas eagles" (S. K. Lothrop 1950, fig. 76c), although it resembles Colombian pendants in its "wings" with spirals, and mushroom-like finials atop the head. Features are visible behind a flattened mask that once covered the face, and two rods (of unknown use, but a constant attribute of the type) are directed to the mouth by hands held at waist level. Most Colombian "Darien" pendants do not have a clear indication of a torso or of shoulders like this, although such pendants found in Costa Rica may have.

In Costa Rica gold replaced jade as the principal elite grave good between about A.D. 600 and 800 (Bray 1981, p. 154); during the transition gold was imported from the south and copied locally. A dozen or more "Darien" style pendants have been excavated in the Atlantic watershed region of Costa Rica, often in association with Cocle style figurines (Balser 1966). The Cenote "Darien" style pendant is clearly a northern copy in which the already conventionalized human form was given a bird-like tail. Like the Cocle figurines, and probably all of the cast *tumbaga* in the Cenote, this pendant almost certainly came from a trading center on the Caribbean coast of Costa Rica.

The head of another "Darien" pendant was found by the 1967 Mexican Cenote expedition (Ediger 1971, color pl. 5).

Terminal Classic (A.D. 800–900)
S. K. Lothrop 1952, p. 95, fig. 88

49. Figurine pendant

Tumbaga; black coating
Cast; burned, crushed, broken
Peabody Museum 10-71-20/C7704, Analysis no. 1259, H. 5.7 cm.

Much of the surface detail was blurred in the wax model of this poor casting. On the front, one eye, the mouth, and the nose have been ruined, and on the back only the two bases of the suspension loop were successfully cast. In order to replace these, enough core was removed so that two holes could be made at the sides of the neck, where pegs had secured the molds. This pendant may be a rare example of a figurine that retains traces of the *outer* clay and charcoal mold (on the face and collar). Maybe the piece was sold as a "second" to foreigners. It was made in the Cocle style, with ear spirals, half-collar, objects in either hand, and characteristic small arms and large thighs.

A drill hole in the back of the left leg was made for an analysis of the *tumbaga* alloy which is 50 percent copper, 47.3 percent gold, and 3.0 percent silver.

Terminal Classic (A.D. 800–900)
S. K. Lothrop 1952, no illustration, table 36

50. Monkey pendant

Tumbaga; black coating
Cast
Peabody Museum 10-73-20/C7726, Analysis
no. 1280, L. 5.3 cm.

"Curly-tailed monkey" pendants are a Cocle
form that was common in Panama in stone
as well as in metal (S. K. Lothrop 1937,
figs. 169, 171). Worn on the chest, the tail of
this pendant would have projected outward,
while danglers probably hung from the
hind feet. Pegholes in this casting are still
plugged, unlike those on some of the other
tumbaga pieces (see no. 44) that may have
been subjected to more heat in the Cenote
offering ritual.

Like the Cocle style cast *tumbaga* figurines, "curly-tailed" animals have been
excavated in the Atlantic watershed of
Costa Rica in contexts suggesting a relatively early date (Stone and Balser 1965).
This monkey probably came from there,
contemporaneously with the figurines
(nos. 44–49).

The *tumbaga* alloy is 54.4 percent copper,
43 percent gold, 2.6 percent silver.

Terminal Classic (A.D. 800–900)
S. K. Lothrop 1952, p. 97, figs. 93c, 108,
table 31

51. Picture plaque

Jadeite, emerald green mottled to white,
black at edges; black coating
Ten perforations near edges; recarving or
thinning; two perforations from ancient
mend; broken; reconstructed
Peabody Museum 10-71-20/C6667,
H. 12.0 cm., W. 13.5 cm., Th. 0.3–0.7 cm.

In his pose, his slender body, artificially
deformed head, and exaggerated nose,
this Maya lord exemplifies the aristocra-
tic sculptural style of Palenque, at about
A.D. 700. He sits within a circular frame
that, with the scrolls at the four corners,
suggests a Late Classic Maya solar cartouche, although the encircling perforated
discs, or *chalchihuitls*, stand for jade and
watery preciousness. In his right hand he
displays a glyphic cartouche of which only
the top third is original—the reconstruction
of the rest is conjectural. As with most Palenque portraiture, this figure wears no
feathers; instead his hair is divided into two
hanks, one hanging backward and one
projecting forward, probably through a jade
tube (see also no. 62).

In front of this figure's face an un-
attached serpentine head levitates—
signifying breath or speech. This unusual
symbolic device is apparently also present,

much larger, in the axial portrait at the top-
most position of the west wall in the Lower
Temple of the Jaguars at Chichén Itzá
(fig. 5). Seated upon a jaguar throne, also
within a Sun disc but of Terminal Classic to
Early Postclassic type, the enthroned figure
from the Lower Temple apparently represents the same Maya "Captain Sun Disc"
(Miller 1977, p. 209) who is depicted on the
west lintel of the Upper Temple of the Jaguars immediately above (fig. 19). These
ninth-century portraits may represent the
ruler of Chichén Itzá who was called Kakupacal (Fire His Shield) (Kelley 1968). The
much earlier, but analogous, portrait on the
jade may portray an earlier, similarly identified, Maya from the south who was perhaps
involved in the legendary founding of Chichén Itzá in the critical Maya katun that
ended at 9.13.0.0.0 8 Ahau (A.D. 672–692),
as recorded in a northern chronicle of Maya
history (Edmonson 1982, p. xvi). This
plaque, with the contemporary bar pendant
from Palenque (no. 52), might have be-
longed to emigrants from the Palenque
region about A.D. 700, and to their descendants who later offered it to the Cenote.

Late Classic (A.D. 650–750)
Proskouriakoff 1974, p. 176, pl. 75:a; 1978,
p. 62; Rands 1965, fig. 44; Ruz Lhuillier
1979, color pl., p. 264

Figure 9. Jade bar, inscription, and figure.
From T. Proskouriakoff 1974, pl. 45:2.

52. Carved bar pendant with fifty-seven-piece jade assemblage

Jadeite, varied
All bored; some burned
Bar pendant: longitudinal bore, two
suspension perforations, ten for
attachments, incised; burned, broken;
reconstructed
Peabody Museum 10-71-20/C6318,
L. 19.4 cm., D. 3.5 cm.
Thirty-one medium round beads:
10-71-20/C6331
Two large round beads: 10-71-20/C6170,
19-37-20/C9258
Twelve banded tubular beads:
10-56-20/C5969 (3), 10-71-20/C6200,
C6269, C6212, C6216, C6275,
19-37-20/C9257 (3), C9263
Twelve small lobed beads: 10-56-20/C5970,
(2), 10-70-20/C6048, C6064,
10-71-20/C6155, C6153 (2), C6168, C6335,
C6342 (3)

The bar pendant worn by the figure incised on this bar is drilled with perforations like the ones on the bar itself, so this assemblage has been constructed in imitation of the one depicted. There is no reason, however, to believe that any of these beads were originally associated with one another. Beads were the commonest jade objects found in the Cenote; thousands, many fragmentary, are represented in the collection. They were worn by the elite—most of the people would not have had any jade.

The figure and the inscription on the bar pendant are incised, while the face is emphasized by sunken relief carving. This stylistic device, the name Chan Bahlum at the top of the second column of glyphs (fig. 9), and the second Calendar Round date, 2 Cib 14 Mol (9.12.18.5.16, in A.D. 690), all tie this pendant securely to the site of Palenque, from which it must have come. Chan Bahlum became ruler of Palenque in A.D. 683 and ruled for eighteen years, so the date on the pendant, which is found twice in the inscriptions of Palenque, refers to an event that occurred seven years into his reign, in his forty-first year (Mathews and Schele 1974). Like the figure plaque carved in Palenque style (no. 51), this bar pendant appears to have been made close to A.D. 692, which was the very important Maya Long Count date of 9.13.0.0.0 8 Ahau, and the date of the founding of Chichén Itzá according to the *Book of Chilam Balam of Tizimín*, a Colonial chronicle of Maya history (Edmonson 1982, p. xvi). These two stylistically distinctive carved jades may have been the personal property of descendants of emigrants from the southern Maya lowlands, who offered them to the Cenote in the ninth century. These is no evidence for rich offerings to the Cenote around A.D. 700 when they were carved, and little reason to believe they were looted from a tomb, since most of the other Early Phase jades appear to be Terminal Classic, or contemporary with their final ritual use.

Late Classic (A.D. 690–725)
Proskouriakoff 1974, pp. 85, 204, 205,
pls. 27, 45:2, fig. 12:2; Willard 1941, facing
p. 90; Tozzer 1957, figs. 623, 624; Rands
1965, fig. 8

53. Head pendant

Jadeite; speckled bright green with gray and black
Circular hollowed back; horizontal bore; nine perforations for attachments; burned, broken; reconstructed
Peabody Museum 10-70-20/C6100, H. 8.4 cm., W. 5.7 cm., Th. 5.1 cm.

On the top and back of this beautifully carved head wearing a jaguar headdress, an incised inscription includes a date (in A.D. 706) that was the katun (twenty-year) anniversary of a ruler's accession at the Usumacinta River site of Piedras Negras, where the inscription may have been added commemoratively to an existing carving. It is possible that the head was taken from a cache or a burial at Piedras Negras, although it could have been taken to Chichén Itzá as an heirloom, perhaps at the time of the convocation of Maya celebrated in the reliefs in the Lower Temple of the Jaguars (fig. 5).

The delicate features, with receding forehead and chin and drooping lower lip, represent a Maya ideal. Such heads were worn as part of collar and belt assemblages (see no. 59); this head was hollowed at the back, probably in part to reduce its weight. The collars, belts, earflares, bracelets, and headdresses worn by the Maya elite would have been very heavy and cumbersome, and in addition to connoting wealth would have emphasized the immobile, purely symbolic role of the ruler.

Late Classic (A.D. 675–725)
Proskouriakoff 1974, pp. 154, 205, color pl. Ia, pl. 60:1, fig. 12:3; 1944; 1960, p. 458; 1978, p. 63; Morley 1946, pl. 91e, f; Easby and Easby 1953, fig. 9; Rands 1965, fig. 14; Kelemen 1969, fig. 241c; Easby and Scott 1970, no. 187; Coggins 1974, no. 191b

54. Pebble head pendant

Jadeite, dark green to black variegated
Horizontal bore; earflares perforated; three perforations at chin; burned
Peabody Museum 10-71-20/C6586, H. 3.7 cm., W. 3.5 cm., Th. 2.0 cm.

A broader Maya face than on the large head (no. 53) is depicted in this idealized portrait carved in high relief on a jade pebble. An abbreviated Long Nose Head headdress, with scroll eyes, is worn, and there were pendants at the chin and ears.

Late Classic (A.D. 650–850)
Proskouriakoff 1974, p. 154, pl. 60:9

55. Head pendant

Jadeite, grayish, olive green
Horizontal bore
Peabody Museum 10-71-20/C6591,
H. 4.5 cm., W. 2.8 cm., Th. 2.5 cm.

The serrated crest on this head recalls a
convention found on dwarfs (nos. 67, 68),
but unlike their large, heavy-jawed heads,
this one has the elongated skull and receding forehead of the Maya elite. While it is
possible that this little head is unfinished,
since the ears are not pierced and the
eyes are without pupils, the closed eyes and
the tongue, or bead (?), between the lips
might be intended to denote death. Rather
than incompletion, the monumentality of
this simple form suggests successful
achievement.

Late Classic (A.D. 700–800)
Proskourikoff 1974, p. 156, color pl. 4,
pl. 62a:3

56. Head pendant

Jadeite, mottled gray-green over dark green
Hollowed back with vertical bore, horizontal
bore, five chin perforations, cheek
perforations; burned, broken; reconstructed
Peabody Museum 10-71-20/C6621,
H. 5.4 cm., W. 4.3 cm., Th. 2.3 cm.

Like the Piedras Negras style head pendant
(no. 53), this one, which personifies the
sun, is hollowed out at the back with many
subsidiary perforations, probably so that it
could serve as part of a collar assemblage.
The solar attributes are "crossed" eyes with
square pupils, an aquiline nose, and teeth
filed into a Tau shape. This pendant is unusual, however, in also having pits that
indicate pupils at the center of the eyes—
not a Classic Period trait. In fact this is a
reworked Late Preclassic bib-helmet head;
the early date is also betrayed by the flange
ear bars, medial head crest, and very large
horizontal bore. Unmodified bib-helmut
head pendants were also found in the
Cenote (see no. 162).

Late Preclassic–Late Classic (200 B.C.–
A.D. 800)
Proskouriakoff 1974, pp. 152, 153, pl. 59c:2

57. Picture plaque

Jadeite, bright green over opaque gray to
black
Horizontal bore; perforations from two or
more ancient mends; burned, broken;
reconstructed
Peabody Museum 10-71-20/C6668,
H. 11.5 cm., W. 14.0 cm., Th. 0.4–1.3 cm.

This plaque depicts an enthroned Maya lord.
When carved with this distinctive technique, such a portrait is described as "Nebaj
type" after the site where a similar jade was
excavated from a cache, with other jades
(Smith and Kidder 1951, fig. 59b). It is interesting that a portrait like this did not
come from a burial; such picture plaques
are not shown as worn in Maya painting or
sculpture, so it is possible they were not the

kind of personal possession that would have
been deposited in burials. The figure is
framed by deity heads; profile heads wearing "jester caps" flank him, and there is a
frontal, "Tau-toothed" solar head below.
These forms have deep grooves doubly outlining them in a convention that designated
the symbolic or supernatural in Late Classic
times. The frontally seated man wears only
a loincloth and a Long Nose Head headdress with drooping feathers behind. Bodily
forms are ample and rounded, lending substance to the seated figure. This effect
comes from the use of the arcs of tubular
drills to outline knees, elbows, hands, and
fingers. The profile head with receding
forehead and chin exaggerates a characteristically Maya canon of beauty in con-
forming to the drill's clean-cutting arcs. The
clarity and brilliance of this style are further

heightened by an impression of movement
in the gesturing hands of this Maya lord.

The plaque may have been traded or carried as spoils or as an offering to Chichén
Itzá from the southwestern Maya regions.
However it traveled, similar events probably
tied the Oaxacan center of Monte Albán to
the Usumacinta River region of its origin. A
fragment of such a "Nebaj" plaque was included in a Monte Albán IIIB cache with a
variety of jades comparable to those found
in the Cenote (Caso 1965, fig. 20). These
suggest a related, eclectic caching activity
that was widespread in the Terminal Classic.

Terminal Classic (A.D. 750–850)
Proskouriakoff 1974, pp. 175, 176, pl. 73:1;
Willard 1933, facing p. 102

58. Picture plaque

Jadeite, brilliant green, white, opaque blue over speckled gray
Horizontal bore, small peripheral perforations; broken; reconstructed
Peabody Museum 10-71-20/C6663,
H. 6.1 cm., W. 5.5 cm., Th. 1.0 cm.

Stylistically this small plaque belongs to the Nebaj type, but it probably pre-dates the later characteristic overuse of arc drilling (see nos. 7, 8, 57). As on more typical examples, the figure has massive, rounded shoulders and assumes a gesturing pose, but here the carving is finer, with the face particularly carefully modeled. Most of the headdress and the enframing scrolls were lost when this plaque was reduced in size.

Late Classic (A.D. 750–850)
Proskouriakoff 1974, p. 176, pl. 73:4

59. Full figure plaque

Jadeite, emerald green splotches on white to black
Horizontal bore, two perforations above; broken; reconstructed
Peabody Museum 10-70-20/C6103A,
H. 12.3 cm., W. 7.8 cm., Th. 0.6 cm.

The feathered jaguar headdress on this plaque has eyes with scrolls in place of pupils, a symbol of underworld beings. Frontal portraits with this type of headdress are found at the Usumacinta River site of Piedras Negras, and the heads depicted on the collar and belt of this figure may have been like the jade head from the Cenote which is believed to have come from Piedras Negras (no. 53). However, the rigid symmetry and little-modulated, low relief of the carving suggest it may have come from elsewhere in the region.

Late Classic (A.D. 750–850)
Proskouriakoff 1974, pp. 160, 161, pl. 67b:3

60. Spangle disc

Jadeite, gray-green to brown
Reworked, perforated
Peabody Museum 10-70-20/C6121,
D. 2.9 cm., Th. 0.5 cm.

This thin, perforated disc, cut down without
regard to design, shows part of the upper
jaw of a feathered jaguar headdress of the
kind commonly worn by frontally presented
Maya lords on jade plaques (see no. 59).
Probably the smooth back was used in a
diadem made up of plain discs.

A square spangle also cut from the upper
jaw of a feathered jaguar headdress was
found in a structural cache at Monte Albán,
Oaxaca, that included five other jades stylistically related to jades from the Cenote
(see nos. 78, 57, 58, 66), and still another
group of similar Maya jades was found
cached at Monte Albán inside a carved
Slate Ware vessel from the Yucatán Peninsula (Caso 1965, fig. 20, p. 906).

Terminal Classic (A.D. 800–900)
Proskouriakoff 1974, p. 89, pl. 48b: 1

61. Head plaque

Jadeite, vivid green and white on black;
black coating
Horizontal bore, ten perforations around
edges, two through earflares; broken;
reconstructed
Peabody Museum 10-71-20/C6646,
H. 8.3 cm., W. 6.3 cm., Th. 1.6 cm.

Imposing high relief, jaguar headdress, and
large earflares dominate this plaque, contrasting with the finely incised features of
the face. Such headdresses, while jaguar in
jaw and nose, generally have feathered eyes
and other bird and reptilian characteristics
that connect them to the allegorical bird-
man-serpent forms so common on the later
architecture of Chichén Itzá.

Late Classic (A.D. 650–800)
Proskouriakoff 1974, p. 160, pl. 67a: 2

62. Picture plaque

Jadeite, bright to olive green and gray
Horizontal bore, two perforations just
below; broken; reconstructed
Peabody Museum 10-71-20/C6674,
H. 7.8 cm., W. 8.8 cm., Th. 0.6 cm.

This frontal, seated figure with an oversized
head provides an example of the extensive
use of concentric and arc drilling to outline
forms, although the technique is not as pro-
nounced as on the Nebaj type plaques
(nos. 7, 57).

Late Classic (A.D. 750–850)
Proskouriakoff 1974, pp. 176, 177, pl. 75b:1

63. Head pendant

Jadeite, dull speckled green, white, black
Hollowed back, two short, horizontal bores,
six holes to front, three small perforations at
bottom; broken; reconstructed
Peabody Museum 10-71-20/C6644,
H. 7.4 cm., W. 8.9 cm., Th. 2.0 cm.

The space surrounding the mask-like face
on this thick pendant has been left empty
or filled with meaningless ornament and
drilled forms. At the bottom the frame suggests the back to back hands found on
Early Classic jades, but this is a mechanical
Late Classic carving of little skill.

Late Classic (A.D. 700–800)
Proskouriakoff 1974, p. 99, pl. 54c:1

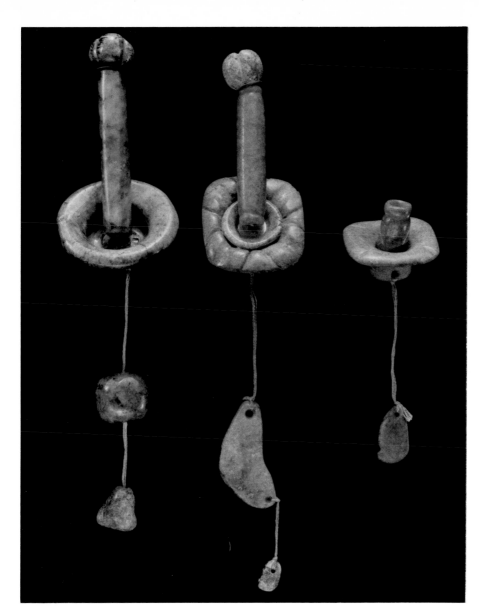

64. Three earflare assemblages

Jadeite, varied
Various bores and perforations
Circular assemblage: flare Peabody
Museum 10-56-20/C5945, D. 4.4 cm.;
10-56-20/C5970; 10-71-20/C6230, C6395;
19-37-20/C9260
Larger subrectangular assemblage: flare
10-71-20/C6470, D. 3.8 × 4.0 cm.;
10-70-20/C6076, C6111; 10-71-20/C6153,
C6208; 63-32-20/22032
Smaller subrectangular assemblage: flare
10-71-20/C6469, D. 3.1 × 3.4 cm.;
10-71-20/C6219, C6392.

These three assemblages are entirely hypo-
thetical, constructed from unassociated
elements in the collection, but they are
modeled on earflares known to have been
worn. Although they were more universally
worn, or at least depicted, than beads, sur-
prisingly few earflares were found in the
Cenote, compared to beads. This may be
because much of what was thrown into the
Cenote was *not* primarily personal posses-
sions, but valuable objects. Most of the
pictorially carved jade from the Cenote is
not shown on the monuments as parts of
costume, and when excavated such jade
has come from caches more than burials.
Beads, however, represented wealth, not
lineage or cultural affiliation.

The circular earflare has a small perforated rosette that fits perfectly into the
throat of the flare. The neck, which fit
through the earlobe, is short, with two holes
for attaching counterweights. This assemblage is styled on several found on
Yaxchilán lintels (Graham and Von Euw
1977), with a "bone Ahau" pendant terminating the back counterweight.

There are fewer square earflares than
round ones depicted in Late Classic Maya
sculpture, but this apparent discrepancy
may only be because most of them are
shown in profile. Like the circular flare
assemblage, the larger square one here derives from the lintels of Yaxchilán, although
it is simpler than most.

The smaller square flare, with two simple
pendants, is modeled on one excavated at
Palenque (Ruz Lhuillier 1973, fig. 227).
Twenty somewhat smaller flares in at least
six different styles, but including four like
this one, formed a diadem worn by the principal occupant of Burial 5 at Piedras Negras
in the middle of the eighth century (W. R.
Coe 1959, p. 124, fig. 48), although it is
likely most were originally intended to be
earflares.

Late Classic (A.D. 750–900)
Proskouriakoff 1974, Ch. 3, pls. 18–37

65. Five plain spangle discs

Jadeite
Perforations; some broken; mended
Peabody Museum 10-56-20/C5937;
10-71-20/C6500, C6501, C6511, C6581,
Max. D. 3.2 cm.

Plain spangle discs were probably used in a
variety of ways, depending on their size and
thickness. Most have a central perforation
and a smaller perforation near the edge,
probably to sew them, overlapping, to a diadem or other parts of a headdress or to a
collar. Forty-one spangles were part of a diadem worn by the occupant of the famed
Sarcophagus at Palenque (Ruz Lhuillier
1973, p. 190, fig. 219).
    One of these spangles (10-71-20/C6500)
is so thin it is translucent, and transparent
at its crumbling ground edge.

Late Classic (A.D. 600–900)
Proskouriakoff 1974, p. 34, pl. 35

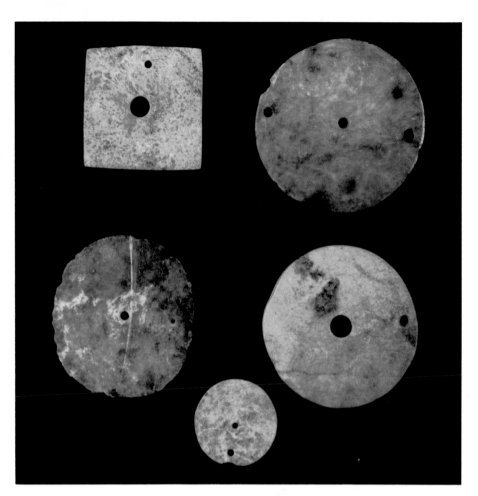

66. Three rosettes

Jadeite
Perforated
Top: Peabody Museum 10-70-20/C6112,
D. 3.6 cm., Th. 0.7 cm.
Bottom left: 10-71-20/C6444, D. 4.2 cm.,
Th. 0.5 cm.
Bottom right: 10-71-20/C6447, D. 5.0 cm.,
Th. 0.4 cm.

Like plain perforated discs, rosettes are
most often shown as diadems, forehead
bands at the base of elaborate headdresses.
Their use is illustrated, in association with
many other types of Maya jewelry found in
the Cenote, on the Late Classic Lintel 26 at
Yaxchilán (Graham and Von Euw 1977).

Late Classic (A.D. 750–850)
Proskouriakoff 1974, pp. 37, 38, pls. 40a:9,
40b:13, 41b:1

67. Dwarf figurine/pendant

Jadeite, emerald green with colorless and
black areas; black coating; red pigment
Horizontal bore, ear perforations
Peabody Museum 10-56-20/C5975,
H. 6.6 cm., W. 3.1 cm., Th. 2.3 cm.

Of the thirteen jade dwarves found in the
Cenote, only two were not broken. Characteristic of the dwarf type are short limbs,
hands at either side of a protruding belly,
and oversized head with aquiline nose and
hair in a serrated crest. Most of these little
figures are drilled horizontally through the
shoulders for suspension, although they
also stand. This dwarf is unusual for a
three-dimensional modeling enhanced by
drilling and cord-sawing used to undercut
the loincloth, separate the arms from the
body, and define the neck with a groove.
Traces of a red pigment are visible on the
loincloth, front and back, and the whole
surface was once covered with a black
coating.

Late Classic (A.D. 750–850)
Proskouriakoff 1974, p. 102, color pl. 1c,
pl. 57:1; Coggins 1974, pp. 243–244, pl. 18

68. Dwarf figurine/pendant

Jadeite, gray-green; red pigment
Two horizontal bores, ear perforations;
burned, broken; reconstructed
Peabody Museum 10-71-20/C6643,
H. 9.0 cm., W. 3.8 cm., Th. 2.7 cm.

This dwarf resembles no. 67 in its stance, in
its simple loincloth apron, and in having its
ears pierced for ornaments, although flares
are indicated on the cheeks as well. All of
the dwarves have a groove at the neck as if
something had been tied there; perhaps
this is why there is a second horizontal
bore, lower than the groove, on this figure. The dwarf has a medial crest of hair,
marked brow ridge, and prominent nose,
but, unlike no. 67, wears a heavy bead
necklace with a long counterweight hanging down the back, and a diadem of rings at
his forehead.

Late Classic (A.D. 750–850)
Proskouriakoff 1974, p. 102, color pl. 4,
pl. 57:5

69. Dwarf figurine/pendant

Jadeite, speckled green, gray to black
Longitudinal bore, horizontal bore; broken;
reconstructed
Peabody Museum 10-71-20/C6640,
H. 6.1 cm., W. 1.9 cm., Th. 2.0 cm.

The protruding belly and buttocks of this
dwarf are confined to the narrow form of
the bead from which it was carved. In its
stance and simplicity it conforms to the
dwarf type already noted (nos. 67, 68), dif-
fering only in having tiny pits drilled on the
right half of its face, perhaps to indicate
tattooing. Like most of the jades in the
Cenote, this one was almost certainly broken as the result of burning, which led to
the crackling and disintegration of the
stone.

No jade dwarf figurine has ever been excavated, but dwarves are represented in
scenes with ruler figures on the monuments and ceramics of the Late Classic
southern lowlands, and it is possible that
they are represented on some jade plaques
as well (see nos. 70, 103).

Late Classic (A.D. 750–850)
Proskouriakoff 1974, p. 102, pl. 57:2

70. Full figure plaque

Jadeite, speckled green and dark gray; black coating
Horizontal bore, six (originally eight) perforations at bottom edge, three perforations through to front; broken; partially reconstructed.
Peabody Museum 10-71-20/C6656,
H. 9.4 cm., W. 8.3 cm., Th. 1.0 cm.

A full figure is depicted on this plaque, but the oversized head and headdress recieve all the attention. As on no. 63, the hands are shown below the head, and the three deeply drilled and perforated circles of the earflares and headdress dominate the composition and characterize the style. A dwarf is suggested by the short legs and prominent belly, although such an elaborate headdress makes this seem less likely. If all such plaques do represent dwarves, then they were much more widespread than has been thought, with perhaps a dozen examples from the Cenote.

Late Classic (A.D. 750–850)
Proskouriakoff 1974, p. 161, pl. 68:6

71. Carved bead

Jadeite, speckled bright green to black
Longitudinal bore, three small perforations on projecting edge; broken; reconstructed
Peabody Museum 63-32-20/21996,
L. 9.5 cm., W. 3.1 cm., Th. 1.5 cm.

This bead resembles Early Classic examples in depicting a full figure drilled longitudinally, but the more sharply defined features and active position of the figure indicate a later date. The form of the stone may have suggested this subject, since the triangular projection corresponds perfectly to the arched body of the figure, which has its feet and legs directly above the head; it was worn horizontally. Three small perforations show that the face looked upward, and pendants once hung below. Next to the central perforation there is a small gash in the exposed chest. This may be a heart sacrifice victim with kicking legs, as on two of the jade rings from the Cenote (Proskouriakoff 1974, pl. 48a:1,3); however, acrobats also assume such poses on Classic Period jades (W. R. Coe 1967, p. 51).

Late–Terminal Classic (A.D. 600–900)
Proskouriakoff 1974, pp. 86, 87, pl. 46a:8

72. Carved bead/pendant

Jadeite, dull variegated gray-green, white, black
Longitudinal bore, horizontal bore; broken; reconstructed
Peabody Museum 63-32-20/23415,
L. 8.6 cm., W. 2.9 cm., Th. 1.6 cm.

This bead is carved in a soft low relief that is typical of Early Classic Maya jadeworking. The figure holds its arms in front of the chest with hands back to back. Facial features are schematically represented by rounded bars, with an inverted T-shaped nose attached to the brow ridge. The headdress conventions are shorthand for a frontal jaguar headdress where the upper jaw is surmounted by a double scroll signifying the jaguar nose (see nos. 59, 61).

 Two closely related jades were excavated from an Early Classic tomb at Nebaj in the Guatemalan highlands and provided Alfred V. Kidder with the basis for a definition of Early Classic Maya jadeworking style (Smith and Kidder 1951, pp. 33–34, fig. 52).

Early Classic (A.D. 400–600)
Proskouriakoff 1974, p. 96, pl. 52c:1

73. Effigy bead

Jadeite, pale green opaque
Horizontal bore, perforation; burned, chipped
Peabody Museum 10-71-20/C6407, W. 2.7 cm., Th. 1.7 cm.

This three-cornered bead is the effigy of a cord-wrapped object. The smallest point, which is perforated for a dangler, would have hung down. No others quite like it are known.

Terminal Classic–Early Postclassic (A.D. 800–1000)
Proskouriakoff 1974, p. 86, pl. 46a:4

The Early Phase of Sacred Cenote Ritual: Part II

It is postulated that the second, longer part of the Early Phase of Cenote ritual is Early Postclassic and probably lasted from A.D. 900 until 1150, becoming sparser and less exotic in character toward the end. During this period the Central Mexican capital of Tula was flourishing, and genuinely Toltec eagle warriors and militarism were exalted at Chichén Itzá, as exemplified by the building of the Temple of the Warriors and three Great Plaza structures: the Venus and Eagle platforms and the Tzompantli, or skull rack.

At this time imported cast gold was worked in the distinctive style of the lower Central American Pacific goldworking region, rather than the gold-copper alloy previously brought to Chichén Itzá. This cast gold, which includes many bells, was probably still transported from the Caribbean coast of Costa Rica, but different routes may have supplanted the earlier ones. Sheet gold was also still imported to be worked locally, but there was much less carved jade offered to the Cenote, and like the cast gold this dimished steadily, while the presence of cast copper increased.

The early "Toltec" intrusion at Chichén Itzá, which had initiated active Cenote ritual with exotic offerings close to A.D. 800, had coexisted for about a century with the politically controlled local Maya order, while absorbing its more sophisticated culture. However, by the tenth century Cenote offerings displayed few Maya characteristics, and the offerings reflect the warrior cult of the Toltec and the extent of their trade network. Two centuries later Chichén Itzá was declining and may have been abandoned by its resident elite population.

74. Figurine pendant

Gold; black coating
Cast; burned, crushed
Peabody Museum 10-71-20/C7702, Analysis
no. 1257, H. 4.9 cm.

This gold figure is worked in what is known
as Veraguas style. It was cast with the
whole back left open, thus simplifying the
work and saving metal. The hole visible on
this figure is from an analysis that showed
the metal to be 96.4 percent gold and 3.6
percent silver—close to the composition of
the other pieces believed to have come from
Veraguas on the Pacific coast of Panama,
west of the Cocle region.

This figure is related to the Cocle ones in
holding two objects and in having ear spirals, but it is simpler in style and execution,
with heavier cast forms.

Early Postclassic (A.D. 900–1150)
S. K. Lothrop 1952, p. 100, fig. 97e, table 32

75. Figurine pendant

Gold
Cast; crushed
Peabody Museum 10-71-20/C7703, Analysis
no. 1258, H. 4.8 cm.

Like no. 74, this figure has characteristics
of the Veraguas style. It is cast with an open
back and wears no jewelry, but it also has
markedly rectangular shoulders and originally had six square projections at the top
of the head, round protruding eyes, and
hands made up of concentric bands, or actually wax threads, before they were cast.
These traits are also found on cast gold figures known to have come from the Diquís
Delta region of southern Pacific coastal
Costa Rica, northwest of Veraguas, Panama
(S. K. Lothrop 1963, pls. 35–40). The Diquís Delta was near a major source of gold
(Bray 1981, p. 158); this may have been
traded south along the coast, since the
three Pacific coastal styles of goldwork
(Veraguas, Chiriquí, Diquís) are closely in-
terrelated, and since most gold has come
from unrecorded looting is not possible to
separate the three styles definitively. It is
safest, therefore, to describe many of these
castings as Diquís-Chiriquí-Veraguas in
style.

Wherever it was made, Pacific style goldwork was surely exported to Yucatán from
Caribbean ports, like the *tumbaga* castings
that probably came from farther north in
the Atlantic watershed of Costa Rica. Pacific goldwork was seen in the southeastern
Talamancan region of Costa Rica in the sixteenth century, and just to the south in
Panama in 1502, when Columbus noted
that gold discs were being traded in Al-
mirante Bay (Bray 1981, pp. 155, 156).

Early Postclassic (A.D. 900–1150)
S. K. Lothrop 1952, not illustrated, table 34

76. Figurine pendant

Gold
Cast; crushed
Peabody Museum 10-73-20/C7718, Analysis
no. 1274, H. 6.2 cm.

This partially open-backed gold pendant
resembles nos. 74 and 75, but its facial features are flattened pellets with slits in them,
and male sex is indicated. There are elements of the Coclé style in the objects held
in either hand and in ear spirals, although
the feather panaches have been conventionalized into rectangular flanges. This
figurine represents the ill-defined Diquís-
Chiriquí-Veraguas style.

Early Postclassic (A.D. 900–1150)
S. K. Lothrop 1952, p. 100, fig. 96b, table 34

77. Heteromorphic figurine pendant

Gold
Cast; crushed
Peabody Museum 10-71-20/C7705, Analysis
no. 1260, H. 6.3 cm.

This figure is identified as a "crocodile god"
by its large mouth with fangs and the conventionalized serpents that emanate from
its body. It is the only cast anthropomorphic
figurine from the Cenote that has animal
characteristics.

The flattened rectangular headdress and
"feet" are closely related to the flat projections characteristic of Veraguas "eagles"
and frogs. It is a rough casting composed of
98.4 percent gold, 1.5 percent silver, and 0.1
percent copper.

Early Postclassic (A.D. 900–1150)
S. K. Lothrop 1952, p. 101, fig. 96a,
table 34; Furst 1964, p. 7

78. Figurine pendant

Gold
Cast
Peabody Museum 10-73-20/C7722, Analysis
no. 1277, H. 3.7 cm.

This little figure is completely flat cast except for a doubled suspension loop at the
back of the neck. It has a number of characteristics that tie it to the Diquís variant of
the Pacific coastal goldworking region.
These are the summarily indicated triangular head flange with "ear spirals" and
hands composed of concentric wires, all in
conjunction with a chinless face (Snarskis
1981, no. 285).

Early Postclassic (A.D. 900–1150)
S. K. Lothrop 1952, not illustrated, table 34

79. Miniature figurine pendant

Gold; black coating
Cast; crushed
Peabody Museum 10-71-20/C7706, H.
2.6 cm.

Wearing a pointed, brimmed hat above simplified ear spirals, this tiny flat male figure
is apparently megaphallic. There is, however, a second unidentified serpentine form
that was crushed down upon its legs. Probably Diquís in origin.

Early Postclassic (A.D. 900–1150)
S. K. Lothrop 1952, p. 100, fig. 97f

80. Frog pendant

Gold
Cast
Peabody Museum 10-71-20/C7710,
L. 2.4 cm.

After "eagles," frogs are the second most
commonly represented animals in the goldwork of Veraguas, Chiriquí, and Diquís, yet
only six frogs were found in the Cenote and
none are bells, nor do any of them have the
large flattened feet characteristic of the Pacific coastal style. No "eagle" pendants were
found either. As with the figurines, these
omissions strongly suggest selection, and
possibly even manufacture, for the export
trade.
    Frogs are symbolically important in Yuca-
tec Maya rain-making ritual (Redfield and
Villa Rojas 1962, p. 142). This simple, ap-
pealing frog was cast with an open back.

Early Postclassic (A.D. 900–1150)
S. K. Lothrop 1952, p. 101, fig. 98a

81. Frog pendant

Gold
Cast; crushed
Peabody Museum 10-71-20/C7710B,
Analysis no. 1266, L. 4.8 cm.

This open-backed cast frog has hind feet that
are also animal heads instead of the flat,
flange-like feet most characteristic of Veraguas style frog pendants. But the scrolls
at its mouth and the globular bell eyes
conform to Veraguas style, and the dorsal
double line may be an early characteristic.

Terminal Classic–Early Postclassic (A.D.
800–1100)
S. K. Lothrop 1952, not illustrated, table 34

82. Turtle pendant

Gold
Cast
Peabody Museum 10-71-20/C7711A,
L. 3.1 cm.

Turtles were symbolically important at the
Puuc site of Uxmal in Terminal Classic
times, and at Mayapán in the Middle Postclassic. In between, at Chichén Itzá, they
are important in the monumental art
in watery basal friezes, and as the turtle
shells worn by Bacabs, or supernatural sky-
bearers. The Maya also identified a turtle
constellation (Kelley 1976, p. 45).

This open-back casting in the Diquís-
Chiriquí-Veraguas macrostyle is in perfect
conditon.

Terminal Classic–Early Postclassic (A.D.
800–1150)
S. K. Lothrop 1952, not illustrated

83. Turtle bell

Gold; black coating
Cast; crushed
Peabody Museum 10-73-20/C7739, Analysis
no. 1283, L. 4.0 cm.

This swimming turtle is modeled in simple,
rounded forms, with unadorned feet, an
elongated nose and globular eyes like early
"eagle" pendants found in the Atlantic watershed region of Costa Rica (Balser 1966,
fig. 5c). It is 88.3 percent gold, 10.1 percent
copper, and 1.6 percent silver.

Terminal Classic (A.D. 800–1000)
S. K. Lothrop 1952, p. 104, fig. 104h,
table 34; Spear 1978, pl. 21

84. Monkey Pendant

Gold
Cast; crushed
Peabody Museum 10-71-20/C7712A,
H. 3.3 cm.

This rough, solid casting from the Pacific
goldworking region represents a monkey
which holds its curling tail in one paw
while holding the other paw to its mouth.
Variations on the encircling tail with paw to
mouth are found on all of the seven gold
monkeys from the Cenote, but the other six
are bells. There are only three other simple
animal figurines in the collection; these are
two frogs and a turtle. Monkeys, frogs, and
turtles all fit easily into the Mesoamerican
environment and religion and would have
been entirely symbolically acceptable in
Yucatán.

Early Postclassic (A.D. 900–1150)
S. K. Lothrop 1952, p. 103, fig. 105b

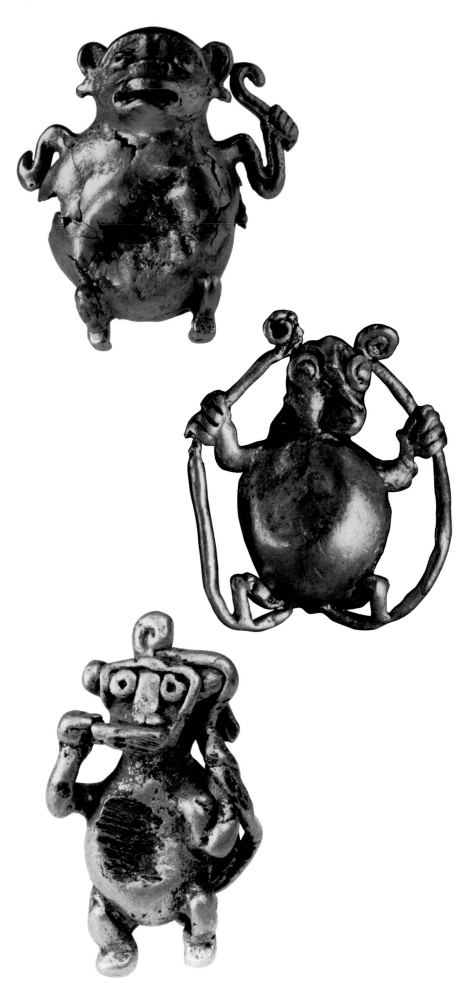

85. Four monkey bells

Gold, *tumbaga*; black coating
Cast; crushed
Peabody Museum 10-71-20/C7712B,
H. 3.0 cm.; 984-2-20/25617, H. 3.6 cm.;
10-71-20/C7713, H. 3.1 cm.; 10-73-20/
C7734, Analysis no. 1281, H. 3.9 cm.

The six crushed monkey bells in the collection represent six different styles, types, metals, and methods of casting, yet they all belong to the genus "monkey bell with tail," as can be seen from these four.

The largest monkey (10-73-20/C7734) has double earspirals and holds its encircling tail in the right paw, with a short rod (?) in the left at its mouth. It is a heavy casting that is 96.4 percent gold with 3.6 percent silver.

The coppery *tumbaga* monkey (984-2-20/ 25617) holds the end of its curled tail in the left paw, but the rest of the tail was never cast and the right limb is vestigial. Two small holes in the back of the neck were used for suspension instead of a loop.

The monkey bell with two encircling tails (10-71-20/C7713) carries the design to a symmetrical conclusion, with the curling ends of the tails doubling as spiral ears. This bell combines open-back casting of the head with full round casting of the bell/body.

The smallest monkey (10-71-20/C7712B) is a rough, heavy casting, very much like no. 84, and it is covered with red-brown pigment. It retains its pellet and, most unusual, it has a cylinder of folded sheet gold inside its suspension loop—probably to make the loop smaller.

Monkey pendants with encircling tails are known from Veraguas, but they are rare. However, monkey bells apparently come only from the Cenote—where, paradoxically, they exhibit a variety of styles. Did every workshop turn out a few bells for export purposes? Or can the Cenote bells be a small sample of a widespread industry that supplied other, still unknown, regions?

Terminal Classic–Early Postclassic (A.D. 800–1150)
S. K. Lothrop 1952, p. 103, fig. 105a, f, g

86. Two plain bells

Gold
Cast; slightly crushed
Peabody Museum 10-71-20/C6372,
D. 1.4 cm.; 10-71-20/C7667, D. 1.4 cm.

There are twenty-two more plain cast gold
bells in the collection, but they are all
crushed flat, and are larger than these. Most
are yellow gold in appearance, but some
have a visible copper content. The smaller,
more coppery, bell here (10-71-20/C6372)
has an unusual flattened form with a wide
shoulder, and the suspension loop, now
closed, was cast open, probably to attach
the bell to a closed cast loop on some larger
object.

More than eighty cast gold or *tumbaga*
bells were found by Edward H. Thompson
in the Cenote, many more than have ever
been found in the Diquís-Chiriquí-Veraguas
region of their presumed origin. This is
probably because these imported bells were
an important part of the regalia of the Mexican warriors who dominated Chichén Itzá
from about A.D. 800 until 1150, and they
were manufactured for export.

Terminal Classic – Early Postclassic (A.D.
800–1150)
S. K. Lothrop 1952, pp. 101, 102, fig. 103b

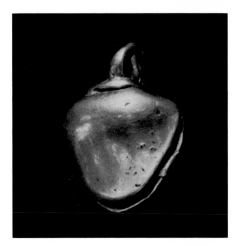

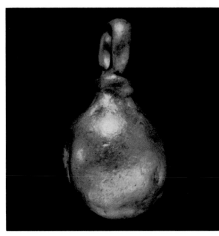

87. Three human head bells

Gold; black coating
Cast; crushed
Peabody Museum 10-71-20/C7665, W.
2.7 cm.; 10-71-20/C7693A, W. 2.6 cm.;
10-73-20/C7733, W. 1.0 cm.

The small head bell, with its face confined
to the shoulder (10-73-20/C7733) was not
crushed and retains its pellet, or voice.

Among the seven crushed head bells in
the collection there is only one (10-71-20/
C7665) that is inverted—a trophy head?
The heavy casting, features, and ear spirals
of this one resemble the figurine pendant
(no. 76), suggesting that the full round
casting of bells occurred in association with
the open-back casting of larger pieces. This
bell has a platform with a three-wire suspension loop.

The third head bell (10-71-20/C7693A) is
of a different form and style. A doubled loop
rises from the spherical body of the bell,
and facial features are carefully detailed
with eyebrows, outlined eyes, and suspension holes at the bottom of relatively realistic ears. This face is like no others in the
collection, but similar ears are found on a
head bell described as coming from Costa
Rica (Spear 1978, pl. 25).

Terminal Classic – Early Postclassic (A.D.
800–1150)
S. K. Lothrop 1952, pp. 102, 103,
fig. 104a, d, e

88. Two feline head bells

Gold
Cast; burned, crushed
Peabody Museum 10-71-20/C7666A,
H. 3.8 cm.; 10-71-20/C7666B, H. 2.2 cm.

These two, of three crushed feline head
bells in the collection, are unlike any others
known from the presumed Diquís-Chiriquí-
Veraguas region of their origin, because, instead of loops, they have two large holes in
the crown of the head for suspension.

Early Postclassic (A.D. 900–1150)
S. K. Lothrop 1952, p. 103, fig. 104i, j

89. Two deer head bells

Gold
Cast; crushed
Peabody Museum 10-71-20/C7666C,
H. 3.8 cm.; 10-73-20/C7736, H. 2.4 cm.

These heavy castings differ from each other
most in having been crushed on opposite
axes. Like felines and frogs, deer are animals that were abundant in Mesoamerica,
with distinct roles in the mythology and ritual of Yucatán.

Early Postclassic (A.D. 900–1150)
S. K. Lothrop 1952, p. 103, fig. 106a, c

90. Small mammal bell

Gold; black coating
Cast
Peabody Museum 10-71-20/C7668,
H. 2.5 cm.

This tiny seated, stub-tailed mammal holds what might be an ear of corn to its mouth in a gesture adopted for monkey effigies as well (see nos. 84, 85). It is an undamaged, clear-toned bell. If intended for suspension, it would have hung through its arms, since there is no suspension loop—otherwise it sits up. Eight small open-back cast gold peccaries from the Diquís region of Costa Rica are stylistically close to this animal, although they are not bells, suggesting a common provenience (Snarskis 1981, pl. 88).

Early Postclassic (A.D. 900–1150)
S. K. Lothrop 1952, p. 98, fig. 94; Spear 1978, pl. 19

91. Two crab bells

Gold; black coating
Cast; one burned, crushed
Peabody Museum 10-71-20/C7716,
W. 2.7 cm.; 10-73-20/C7740, Analysis
no. 1284, W. 5.9 cm.

The large, heavy cast crab has eyebrows, a
snout, and a mouth with teeth in it which is
bent under at the forward edge of its upper
shell. Two suspension loops are located behind the large claws so that the crab would
have hung "face" down. The possibility that
this bell might have been made for export is
suggested by the unique presence of a face
and of an incised design on the bottom of
the shell. The design consists of a circle in
which a cross and a square are inscribed.
This is not an immediately recognizable
Mesoamerican symbol, nor are such signs
Costa Rican; it is, however, unlikely to be
purely decorative.

Crabs are represented in the monumental
sculpture of Escuintla, on the Pacific coast
of Guatemala, and on a jade in the Cenote
that came from that region (see no. 39);
otherwise they are rarely given symbolic
importance in Mesoamerica. Crabs are,
however, shown swimming with other
marine creatures in the sea painted on
the walls of the Temple of the Warriors at
Chichén Itzá (Morris, Charlot, and Morris
1931, pls. 139, 159). This casting is 95.8
percent gold and 4.2 percent silver. One
published cast gold crab bell is thought to
have come from the Diquís region of Costa
Rica (Snarskis 1981, no. 258), and the
smaller crab bell from the Cenote may
come from there as well. It retains its metal
pellet, and would have hung "face" up.

Terminal Classic–Early Postclassic (A.D.
800–1150)
S. K. Lothrop 1952, p. 104, figs. 106d, 107,
table 32

92. Bell surmounted by male figure

Gold; black coating
Cast; crushed
Peabody Museum 10-71-20/C7661,
H. 5.9 cm.

A small naked man stands atop the platform of this bell. He holds a staff in his right hand while his left, with the arm broken off, reaches to ward off, or to steady, the bird that has alighted on his head. This anecdotal scene is unique in the collection of cast objects. It probably refers to an episode in the mythology of the Diquís-Chiriquí-Veraguas goldworking region, but was universal enough to be acceptable for export.

Early Postclassic (A.D. 900–1150)
S. K. Lothrop 1952, p. 102, fig. 101c

93. Two bells surmounted by crocodile men

Tumbaga; black coating
Cast; burned, crushed
Peabody Museum 10-71-20/C7663B,
Analysis no. 1237, H. 5.6 cm.;
10-71-20/C7663C, H. 5.4 cm.

Crocodilian-headed men are seated on the platforms of these two bells. They wear tall, brimmed hats and hold rods (?) to their mouths in either hand, like the "Darien" pendant figure (no. 48). The bells probably come from the same Diquís-Chiriquí-Veraguas workshop, but there are differences between them. The more burned bell (10-71-20/C7663C) has a three-wire border below the platform, while the other is plain. More interesting, however, is the fact that the more golden of the two was mis-assembled with the suspension loop between the figure's knees and with his head on backward—when compared to the other, more orthodox one.

The shinier bell is 61.6 percent gold, 34.4 percent copper, and 4.0 percent silver.

Early Postclassic (A.D. 900–1150)
S. K. Lothrop 1952, p. 102, figs. 102a, e, table 31

  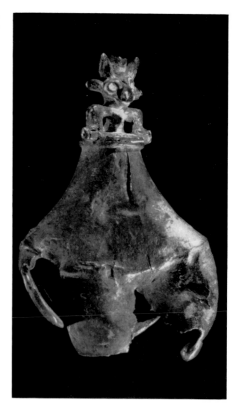

94. Bell surmounted by "eagle"

Gold; black coating
Cast; crushed
Peabody Museum 10-73-20/C7742,
H. 4.2 cm.

This "eagle" with wings spread has more
surface detailing than most of the cast gold
bells in the collection. The wings have a
border of circles, there are three small loops
at the front, and wire spirals are placed just
below the platform. It is more realistic than
most of the large flat pendants with birds
known as Veraguas eagles (see no. 95), but
like the other cast bells, it was probably
made in the Diquís-Chiriquí-Veraguas goldworking region and exported to Yucatán
from the Caribbean coast.

Early Postclassic (A.D. 900–1150)
S. K. Lothrop 1952, pp. 101, 102, fig. 99c;
Spear 1978, fig. 253

95. Bell surmounted by "eagle"

Gold
Cast; slightly crushed
Peabody Museum 10-73-20/C7729,
H. 4.2 cm.

Here the classic flat Veraguas "eagle" found
on pendants has been adapted to a bell, and
uncharacteristically shown diving. Perhaps
this descending position and the bell itself
were made specifically for trade to Chichén
Itzá, where diving birds and bells were
important elements in the regalia of the intrusive Toltec warrior elite. Except for the
figurines (nos. 76, 77) which have small
flattened appendages and the "Darien" pendant (no. 48), this bell and another like it
are the only Cenote examples of the flattened wings and tail so characteristic of the
Veraguas style bird imagery.

Terminal Classic–Early Postclassic (A.D.
800–1150)
S. K. Lothrop 1952, pp. 101, 102, fig. 99e

96. Bell surmounted by owl

Gold; black coating
Cast; crushed
Peabody Museum 10-71-20/C7663H,
H. 4.5 cm.

Six of the twenty-odd crushed bird bells in
the collection are anthropomorphic owls
which, like this one, may have wings, or
arms, and emphasize the feather tufts and
large eyes of the owl. In Mesoamerica and
elsewhere, owls have sinister, nocturnal
connotations.

Early Postclassic (A.D. 900–1150)
S. K. Lothrop 1952, p. 102, fig. 101d

Figure 10. Gold Disc L.
From S. K. Lothrop 1952, fig. 41.

97. Bell surmounted by owl

Gold
Cast; crushed
Peabody Museum 10-73-20/C7727,
H. 4.6 cm.

This owl has no head tufts, unlike no. 96,
but it is a more realistic, full-figure bird with
wings spread, that looks as if it has just
alighted. The bell represents the Diquís-
Chiriquí-Veraguas style.

Early Postclassic (A.D. 900–1150)
S. K. Lothrop 1952, pp. 101, 102, fig. 99g

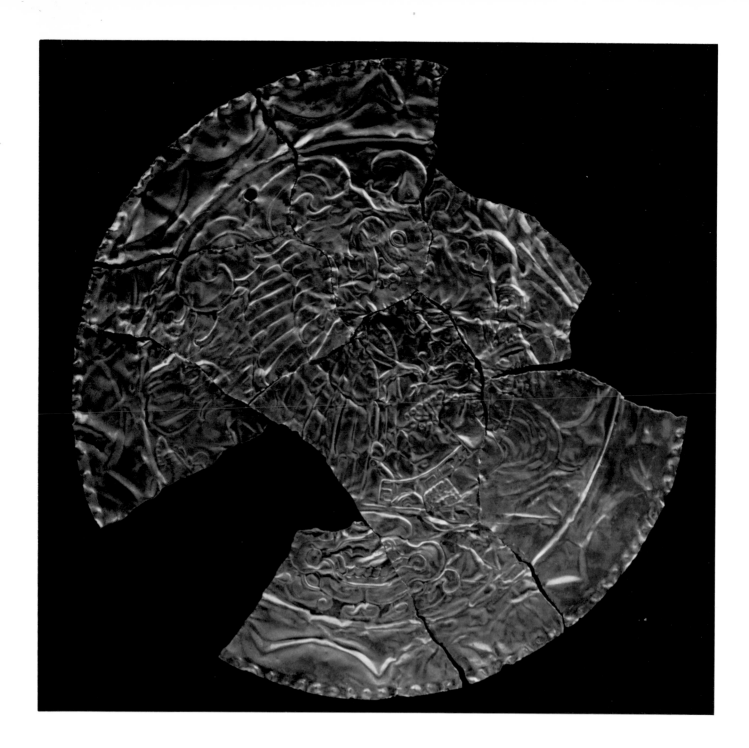

98. Disc L, eight fragments

Sheet gold; black coating
Hammered, cut; embossed; perforation;
cut, crumpled; reflattened, partially
reassembled
Peabody Museum 10-71-20/25611,
Est. D. 16.9 cm.

On this disc a face with a long, bulbous
nose and nose bead looks down upon its
Maya victim from the open beak of a warrior eagle, or eagle warrior (fig. 10). This
raptorial figure and the frontal earth monster below resemble similar elements on
later structures at Chichén Itzá, like the

Temple of the Warriors. The Maya wears a
feathered backdress like the ones worn by
the captives on Disc F (no. 14), and even
though he has a mustache, his nose bar
and receding forehead clearly identify him
as Maya. It is perhaps significant that the
face and eye of the fallen Maya were cut
through in the destruction of this disc,
whereas the eagle warrior's face was left
intact.

Samuel K. Lothrop suggests that gold
discs were worn only by eagle warriors,
since the later complementary Aztec order
of jaguar warriors is never represented on
the discs. The association of eagles and of
gold with the Sun make this an interesting

possibility, but it is likely that jaguar warriors did not exist at Chichén Itzá, since
they are never represented there. If the disc
is viewed from the back, with the design
reversed, one can see that larger forms
were embossed from this side, while finishing details were worked from the front. A
pointed stone or bone tool was probably
used while the sheet gold rested on a re-
silient surface like heavy leather, or sand.

Early Postclassic (A.D. 950–1100)
S. K. Lothrop 1952, pp. 41, 42, figs. 10k, 41;
Tozzer 1957, fig. 437; Covarrubias 1966,
fig. 124; Kubler 1975, fig. 72; Cohodas
1978a, fig. 105

99. Mask

Sheet gold; black coating
Hammered; cut, embossed; two small, six
large perforations; torn, crumpled, folded in
half; reflattened
Peabody Museum 10-71-20/C7689A,
Analysis no. 1326, H. 13.4 cm., W. 11.6 cm.

The interlaced elements on the eyelids of
this mask signify gold in the Mexican codices, and the metal of which it is made is
99.8 percent gold, with a trace of silver.
There is no known Maya glyph for gold.
The long face and narrow nose of this mask
appear neither Maya nor Mexican, although
bumps at the bridge of the nose and around
the mouth may represent scarification like
that seen on ceramic figurines from the
Maya island of Jaina. The eyebrows are
clearly designated, but it is difficult to be
sure whether the framed areas with the
gold signs are eyelids, or might be open
eyes with the lashes below; probably they
are eyelids. (The published drawing errone-
ously places the gold signs on the cheeks,
with shading added above to suggest protruding eyes that do not exist.)

Early Postclassic (A.D. 900–1100)
S. K. Lothrop 1952, p. 64, fig. 46a, table 31;
Tozzer 1957, p. 96, figs. 91–93

100. Mask

Sheet gold
Hammered; cut, embossed; four small, four
large perforations; crumpled; reflattened
Peabody Museum 10-71-20/C7689B,
H. 7.8 cm., W. 8.6 cm.

This small gold mask with open mouth, and
closed eyes signifying death, was attached
to a backing and may have been part of a
collar, belt, or shield. As on no. 99, there are
tears in the rim near the tiny perforations,
suggesting that the masks may have been
wrenched from their backings.

If Maya face masks existed, they must
have been made of perishable materials,
since with the exception of some realistic,
stone mosaic mortuary ones they are unknown archaeologically. In Maya studies
the word "mask" refers, instead, to the head
or face of a mythological being depicted as
part of a costume or the frame or furniture
of a scene. In Central Mexico, face masks,
which are generally of unknown provenience, are thought to have been mortuary
in purpose as well. There is no evidence for
funerary, as opposed to sacrificial, rites at
the Cenote, so these gold masks probably
served some other purpose.

Early Postclassic (A.D. 900–1100)
S. K. Lothrop 1952, p. 64, fig. 48b; Willard
1941, facing p. 93

101. Eight miniature masks

Sheet gold
Hammered; cut, embossed, perforated;
crumpled, folded; reflattened
Peabody Museum 10-71-20/C7691A–H,
Max. W. 3.1 cm., Min. W. 2.0 cm.

Fifteen of these little gold masks were
found in the Cenote (five were presented to
Mexico in 1959). Most resemble the larger
mask (no. 100) in having a marked brow
ridge, an open mouth, a prominent narrow
nose with flaring nostrils, and perforated
earlobes. All but one were crumpled or
folded, suggesting that they were treated
individually as offerings, even though they
might have been attached to a single backing. Although they are stylistically similar,
as many as five artisans seem to be represented among the ten masks still in the
collection.

Early Postclassic (A.D. 900–1100)
S. K. Lothrop 1952, p. 66, fig. 50

102. Two bells surmounted by parrots

Gold; black coating
Cast; crushed
Peabody Museum 10-71-20/C7658A,
H. 7.0 cm.; 10-71-20/C7658B, H. 8.2 cm.

Both of these bells have diving birds on
their platforms. These are probably parrots,
but other diving birds, birds of prey, were
worn at the front of the headdress by the
Mexican warriors at Chichén Itzá who also
wore bells at their calves. Thus these bells
might have been particularly desirable to
the warrior elite involved in Cenote ritual.

But if these unusually large, heavy bells
should date from a later period than most of
the others, they might have signified Kinich
Kakmo (Sun-Eyed Fiery Macaw) who "was
a sort of sun god whose rays descended and
consumed sacrifices" (Roys 1933, p. 141) in
later Postclassic Yucatán.

Whenever they were made, they probably
come from the same Diquís-Chiriquí-
Veraguas region as most of the other gold.
Marks from the instrument used to crush
the larger bell are visible on the back. The
smaller bell retains its pellet.

Early–Middle Postclassic (A.D. 900–1300)
S. K. Lothrop 1952, pp. 101, 102, figs. 99h,
100a; Spear 1978, pl. 18.

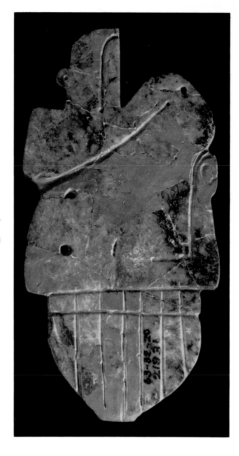

103. Full figure plaque, carved on two sides

Jadeite; splotchy emerald green, black;
black coating
Horizontal bore, one edge perforation;
recarved, two suspension holes; broken;
reconstructed
Peabody Museum 63-32-20/21931,
H. 12.7 cm., W. 6.6 cm., Th. 0.9 cm.

This plaque may possibly represent a dwarf,
like no. 70. It shares many of the same
bodily conventions, as well as the common
late use of three circles to frame the head
and organize the headdress. The central
circle may represent a schematic jaguar
nose (see nos. 59, 60, 61) or a jade tube
through which hair is drawn forward as
shown in profile on an earlier picture plaque
(no. 51).

This plaque was later cut down and the
back recarved in a crude style to represent a
turkey or vulture.

Late Classic–Early Postclassic (A.D.
750–1100)
Proskouriakoff 1974, p. 174, pl. 71a:1

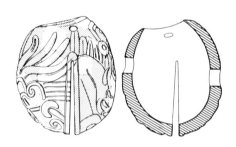

Figure 11. Jade globe.
From T. Proskouriakoff 1974, pl. 46b:1.

104. Carved globe

Jadeite, speckled gray, green
Hollowed, slit, large circular hole, four
smaller perforations; burned, broken;
reconstructed
Peabody Museum 10-70-20/C6086,
H. 4.3 cm., D. 5.3 cm.

Fragments of eight globular jade bells (?)
are in the collection. The extensive restora-
tion of this one is conjectural, but includes
a goggle-eyed human face below the feathered legs of a jaguar-bird-serpent, or earth
monster (fig. 11). Although here rear-
ranged, these same symbolic pictorial
elements are found at the base of columns,
and elsewhere, at Chichén Itzá (Tozzer
1957, figs. 314–320).

This bell shape was hollowed by using
tubular drills. The globes could have had
clappers suspended inside, but the five
holes of varying size are unexplained. Such
a hollowing of spherical jade is unknown
elsewhere in Mesoamerica.

Terminal Classic–Early Postclassic (A.D.
800–1000)
Proskouriakoff 1974, p. 87, pl. 46b:1

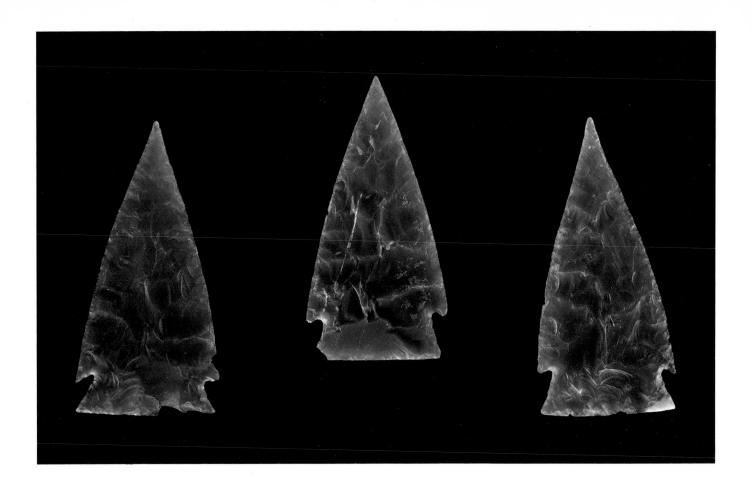

105. Three corner-notched projectile points

Jasper, green; red pigment; hafting resin
Bifacially flaked
Peabody Museum 10-4-20/C5291 (2);
83-42-20/30576, L. 4.8–5.0 cm.,
W. 2.3–2.4 cm., Th. 0.2–0.3 cm.

Six of the seven green jasper points that
Augustus Le Plongeon excavated from the
Chac Mool cache in the Platform of the
Eagles are now in the Peabody Museum
(see also nos. 11, 106). These unique points
and those in no. 106 are included in this
section as rare examples of non-Cenote ritual activity from Early Postclassic Chichén
Itzá. These are made of three slightly different stones; two yellowish green of which
one is banded, and the third blue-green.
This jasper is very rare archaeologically, and
of unknown provenience. The finest workmanship produced these delicate points,
presumably for ceremonial purposes, although they retain traces of hafting resin
along the bases, as do the other points from
the same cache.

Early Postclassic (A.D. 900–1100)
Salisbury 1877, p. 74 and facing plate;
Proskouriakoff 1962b, fig. 53f; Sheets,
Ladd, and Bathgate n.d.

106. Two corner-notched projectile points

Chert, gray, red/orange marbled
Bifacially flaked
Peabody Museum 10-67-20/C5401 (2),
L. 4.0, 4.1 cm., W. 2.8 cm., Th. 0.3 cm.

These two examples of fine chert are worked
as beautifully as the green jasper and chalcedony points that came from Augustus Le
Plongeon's excavation of the Chac Mool
statue in the Platform of the Eagles at
Chichén Itzá (see nos. 11, 105). These were
presented to the Peabody Museum by Edward H. Thompson, who reported having
obtained them "from an old Indian who
kept them in the shrine of a saint, [having
taken] them from the ground when the Dr.
[Le Plongeon] was looking at the other work-
men." Like the ones more surely known to
be from the Chac Mool cache, these retain
traces of both red pigment and hafting
resin.

Early Postclassic (A.D. 900–1100)
Sheets, Ladd, and Bathgate n.d.

107. Polychrome-decorated Slate Ware jar

Fired buff and red-slipped clay; post-fire
smudging; post-fire stucco decoration: blue,
yellow, white, black pigments
Hand-built; broken; partially restored twice
Peabody Museum 07-7-20/C4752,
H. 22 cm., Max. D. 22.5 cm.

What remains of this Slate Ware olla reveals
an extraordinary complexity of ceramic decoration. Unusual both in its pre-fire and its
post-fire decoration, this Balam Canche
Red-on-slate vessel was painted with a
sparkling specular hematite red slip *over* a
fugitive Black-on-buff smudged design,
suggesting the unlikely possibility that the
vessel was fired more than once. On top of
these the olla was finally completely decorated with a technique known as "pseudo-
cloisonné" (Castillo, 1968, Ch. 3). In this
example of the technique the jar was apparently covered with large areas of pink and
blue/green tinted stucco that approximated
the shape of the design elements; then this
base coat was cut away to the surface of the
vessel to outline the pictorial forms; these
wide grooves were filled with dark gray
stucco and became the outlines. This unusual variation on the technique, involving
outlining pre-existing forms instead of fill-
ing in pre-existing outlines, is described for
several Classic Period examples (Holien
1977, pp. 126–128). The white and yellow-
surfaced white areas were filled in last.

It has long been suggested that the ceramic pseudo-cloisonné technique was the
forerunner of the modern "lacquering" of
gourds in western Mexico, and that an
organic binder must have been used, although others have maintained that only
inorganic materials were involved. It is unlikely that this example and the pseudo-
cloisonné decorated gourds (no. 108) could
have survived the waters of the Cenote
without some resinous, water-resistant vehicle (Holien 1977, Ch. 2).

The serrated and feathered-serpent
bodies that once covered this vessel resemble serpents in the murals excavated in
the early Temple of the Chac Mool at Chichén Itzá (Morris, Charlot, and Morris
1932, pl. 132). This suggests an early Early
Postclassic date for this vessel, as does
George Brainerd's association of such Red-
on-slate ware vessels with ceramics excavated at Xochicalco and Tula in Central
Mexico (Brainerd 1958, p. 56, fig. 75).
"Pseudo-cloisonné" decorated ceramics
have similar northern affinities.

Early Postclassic (A.D. 900–1100)
Ball and Ladd n.d.

108. Three polychrome-decorated fragments

Gourd; clay and resin (?); beige, black,
blue, green, red pigments; paraffin
impregnated
Cut, broken
Peabody Museum 10-71-20/C6782 (3),
Max. H. 4.7 cm., Th. 0.3–0.7 cm.

The three "pseudo-cloisonné" (see no. 107)
decorated gourd fragments in the Peabody
collection apparently come from three different gourd vessels. One of them, with
the finned body of a fish, is probably part of
the same decorated gourd the Mexicans
found a piece of in 1967 (Piña Chan 1968,
photo 9); they found many such gourds,
worked in several different pictorial styles,
including Late Classic figural scenes (Ediger 1971, color photos 20, 23).

These three fragments are stylistically
and technically similar, but they differ
slightly in the use of line and detail. All
have raised black outlines which represent
a base coat that was cut away, leaving outlined forms to be filled in, or inlaid. The
inlay was a white material that had been
tinted with various pigments and formed
hard, bright, opaque surface layers that are
still largely intact.

The claw and leg of a bird stand upon a
blue-green band on the third fragment. Behind the claw the wing was once inlaid with
color; the background was red. On the
second there may be depicted a load, or
bundle, in a net with a tumpline (a carrying
strap worn across the forehead). The load is
set down upon the three-color band dividing
the design.

All three gourds were coated inside with a
black resinous, presumably waterproof,
material. Paraffin used to preserve these
fragments darkened the pigments; these are
closer to the original, lighter hues where
the paraffin has recently been reduced or
removed.

Terminal Classic–Early Postclassic (A.D.
800–1200)
Coggins and Ladd n.d.

109. Serpentine scepter

Wood; yellow stain (?); paraffin
impregnated
Carved; battered; cut; partially restored
Peabody Museum 10-71-20/C6751,
L. 38.4 cm., W. 4.9 cm.

This small serpentine scepter recalls the
Maya figures portrayed on the walls and
columns of the Temples of the Chac Mool
and of the Warriors at Chichén Itzá. These
figures hold both serpents and serpentine
staffs of office (Tozzer 1957, figs. 655–662),
although they all have more realistic snake
heads than this stylized example with its
elongated, fanged upper jaw and headdress
with a large bow at the back.

Serpentine scepters were probably carried
by Maya at Chichén Itzá at all periods (see
nos. 123–127). This one, and another like it
in the collection, are difficult to date.

Early–Middle Postclassic (A.D. 900–1450)
Coggins and Ladd n.d.

110. Intertwined serpent staff or scepter

Wood; red, white pigments, stucco (?); thick dark coating; burned; wax impregnated
Carved; battered
Peabody Museum 10-71-20/C6694,
L. 58.4 cm.

The two serpents at the end of this staff or scepter are intertwined and reversed like those forming the handle of the sacrificial knife (no. 26), but in this case a shaft emerges from one of the open mouths, instead of a chert blade. The staff is made of a very heavy wood that is battered as if it had seen considerable use, but the dents are all over, not concentrated at the end.

Round black, white, and red stucco (?) spots are located on the top of the snouts, behind the stucco eyes, and on the bottom of the jaws; the teeth are modeled in this same white substance. Black coating is found on top of this once-bright colored decoration.

Early Postclassic (A.D. 900–1100)
Coggins and Ladd n.d.

111. Serpentine atlatl tip

Wood; red pigment; dark coating; paraffin impregnated
Carved, polished; cut; partially restored
Peabody Museum 10-71-20/C6738,
L. 17.5 cm.

This is the distal or throwing end of an atlatl and, like the scepters carried by Maya depicted at Chichén Itzá (Tozzer 1957, figs. 660, 661), this atlatl tip displays an upturned snake head that is relatively realistic, with reticulated skin and fangs. Red pigment remains on the eyes and collar.

On the back side of this carefully smoothed shaft there is a red-painted longitudinal groove that ends with a recessed hook for engaging the end of a dart. The fragile wood and fine finish of this weapon, however, suggest a ceremonial use which culminated in cutting the shaft into sections. It was then offered to the Cenote.

Early–Middle Postclassic (A.D. 900–1400)
Coggins and Ladd n.d.

112. Serpentine atlatl tip

Wood; blue/green pigment; dark coating;
burned; paraffin impregnated
Carved; cut
Peabody Museum 10-71-20/C6739,
L. 15.4 cm.

A complex design including feathers,
scrolls, bands, and other forms covers the
back of this atlatl/scepter tip, but it is not
decipherable because of the twenty-one
holes for inlays that interrupt it. Traces of
blue/green pigment remain on the feathers,
and some of the inlays may have been red,
like the raised spots on the body of the intertwined serpent scepter (no. 110). The
belly of the serpent is hollowed longitudinally, as on the other atlatl tip (no. 111), and
terminates similarly in a recessed hook at
the back of the upturned head.

　With the serpent heads held downward,
these resemble scepters in the hands of
Maya dignitaries represented at Chichén
Itzá. If they were functional atlatls, the
hooks would be held upward in order to
throw darts.

Early–Middle Postclassic (A.D. 900–1400)
Coggins and Ladd n.d.

113. Small bench

Wood; black coating; jade/turquoise,
obsidian; paraffin impregnated
Carved; broken; split
Peabody Museum 10-71-20/C6705,
L. 14.2 cm., H. 6.0 cm.

This graceful little bench with tapering legs
was once decorated with mosaic. A sixteenth-century source relates that wooden
idols were placed on small, leaf-entwined
stools (Tozzer, ed., 1941, p. 94, n. 413). This
bench may have served such a purpose, but
if it did, the wooden idols were probably
more carefully made than the preserved
ones that were thrown late into the Cenote
(nos. 174–176).

　Another small wooden bench that has a
projecting serpent head with a human head
in its open jaws was found, in 1967, by the
Mexicans in their lowest stratum (Piña
Chan 1980, photo 105).

Early Postclassic (A.D. 900–1200)
Coggins and Ladd n.d.

114. Two jaguar tooth effigies

Wood; dark coating; jade/turquoise; paraffin
impregnated
Carved; two perforations in plain one
Peabody Museum 10-71-20/C6716,
L. 4.7 cm.; 10-71-20/C6717, L. 5.8 cm.

The undecorated canine tooth effigy has opposed perforations for suspension. It was
covered with an adhesive coating that
probably once held a gold overlay, since a
bit of gold remains on one of the four of this
type, and gold-plated wooden teeth are reported by T. A. Willard (1926, p. 142). They
may have been part of a necklace. The
mosaic-incrusted wooden canine was cut
down from a longer, angled one, probably
with perforations, like the other. It is similarly hollowed, but this hollow is filled with
a black resinous substance that probably
served as an adhesive. Since this tooth was
not a pendant, it may have been the projecting canine of a mosaic-incrusted mask.

Postclassic (A.D. 900–1520)
Coggins and Ladd n.d.; Saville 1922, fig. 10

115. Carved Redware jar

Fired red-slipped clay
Hand-built, pre-slip carved; broken;
partially restored twice
Peabody Museum 10-56-20/C5923,
H. 23.2 cm., D. 24 cm.

Working in imitation of imported Silho Fine
Orange and Tohil Plumbate vessels, the
Yucatecan potter has here failed to control
firing for a uniform color, failed to achieve
the fluency of much Fine Orange decoration, and apparently decided against
the appropriate bulbous tripod feet, even
though emplacements had been grooved for
them at the base of the wall. The top band
that decorates the shoulder of this olla, as
often on Fine Orange vessels, consists of a
row of *chalchihuitls*, or signs for 'precious'
and 'water' that resemble perforated jade
discs. Below these, two (originally four)
feathered serpents pursue each other
around the vessel. These have large upper
jaws with a row of molars and with flexible
snouts that curl upward; each has an eye
with a hook in place of the pupil and a
feather crest. A pendant with a face hangs
from beads perhaps worn by a serpent at
the left of the remaining design. The truncated serpent bodies terminate in feathers.
These stylized and abbreviated beasts, typical Postclassic serpents, have survived
principally on pottery.

Early–Middle Postclassic (A.D. 1000–1200)
Ball and Ladd n.d.; Brainerd 1958, fig. 85a

116. Three spherical bells

Two copper, one *tumbaga* (?)
Cast
Peabody Museum 07-7-20/C4871,
D. 2.6 cm.; 07-7-20/C4872, Analysis no. 48,
D. 1.4 cm.; 10-70-20/C6007, D. 1.5 cm.

The skeletal death god of the Maya is shown on Late Classic pottery and in the Post-classic Dresden and Madrid codices wearing bells at neck, ankles, wrists, and at the top of the skull; however, this convention evolved before copper bells were known in Mesoamerica and it is likely that the Classic ones were pottery, wood, or seedpods that suggested the rattling of bones. Copper bells first appear in Maya burials early in Postclassic times—as wide-spread trade in Plumbate and Fine Orange pottery and sheet gold suggest new economic and political relationships. Toltec warriors are depicted wearing bells at this time (nos. 14, 25), and it may be in this connection that their use spread.

All of the copper and gold bells recovered from the Cenote were cast by the lost-wax process. In this metal-working technique molten copper was poured into a mold containing a wax model of the bell; this had been formed over a clay and charcoal core, probably by dipping it into molten wax. The hot copper melted and replaced the wax model, which was "lost." Copper spurs on the top of the suspension loops of these bells are pouring spouts that were not filed off in a finishing operation when the outer mold and a friable inner core were chipped away. Most of the bells from the Cenote have lost the metal pellets that were inside the inner core when the bells were cast; these were perhaps removed in the offering ritual, to silence them, since the copper bells, unlike the gold ones, were not crushed or burned.

Copper bells became increasingly common in Postclassic times, and in the sixteenth century they were a medium of exchange. The vast majority of the bells found in the Cenote probably belong to the later phase of offering ritual, beginning in the Middle Postclassic. Most of the thousands dredged from the Cenote by Edward H. Thompson were lost when his hacienda was burned in 1920. Bells of this common globular form are Samuel K. Lothrop's style A. The smaller copper bell (07-7-20/C4872) has silver, tin, iron, lead, bismuth, and arsenic impurities, a composition that most clearly resembles analyzed bells from Oaxaca (Proskouriakoff 1962b, p. 397, table 6). There are no native metals in Yucatán, so any found there must have come from elsewhere—though an itinerant smith might have worked the metal he carried to order, at his market.

Postclassic (A.D. 900–1520)
S. K. Lothrop 1952, pp. 86, 88, figs. 75, 76, table 24; Willard 1926, facing p. 140; Pendergast 1962, p. 526, fig. 5; Bray 1977, p. 370, fig. 2:1–4; Spear 1978, fig. 254; Piña Chan 1980, fig. 111

118. Four decorated pear-shaped bells

Copper; one surface stripped
Incised; cast; three metal pellets
Peabody Museum 07-7-20/C4861,
D. 2.1 cm.; 10-56-20/C5999, Analysis
no. 81, D. 1.8 cm.; 10-70-20/C6003,
D. 3.5 cm.; 10-70-20/C6015, Analysis
no. 29, D. 1.9 cm.

Decoration on the shoulders of these pear-shaped bells puts them in Samuel K. Lothrop's catchall style D4. The large, heavy burned bell has a simple pattern of short vertical bands between encircling horizontal ones, with neither platform, nor wire bordering the mouth. Its pellet is a ragged chunk of golden metal.

The two smaller bells without wire-bordered mouths do have platforms, and a more complex design of incised verticals and horizontals. Their pellets are made of doubled metal wire rolled into a ball; the surface of one of them has been chemically stripped in recent years.

The bell with both a platform and a bordered mouth is from a group of seven in the collection that have simple incised designs consisting of circles, dots, zigzags, and crossed lines. They are poor castings with thin walls, holes, and miscast areas, as for instance the half-open mouth of this bell, which probably could not hold a pellet.

Although style D4 bells are widespread, excavations at Dzibilchaltún, Yucatán, and Lamanai, Belize, have dated some members of the class securely to the Early Postclassic (Taschek n.d.; Pendergast, personal communication).

Postclassic (A.D. 1000–1539)
S. K. Lothrop 1952, p. 90, figs. 83c, 84g, table 28; Pendergast 1962, p. 527, fig. 5; Bray 1977, p. 372, fig. 2:3–15; Piña Chan 1980, fig. 111

117. Three open-work decorated pear-shaped bells

Copper
Cast
Peabody Museum 10-56-20/C5992,
D. 1.1 cm.; 10-70-20/C6008, Analysis
no. 27, D. 1.7 cm.; 10-70-20/C6018,
D. 1.7 cm.

These bells all have open-work shoulders, but two distinct types of Samuel K. Lothrop's style D5 are represented. The largest bell has a "wirework" design of open scrolls and panels joining the top and bottom, while the smaller, more slender bells have graceful, flattened loops for this purpose.

Two bells of this latter type were excavated from an Early Postclassic tomb at Tonina, Chiapas (Becquelin and Baudez 1982, pp. 149–150), although they are rounder than the ten Cenote examples and have wire-bordered mouths like only three from the Cenote. It is not clear how important such "wire" borders are for the classification of bells. Perhaps a thread of wax was added to the edges of the long mouth cut out of the wax model to strengthen the edges, occasionally to hide a ragged cut, or possibly as a stylistic device to identify the work of a metalsmith, or metalworking region.

Postclassic (A.D. 900–1539)
S. K. Lothrop 1952, pp. 90, 91, figs. 83a, 84b, f, table 28; Pendergast 1962, p. 526, fig. 5; Bray 1977, p. 373, fig. 2:22–24

119. Plano-convex disc

Green obsidian
Ground, polished
Peabody Museum 10-70-20/C6036,
D. 2.7 cm., Th. 0.6 cm.

Most, if not all, of the green obsidian exported throughout Mesoamerica in the Classic and Postclassic periods was exported from the mines at Pachuca, Hidalgo, in the central highlands of Mexico. In the Early Postclassic, when this green obsidian disc was probably made, the Toltec capital at Tula, Hidalgo, controlled the mines and maintained contact with their southern capital at Chichén Itzá.

However, beyond its greenness, there is little to suggest a date for this disc, which has a polished convex face with a flat ground back and beveled edge. It may have served as the eye of a skull (see no. 199), although more than one use is suggested by chips in the stone around the back rim which are covered by traces of green stucco.

Early Postclassic (A.D. 900–1150)
Moholy-Nagy and Ladd n.d.

120. Atlatl finger grip

Marine shell; burned
Carved, incised; broken
Peabody Museum 10-70-20/C6040,
W. 3.9 cm., Est. Hole D. 1.5 cm.

In Postclassic Mesoamerica, finger grips, often made of shell, were lashed on to the lower third of an atlatl shaft when finger holes were not an integral part of the wooden weapon (Ekholm 1962). They were made in pairs and the mate for this one was found in the Cenote by the Mexicans in 1967, along with half of a similar pair. All three shell grips have intertwined serpents with scaly bellies, open-fanged jaws, and eyeholes that may have held inlays.

Postclassic (A.D. 900–1539)
Moholy-Nagy and Ladd n.d.; Merwin and Vaillant 1932, pl. 35y

121. *Macuahuitl* effigy (?)

Wood; red pigment; dark coating; burned; paraffin impregnated
Carved, incised; battered; worm-eaten (?)
Peabody Museum 10-71-20/C6693,
L. 48.8 cm.

This heavy, collared club has always been thought to be an effigy of the obsidian-edged Mexican weapon known in Nahuatl as a *macuahuitl* (Tozzer 1957, p. 172). But if the cross-hatching and thick red paint that completely covered the carved top were part of the original design, then the effigy obsidian blades that project around the edge were also supposed to have been red and cross-hatched. Whatever its significance, this staff saw heavy use. It is scarred and battered and its end was burned off, perhaps just before it was thrown into the Cenote.

Postclassic (A.D. 900–1539)
Coggins and Ladd n.d.; Follett 1932, fig. 17; Piña Chan 1980, fig. 106

122. Long-handled open-work censer

Fired specular hematite red-slipped clay;
blue pigment; burned
Hand built, perforated, incised; broken;
partially reconstructed
Peabody Museum 07-7-20/C4738,
Rim D. 14.8 cm.

This type of long-handled open-work censer, with hollow globular feet, is generally described as "Mixtec" because it resembles censers that were common in the Oaxaca-Puebla region in Postclassic times, whereas they were rare elsewhere. Three complete ones and twenty-four sherds, including two with specular hematite red slip like this one, were excavated at Zaculeu, in western Guatemala (Woodbury and Trik 1953, pp. 153–155), and a post-fire painted one at Los Naranjos, Honduras (Baudez and Becquelin 1973, fig. 130h, pp. 340–341). These all have Plumbate pottery associations which make them important elements in the Early Postclassic Mexican expansion that carried Plumbate and Fine Orange ceramics, and the earliest copper bells to Chichén Itzá. A cruder, unslipped censer of this type also came from the Cenote, and another was recently excavated from a burial at Chichén Itzá (Callaghan and Gallereta N. 1976, photo 25, fig. 13), suggesting that these may have been local copies. This one differs from the other two Chichén censers in red slip, a fine paste, and a recognizable design in the holes cut in the wall of the vessel. The design consists of *chalchihuitls*,

frets, and interlaces with a face on each side. The incised design was added after the perforations were cut in the wall, after slipping, and after firing. This incised design explains the apparently meaningless shapes of the cut-out holes on this vessel, and by analogy it explains the similar oddly shaped holes on other unslipped and unincised censers of this type.

There was burning inside the vessel, as would be expected of a censer, and it looks on the outside as if it had been set upon a fire. The long handle, which is unlike any others of the type, has a delicately constructed, thin-walled finial with a knob at the end that almost resembles a bud, with folded petals painted alternately red and blue. This handle is also the vessel's third foot and was probably a rattle like the bulbous feet.

Early Postclassic (A.D. 900–1150)
Ball and Ladd n.d.; Brainerd 1958, fig. 97h

The Late Phase of Sacred Cenote Ritual

The Late Phase of Cenote ritual is Middle to Late Postclassic, lasting from A.D. 1250 to 1539 at most. After a century or more of depopulation and diminished ceremonial activity, Chichén Itzá became the goal of pilgrimages, and the Sacred Cenote became the focus of a more purely Maya ritual and the repository of different kinds of offerings. This renewed activity was under the control of the city of Mayapán to the southwest, which, while having supplanted Chichén Itzá as northern capital, still drew its legitimacy from custody of the ancestral shrines and the Sacred Cenote at Chichén Itzá.

Late Cenote ritual was much more clearly concerned with deities than was the earlier warrior cult, and although the offerings still reflect an elite ceremonialism, this later Maya society was poorer and more provincial. Wooden "idols" were offered, and great quantities of copal incense and rubber in tripod bowls were cast in. Jade was rare in later Postclassic Mesoamerica, and there are no characteristic Maya jade carving styles; instead, plain jade beads and ancient carved jades, probably found in structure caches at Late Preclassic sites, were offered to the Cenote.

Among the deities invoked at the Cenote was Ek Chuah, god of the merchants, suggesting the cultural importance of long distance trade for the later Postclassic Maya. Some gold-foil-covered objects and a lot of cast copper were traded north to Chichén Itzá and found their way, usually undamaged, into the Cenote, as did thousands of cotton textile fragments which represented one of the major export goods of northern Yucatán.

A third component of this late Cenote ritual had to do with lineage, as exemplified by wooden manikin scepters of a Postclassic type that apparently associated the ruler with the descent of celestial bodies. A lineage ceremony may have tied Mayapán and other related centers to Chichén Itzá by virtue of its empowering, ancestral role and of its possibly reinterpreted Toltec imagery of serpentine descent. Offerings were still made to the Cenote at the time of the Conquest and later, according to sixteenth-century accounts, but only the greatest sacrifice, human life, is specifically described at this late date.

123. Kneeling figure scepter

Wood; yellow stain or paint; jade/turquoise,
obsidian; dark blue-green pigment; sheet
gold, red pigment; black coating; paraffin
impregnated
Carved; cut; broken; partially restored
Peabody Museum 10-71-20/C6754,
L. 28.8 cm.

"And so if this country had possessed gold it
would be this well that would have the
greater part of it," the Bishop de Landa
predicted in the 1560s (Tozzer, ed. 1941,
p. 181). Inspired by Landa's speculation,
Edward H. Thompson proved that the Maya
did have gold, and that they had thrown
some of it into the Sacred Cenote when he
found this gold-masked scepter in 1904, in
the second month of dredging.

The kneeling figure was painted or
stained yellow, and traces of an intense
blue-green pigment remain on the left earflare and knee. It holds what may be a fan
in its right hand, and a small rattle or
scepter in the left (see no. 124). The red-
painted gold mask was held to the wooden
face with a black, resinous adhesive that
covers its carved features. A dark adhesive
was also used to cement the five greenstone
and obsidian mosaic tesserae that remain
on the headband. This figure has an elaborate backdress that consists of a complex
bow and a plaited "mat sign," a knot that
resembles the ones used repeatedly in the
borders of the contemporary wall paintings
at Tulum (Miller 1982, pls. 28, 37). Like the
other three figural scepters, this one has a
chamber behind the figure, and, as with
two of them, the chamber probably had a
cover, since there are perforations at the
rim. There is clear evidence of burning
inside, and there are bits of copal at the
broken edges.

The shaft was cut and broken in three
places, perhaps long before the scepter's
consignment to the Cenote, since the
breaks had been mended by boring a hole
through the shaft to splint them together
and were cemented with black adhesive.
The nonfunctional atlatl hook was very
likely broken earlier as well.

Postclassic diving figure scepters and
Classic Period manikin scepters all represent supernatural beings which are
probably related to lineage and the legitimacy of rulers, so it is unlikely that this
gold- and jade-bedecked personage is an
ordinary mortal, even though he kneels and
has no clearly divine attributes. Perhaps the
gold mask denotes a deity impersonator.

Middle Postclassic (A.D. 1300–1450)
Coggins and Ladd n.d.; S. K. Lothrop 1952,
fig. 53; Tozzer 1957, fig. 99

124. Rattle (?)

Wood; dark coating; jade/turquoise, gold;
paraffin impregnated
Carved; scratched; split
Peabody Museum 10-71-20/C6695,
L. 22 cm., Rim D. 4.2 cm.

This object resembles one carried in the left
hand of the kneeling figure on the cham-
bered scepter (no. 123). A style D bell (see
no. 27), with a pellet but lacking a loop, was
found inside the chamber of this small
scepter, although it falls out easily and may
not belong to it. The chamber is open at the
back and through the flaring top, with charring inside and at the rim, so this may have
been a simple copal-burning scepter that
was later converted to a rattle.

The collared shaft is covered with
scratches which enhanced the adhesive-
ness of a resinous coating that probably secured a thin sheet of gold foil and glued
mosaic to the chamber wall; two green
stone tesserae remain, and there is a tiny
fleck of gold on the flare.

Middle Postclassic (A.D. 1300–1450)
Coggins and Ladd n.d.; Saville 1922, pl. 3A;
Piña Chan 1980, fig. 106

125. Diving figure scepter

Wood; dark coating; jade/turquoise (?), red pigment; paraffin impregnated
Carved; cut, broken; warped
Peabody Museum 10-71-20/C6753,
L. 39 cm., W. 8.1 cm.

The lower end of this staff of office originally had the recurved tip of a dart-thrower, or atlatl. As on some Classic Period manikin scepters, this vestigial hook refers to the origin of the Maya scepter form in atlatls that were once held as personal and national insignia by Central Mexican warriors abroad.

For the Maya, such scepters became symbols of lineage (Coggins 1979, p. 40). This "diving" figure scepter, with a large bow at the forehead and a simple rounded collar, descends holding balls that may represent copal. Smoke from burning copal probably poured from the chamber between its bent legs. Small perforations near the rim suggest that a lid may have directed the smoke out the side slots and through the lattice at the back.

Descent from the heavens is one of the dominant symbolic themes at Chichén Itzá throughout the Postclassic Period. Descending serpents grace the columns and balustrades of Early Postclassic structures, and birds descend at the front of Toltec warrior headdresses (fig. 5). Anthropomorphic diving figures became important in later Postclassic Maya religion, and the Bishop de Landa described the sixteenth-century Maya feast of Em Ku—the descent of the god (Tozzer, ed. 1941, p. 106, n. 686). In the late Mixtec and Maya manuscripts, descending figures often represent heavenly bodies, and copal-burning ones might be *buts' ek'*—smoking stars, or comets (Barrera Vásquez 1980). "Diving gods" are also found on the façades of the Middle Postclassic temples at Tulum, on the east coast, and this scepter may be contemporary with an early Tulum wall painting that depicts a similar mosaic-masked figure (Miller 1982, pl. 21) and with the florescence of the site of Mayapán, where diving figures are found in stone and ceramic sculpture (R. E. Smith 1971, fig. 64e, f; Proskouriakoff 1962b, fig. 3). A fragmentary ceramic diving figure, like the Mayapán ones, but painted in the white, blue, and black colors characteristic of Tulum wall painting (see no. 192), was found in the Cenote by the 1967 Mexican expedition (Ediger 1971, color photos 15, 17).

Throughout the approximately seven centuries (A.D. 800–1500) of its ceremonial use, objects offered to the waters of the Cenote, twenty meters below, descended from above like the copal offered by this figure. Like the falling copal, which was offered in flames, perhaps the sacrificial objects emulated the setting of brilliant heavenly bodies.

There are traces of red pigment around the mouth and eyes, and more than one hundred tiny jade, and possibly turquoise, mosaic tesserae remain on the face.

Middle Postclassic (A.D. 1300–1450)
Coggins n.d.; Willard 1926, opposite p. 125;
Saville 1922, pl. 3a

126. Diving figures scepter

Wood; blue-green pigment, white stucco;
traces of black coating; paraffin
impregnated
Carved
Peabody Museum 10-71-20/C6698,
L. 28.0 cm., Flare D. 3.5 cm.

On August 4, 1904, when Edward H.
Thompson dredged this perfectly preserved
object from the Cenote, he was convinced
that it was a flute—probably because the
upper half is hollow. However, it is one of
three diving figure scepters that he found,
and it differs from the other two in having
two figures that dive along the shaft instead
of one; the descending figure at the base
wears a large serpent helmet and the one
above carries balls of copal (?) while wearing a plain round collar and a headdress
with diverging panaches like the mosaic-
masked diving figure (no. 125).

The arms of the upper figure are feathered, and its body is hollowed out to form
a chamber that is open at the back and
through the flare at the top. There is faint
evidence of burning inside this chamber.
The butt of the shaft inside the lower figure
is also hollow, perhaps to hold the scepter
upright when not in use.

Traces of dark resinous and white stucco
coatings and of blue-green pigment on the
headband suggest that this scepter was
once colorfully decorated. There is no evidence of damage associated with offering to
the Cenote.

This scepter is extraordinary for the crisp-
ness of its carving and for an iconographic
clarity that resembles the sharp-featured
gods of Chen Mul Modeled incense burners
(J. E. S. Thompson 1957), although the
principal clues to identification have been
lost with the paint. The two diving figures
may signify the descent of two associated
celestial bodies, but, like the figures on nos.
123 and 125, they also refer to the ancient
atlatl scepters in having a hook that is
formed by the upper jaw of the serpent
headdress of the lower figure.

Middle Postclassic (A.D. 1300–1450)
Coggins and Ladd n.d.; Pijoán 1964,
fig. 811; Easby and Scott 1970, no. 255;
Piña Chan 1980, fig. 106

127. Diving figure scepter

Wood; dark coating; paraffin impregnated
Carved; broken; partially restored
Peabody Museum 10-71-20/C6697,
L. 35.0 cm.

The serpentine shaft of this scepter is inverted so that the open jaws of a serpent are at the top of the handle to receive the descending figure, rather than at the bottom, terminating in a hook/serpent head, as on nos. 123, 125, and 126. What may be a ball of copal is clasped in this figure's large hands, below feathered arms, as it descends. Perforated discs encircle the headband, and an open-jawed animal, now broken, was in the headdress above. At the top of the scepter there is a spherical basket that probably had a lid, suggesting that smoke may have poured through the open "weave," although there is no charring visible inside. Tozzer believed these scepters were "aspergilla," or sprinklers of holy water, like some described by Landa (Tozzer 1957, p. 198), but it is hard to see how any of them could have held water. On the back of the shaft, just below the serpent's lower jaw, there are six horizontal grooves that could have served as rasps, or as a tally for the occurrence of the astronomical event that the scepter itself may represent.

The three descending figure scepters are made of three different woods. They are carved in three different styles, and they vary in iconography, but all three have figures that carry round objects, wear the same simple collar, and have analogous headdresses. The differences may represent the participation of different towns or regions in Cenote rituals—possibly in only one Cenote ritual—whereas the similarities speak for their contemporaneity—during the period of the florescence of Mayapán, when that city governed a league of towns and their lords (Tozzer, ed. 1941, pp. 25, 26).

Middle Postclassic (A.D. 1300–1450)
Coggins and Ladd n.d.

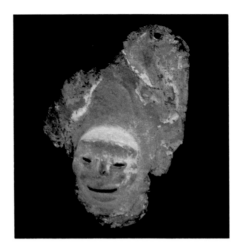

128. Diving god pendant fragment

Sheet copper, gilt; black coating
Hammered, embossed, cut; perforation for suspension
Peabody Museum 10-71-20/C7692,
H. 4.1 cm.

Diving gods were an important symbolic form for the Maya in Middle and Late Postclassic times (see nos. 125–127). Here a face is modeled in high relief below frog-like legs embossed in low relief. A dark coating, possibly an adhesive, covers the triangular area of the headdress and the face, which was worked over a three-dimensional form, with eyes and mouth cut out; this high-relief technique is otherwise unknown.

A suspension hole at the rounded upper edge suggests that this was a disc, possibly worn as a pectoral or at the front of a headdress.

Middle–Late Postclassic (A.D. 1400–1539)
S. K. Lothrop 1952, p. 72, fig. 57b

129. Two earflares

Sheet copper, gilt; black coating; burned
Hammered, cut; two perforations
Peabody Museum 10-71-20/C7418B,
D. 4.0 cm.; 10-71-20/C7418, D. 7.9 cm.

The manufacture of these earflares involved a degree of virtuosity unknown in other kinds of Mesoamerican sheet metal work. The flares must have been hammered over a form, from a single flat sheet, since no seams are visible. Only the face of the flares was gilt. The stem was passed through a hole in the earlobe and held in place behind the ear by a weight hung from a cord passed through the two perforations in the stem. This is the same construction found on Classic jade earflares (see no. 64).

Edward H. Thompson found six copper earflares, including a pair, in the Cenote; one of these was presented to Mexico in 1959, and the Mexicans found more in 1967 (Piña Chan 1970, photo 38).

Late Postclassic (A.D. 1400–1539)
S. K. Lothrop 1952, pp. 79–80, fig. 66; Bray 1977, p. 378, fig. 5:13

130. Finger ring with mask

Copper
Cast
Peabody Museum 10-56-20/C5982,
D. 2.0 cm.

Only prominent canines, suggesting venerability, serve to identify this face, which is surmounted by an imperfectly cast feather (?) headdress. Cast loops that may have held cast danglers form the nose and ears. The face was carefully modeled in wax before the "wirework" details, including "feathers," were added; at the sides of the headdress these "feathers" are loops, whereas the vertical ones terminate in tiny blobs. The ring resembles gold and silver ones found in the Late Postclassic Tomb 7 at Monte Albán in its "false filigree" technique with bird head panels (Caso 1969, fig. 97), although on this poor casting the open-work is not completely successful. "False filigree" uses wax threads to create a tracery which is replaced by molten copper in the lost-wax casting (see no. 116).

Late Postclassic (A.D. 1400–1539)
S. K. Lothrop 1952, pp. 83, 84, figs. 71, 72c

131. Open-work finger ring

Copper
Cast
Peabody Museum 10-56-20/C5981,
D. 1.9 cm.

The "false filigree" loops and scrolls on this ring suggest Oaxacan workmanship, as they do on the mask ring (no. 130), on four more open-work rings in the collection, and on five found in the Cenote by the 1961 Mexican expedition (Littlehales 1961, p. 550). There are also sixteen plain cast rings in the Peabody Museum Cenote collection: cylinders, biconical and barrel shapes (one with a twisted border), and double and triple and convex forms. Several were covered with gold foil.

Postclassic (A.D. 1000–1539)
S. K. Lothrop 1952, pp. 83–85, figs. 71, 72a, 73b; Piña Chan 1980, fig. 111

132. Two "wirework" bells

Copper
Cast
Peabody Museum 07-7-20/C4855, Analysis
no. 140, D. 2.6 cm.; 07-7-20/C4856,
D. 1.4 cm.

The wire-like decoration on these bells is
the cast copper impression of wax threads
that were wound around the shoulder of the
wax model of the bells, with final wax
threads added in a zigzag pattern, to outline
the mouth and to form the single-wire loop.

These two variations on this technique
reveal different degress of skill. The "wires"
encircling the large bell are somewhat
irregular in thickness and placement,
whereas the elongated bell has evenly
placed threads that measure two to a milli-
meter. It is hard to imagine how the wax
could have been extruded, or conceivably
rolled, so fine, or how the bell was turned so
regularly to cover the dipped wax model.

There are twenty-two wirework bells in
the collection; nineteen are elongated and
three biconical. Most have broken loops and
lack pellets, although three retain small
stones inside.

Wirework bells like these have been
excavated in the Valley of Mexico and
Michoacán in Late Postclassic contexts, and
it is likely that they were imported from
there, perhaps after the fall of Mayapán,
since none were found at that city, which
was the successor to Chichén Itzá as northern capital.

Late Postclassic (A.D. 1450–1539)
S. K. Lothrop 1952, pp. 91–93, fig. 86, table
30; Pendergast 1962, pp. 527, 528, fig. 5;
Bray 1977, p. 373, fig. 2:20, 21

133. Two "button" bells

Copper; one surface stripped; metal pellets
Cast; one incised
Peabody Museum 07-7-20/C4866,
D. 4.1 cm.; 07-7-20/C4868, D. 2.7 cm.

With flattened shoulders and rounded
bases, these bells resemble large buttons.
The larger bell is a smooth, thin casting,
whereas the smaller one, which has been
chemically stripped of its patina, has a
rough surface with a quadripartite design
incised on the shoulder. Neither bell has a
platform or a wire-bordered mouth. Sharply
angled button bells are not known north of
the Maya regions, but have been found in
more than one location in Honduras (Bray
1977, p. 370).

"Button" bells are Samuel K. Lothrop's
style B. After spherical and pear-shaped
bells, they are the most numerous.

Middle–Late Postclassic (A.D. 1300–1539)
S. K. Lothrop 1952, p. 88, figs. 77, 78,
table 26; Bray 1977, fig. 2:5; Spear 1978,
fig. 256; Piña Chan 1980, fig. 111

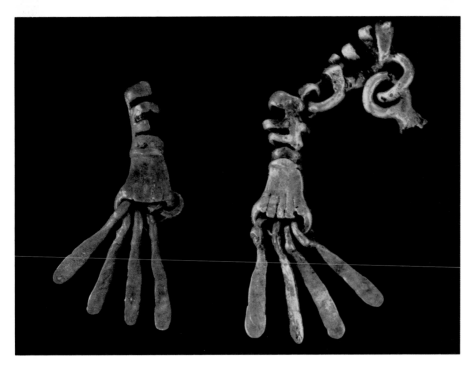

134. Two jointed pendants

Tumbaga (?); black coating on one, the other cleaned
Cast (?); crushed, broken
Peabody Museum 10-71-20/C7671,
Max. L. 9.5 cm.

Cast figural pendants with rows of open cast rings for danglers are well known in the Diquís region of Costa Rica (S. K. Lothrop 1963, pls. 37–43), but none of these has sequences of joints; nor do the danglers have complex shapes. These two incomplete pendants probably came from Oaxaca, where multiple-element danglers were made (Caso 1969, figs. 250, 251). They may have been part of a single pectoral, unless they were made as ear ornaments by an indigenous Central Mexican goldsmith after the Conquest—an unlikely scenario, but their sliced tubular form with spatulate danglers is otherwise unknown.

Late Postclassic (A.D. 1400–1600)
S. K. Lothrop 1952, p. 73, fig. 58

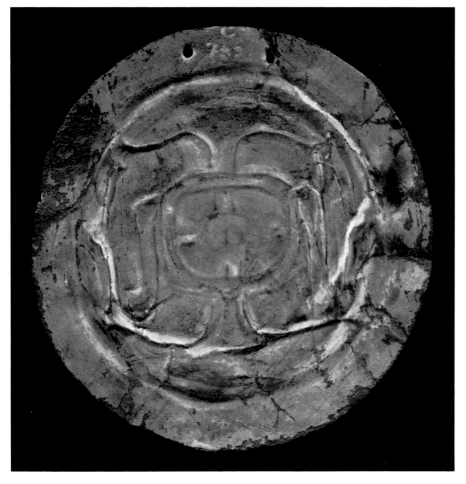

135. Sun Disc

Sheet copper; gilt
Hammered, cut, embossed; two perforations for suspension
Peabody Museum 10-71-20/C7651,
D. 8.1 cm.

Once covered on both sides with gold foil, this disc bears the *kin* glyph signifying "the Sun" and "a day" (fig. 12).
   The disc may have been half of a pair in which the second had a moon glyph and was made of some "white" metal, like tin (see no. 136), lead, or silver, although no silver has been found in the Maya lowlands. Very large, heavy pairs of Sun and Moon discs made of gold and silver were described by sixteenth-century Spanish historians in both Mexico and Peru; presumably they were melted down, and these simple Maya pendants are the only surviving examples of the form. A gilt copper pair of Sun and Moon discs in the collection was presented to Mexico in 1959.

Late Postclassic (A.D. 1450–1539)
S. K. Lothrop 1952, pp. 77–79, fig. 62b;
Tozzer 1957, fig. 277b

136. Moon Disc pendant with wooden support

Tin: hammered, embossed; cut;
disintegrated
Wood: paraffin impregnated; perforated;
stained
Peabody Museum 10-71-20/C7647,
D. 6.4 cm. (tin), 6.0 cm. (wood)

This Moon disc may have been paired with
the Sun disc no. 135 (fig. 12); it is likely
that this pair and a set of gilded copper ones
from the Cenote (presented to Mexico in
1959) were analogous. Here the Sun and
Moon symbolism is Maya—but the blank
copper and (rare) tin discs were probably
imported from central or western Mexico to
be worked in Yucatán.

   Although the wooden disc is smaller in
diameter, the perforations match those in
the tin one, and the disintegrated area at
the edge of the tin matches the stain on
the wood.

Late Postclassic (A.D. 1450–1539)
S. K. Lothrop 1952, pp. 77–79, fig. 62

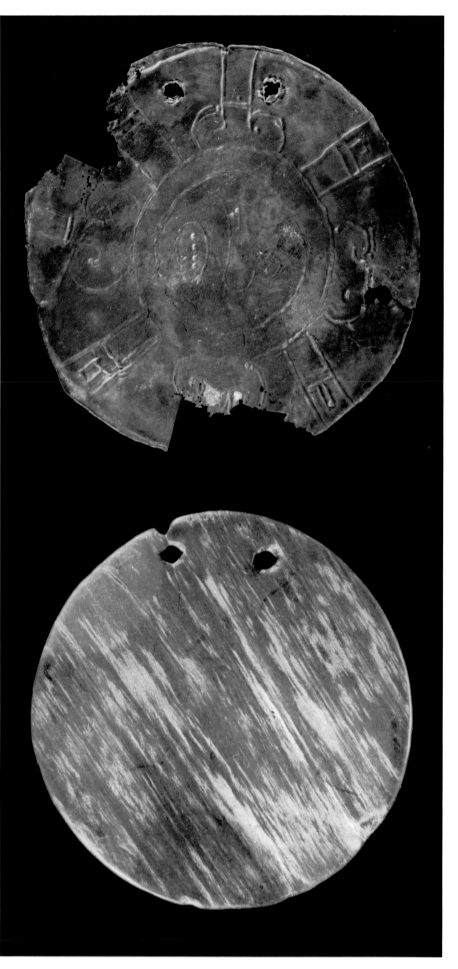

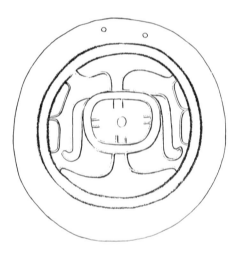

Figure 12. Gilt copper Sun (above) and tin
Moon discs. From S. K. Lothrop 1952, fig.
62.

137. Embossed disc

Sheet copper; gilt; burned
Hammered, cut; embossed; two
perforations for suspension; two
perforations for mend with metal strap; torn
Peabody Museum 10-71-20/C7648, Analysis
no. 99, D. 22.6 cm.

Figure 13. Copper disc with deity figure.
From S. K. Lothrop 1952, fig. 60.

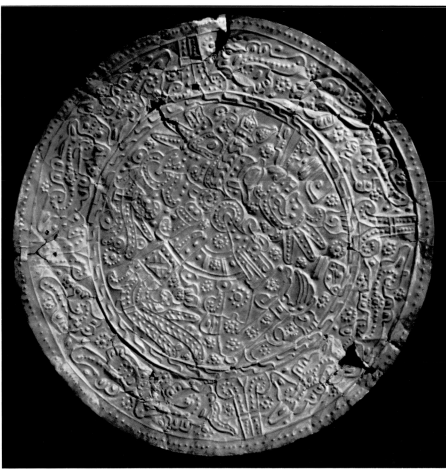

This disc (fig. 13) represents Ek Chuah, the merchant god, with a combination of Late Postclassic Maya and Mixteca-Puebla traits that are also characteristic of the wall paintings at Santa Rita, Belize (J. E. S. Thompson 1966; Gann 1900). Although he does not have the exaggerated nose usually shown for the merchant god, this embossed image has many other important attributes which are shown for Ek Chuah in the Maya ritual manuscript, the Madrid Codex. These include a beard that encircles the mouth, fangs, "fish-tail" eye surrounds, a *mecapal*, or plaited tumpline, with one or two knots (?) at the front, and a quetzal bird or feathers on top of the headdress (Villacorta C. and Villacorta R., eds. 1930, Madrid Codex, pp. 51–55). The tumpline refers to the prime role of Ek Chuah (Black Porter) as the carrier of exotic goods in commerce; the two projections at the front of this *mecapal* are also present in both the Santa Rita and the Madrid Codex depictions of Ek Chuah, and perhaps on a cast copper example from the Cenote (see no. 139). The quetzal may be symbolic of the great value of the long, green quetzal feathers, and of their importance in long distance trade.

Outside the *mecapal*-like border that encircles the bust of Ek Chuah, an outer band is divided into four quarters by paired scrolls or rays. These denote a celestial body (see no. 136) and may in this case refer to Ek Chuah's first name, which means "star" as well as "black." The quadripartition of this small cosmos may also refer to the directional ceremonies described for Ek Chuah in the Madrid Codex, where he is repeatedly surrounded by glyphs for "east," "north," "west," and "south" (pp. 50, 51). In the codex the god is also associated with calendric day signs like the "10 Lamat" and "11 Muluc" that are placed in front of him in the circle.

Between the divisions of the border there are two kinds of floating blobby forms with tabs and dots. These probably are not the somewhat comic animal forms that our modern eyes may see in them, although their identity is uncertain. Rosettes that fill empty spaces are a device also found in the paintings of Santa Rita, although it seems likely that such punctate designs derive from the embossing of metal.

Plain sheet copper discs were probably imported to the Santa Rita region, where they were worked and perhaps carried to Chichén Itzá as offerings by merchants who relied on the beneficence of Ek Chuah.

Late Postclassic (A.D. 1450–1539)
S. K. Lothrop 1952, pp. 74–77, fig. 60, table 22; J. E. S. Thompson 1966, fig. 2b; Kubler 1975, fig. 75

138. Embossed disc

Sheet copper; gilt; burned
Hammered, cut, embossed; two
perforations
Peabody Museum 10-71-20/C7412A,
D. 13.9 cm.

Figure 14. Copper disc with bird head.
From S. K. Lothrop 1952, fig. 59a.

This copper disc (fig. 14) is a variation on the same Ek Chuah, merchant god, theme found on the larger one (no. 137), and it was probably also embossed at or near Santa Rita, Belize. Here, however, the symbolism has been reduced to the quetzal bird from the god's headdress which is, similarly, encircled by the plaited *mecapal*, or tumpline, of Ek Chuah. Alfred M. Tozzer has suggested that this is an eagle, like heart-devouring ones depicted at Tula (1957, p. 132), but this disc was made centuries after there is any evidence for an eagle warrior cult in Yucatán. Both copper discs also include glyphs alluding to days in the 260-day ritual calendar, in this case "2 Ahau," and both have borders that are quartered by the rays of heavenly bodies.

A second disc embossed with a quetzal head was presented to Mexico in 1959 (S. K. Lothrop 1952, fig. 59b); although variant, it probably represents the same motif. A fourth embossed copper disc taken from the Cenote by the Mexicans in 1967 may allude to another aspect of the Ek Chuah theme (Bray 1977, fig. 10). This disc has a rare frontal portrait of "God C," or Xaman Ek, who is the North Star and thus closely associated with celestial "navigation" and with merchants, who must travel, perhaps at night.

Late Postclassic (A.D. 1450–1539)
S. K. Lothrop 1952, pp. 74–77, fig. 59a;
Tozzer 1957, fig. 276

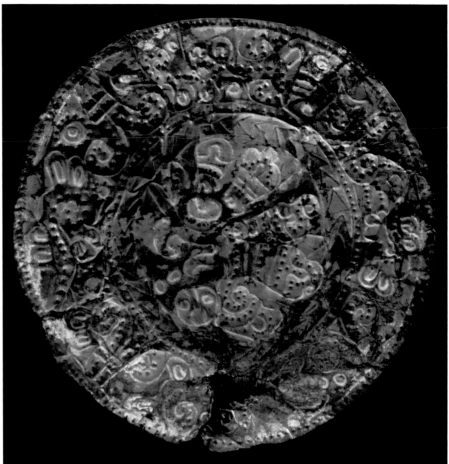

139. Merchant god head effigy bell

Copper
Cast
Peabody Museum 07-7-20/C4848,
H. 2.9 cm.

This somewhat crudely cast bell probably represents Ek Chuah (Black Porter), the Maya patron of trade who is characterized by a large and projecting nose, often with a drooping lower lip or chin. There is no representation of Ek Chuah in the monumental painting and sculpture of Chichén Itzá, where so many exotic objects were taken in trade, and none from the Cenote before Middle Postclassic times. This omission suggests that between about A.D. 800 and 1200 Cenote ritual, and perhaps ceremony at Chichén itself, had little to do with commerce and its institutions. Ek Chuah masks are found in the Guatemalan highlands in stone, pottery, and copper (Smith and Kidder 1951, fig. 89), and in the northern lowlands he is represented in the Late Postclassic Maya Madrid Codex (Villacorta C. and Villacorta R., eds. 1930) as well as in the wall paintings at Santa Rita, Belize (Gann 1900, pl. 22). Two copper discs from the Cenote probably allude to him as well (see nos. 137, 138). The two knobs at the front of this head may represent two projections that are regularly shown at the front of Ek Chuah's plaited tumpline.

Middle–Late Postclassic (A.D. 1350–1539)
S. K. Lothrop 1952, not illustrated; Spear 1978, fig. 267

140. Nine death's head pendants

Copper
Cast
Peabody Museum 07-7-20/C4851A–F,
H. 3.0–3.6 cm.; 10-70-20/C6027A–C,
H. 4.5 cm.

These skull effigy pendants are open-backed and crudely cast with carelessly incised detail. They are surmounted by "wirework" through which the wax was poured, as can be seen from the pouring spouts left at the top of each one. There are no suspension loops. Instead there are slits at each side of the masks, so they might be strung on a ribbon and possibly worn on a collar or headband. The larger masks have cross-hatched "beards," and one has the remains of an eyebrow. All have the round eye sockets and triangular nose hole characteristic of skulls (see no. 199).

Skulls are symbolically important at Chichén Itzá from Terminal Classic times when they are centrally located on the balls in the reliefs in the Great Ball Court. In the Early Postclassic this death motif is most clearly expressed on the Tzompantli, or skull rack platform, in the Great Plaza. Skull-shaped portable objects are, however, more common later in the Postclassic. The unusual shape of these pendants derives from that of the oliva shell; plain oliva shells were depicted worn as "tinklers" on the belt in Late Classic sculpture, whereas in Postclassic Yucatán oliva shells were occasionally carved to represent death's heads (Eaton 1978, pp. 59, 60, fig. 32c).

Two of the smaller death's heads were presented to Mexico in 1959.

Middle–Late Postclassic (A.D. 1400–1539)
S. K. Lothrop 1952, p. 83, fig. 70;
Pendergast 1962, p. 531, fig. 12; Bray 1977, p. 384.

141. Three effigy ornaments

Jadeite (?), white, green, brown
Horizontal bores, small perforations
Peabody Museum 10-70-20/C6124,
L. 3.0 cm., W. 1.6 cm.; 10-71-20/C6414,
L. 2.9 cm.; 10-71-20/C6419, L. 2.5 cm.

There were ten of these small grooved pendants in the Cenote collection (three were presented to Mexico in 1979). They are all bored, so that the narrowest end hung down, with terminal perforations. The smallest of these most resembles the insect bodies that Proskouriakoff suggests they represent, with subsidiary holes serving to attach wings, feelers, and legs. The two larger ones may represent rattlesnake rattles, which assume this general, tapering appearance at about two years of age. In view of the extraordinary importance of rattlesnakes in the imagery of Chichén Itzá, and later at Mayapán (Proskouriakoff 1962a, fig. 6a–h), it is possible such small effigy pendants were serpent talismans.

Postclassic (A.D. 1000–1539)
Proskouriakoff 1974, pp. 92, 93, pl. 50c:2, 7, 9

142. Pebble head pendant

Speckled gray stone
Two biconical perforations
Peabody Museum 10-70-20/C6099,
W. 4.5 cm., H. 4.1 cm.

Triangular in horizontal section, this pebble
was worked to suggest a face; eyes were
lightly drilled at either side of the projecting
ridge, or nose, while a short horizontal
groove below indicates the mouth. Such
formal abstraction is entirely foreign to the
Maya, who, when they modify a pebble, still
try to make a Maya face (see no. 171).
Although it is simpler, this more closely resembles the stonework of the Postclassic
Mezcala style in Guerrero (Gay 1967). However, a better clue to its origin may be found
in the fact that the eyes and the two perforations at the upper corners were made
with a tubular drill; the "penates," small
stone figurines, of Postclassic Oaxaca were
characteristically worked with tubular drills
(Caso 1965, p. 908)—suggesting a provenience for this piece.

Middle–Late Postclassic (A.D. 1200–1539)
Proskouriakoff 1974, p. 94, pl. 51b:6

143. Bird head effigy bell

Copper
Cast
Peabody Museum 10-56-20/C5996,
L. 2.4 cm.

This is the smaller of two cast bird head
effigy bells in the collection. Both have
curly crests and short beaks, but they differ
in the weight of their metal, in placement
of the loop, and in the type of eyes, which
are pierced on the larger bird and added
beads on the smaller one. Nevertheless,
both probably represent the female great
curassow.

Late Postclassic (A.D. 1450–1539)
S. K. Lothrop 1952, p. 91, fig. 85b; Piña
Chan 1980, fig. 111

144. Three feline head effigy bells

Copper
Cast
Peabody Museum 07-7-20/C4842, Analysis
no. 68, D. 1.9 cm.; 07-7-20/C4845,
D. 2.4 cm.; 984-2-20/25615, D. 1.2 cm.

Cast copper feline effigy head bells, possibly
representing jaguars, are known only from
the Cenote; there were twenty-nine in the
Peabody collection, and more were found by
the Mexicans in 1961 (Littlehales 1961,
p. 550). Unlike all other tested classes of
bells, these lack iron, gold, or antimony in
their copper; a composition that might provide a clue to their origin. The heads are
spherical bells with the features cut out, or
added in wax to plain spheres. The double
wire suspension loops all retain a projection
at the top; this is the neck through which
copper was poured into the mold.

Late Postclassic (A.D. 1450–1539)
S. K. Lothrop 1952, p. 91, figs. 84i, 85d,
table 29; Spear 1978, fig. 257; Piña Chan
1980, fig. 111

145. Three monkey (?) head effigy bells

Copper
Cast
Peabody Museum 07-7-20/C4849A–C,
H. 2.5–1.9 cm.

Like the other animal head effigies, these anthropomorphic bells have no known excavated counterparts, and at least one more of this type was found in the Cenote by the 1961 Mexican expedition (Littlehales 1961, p. 550). A fourth one in the collection has a circular mouth and a loop in place of the nose (S. K. Lothrop 1952, fig. 85a). These are all detailed castings made of a heavy copper, with pierced eyes and scrolls at the side of the head. This use of scrolls suggests a southern, possibly Costa Rican, origin for the detail (see no. 47), but the workmanship may well be Oaxacan; such bells might, however, have come from Veracruz, of which little is known.

Late Postclassic (A.D. 1450–1539)
S. K. Lothrop 1952, p. 91, figs. 84d, 85e;
Spear 1978, fig. 266

146. Two opossum head effigy bells

Copper
Cast; metal pellets
Peabody Museum 07-7-20/C4840,
L. 3.5 cm., 10-70-20/C6025, L. 3.5 cm.

Like the feline head effigy bells (no. 144), these are unique in the corpus of Mesoamerican bells. There are, in addition, four small ones and a third large one in the Cenote collection, and at least one more was excavated by the Mexican expedition in 1967 (Ediger 1971, color photo 3). Unlike the globular feline heads, these bells were specifically shaped as animal heads, although their form is related to that of elongated bells.

The Yucatec Maya word for "opossum" is *och*; this word also refers to small opossum effigy bells worn by children in Colonial times (Barrera Vásquez 1980). Opossums were probably represented in Early Postclassic Plumbate pottery vessels (Shepard 1948, figs. 14j,k, 15a) and in the later Chichén Itzá effigy figure (no. 198), and they are important in the Dresden Codex (pp. 25–28), where four anthropomorphic opossums play the role of year-bearers (J. E. S. Thompson 1972).

Middle–Late Postclassic (A.D. 1350–1539)
S. K. Lothrop 1952, p. 91, fig. 84c

147. Metal sandal

Sheet copper, gilt; coating
Hammered, cut; embossed; perforated, slit,
clinched together
Peabody Museum 10-71-20/C7419. Analysis
no. 94, L. 15.0 cm.

Was this sandal worn? There are no signs of
wear, although only traces of the gilding remain beneath the black coating on the sole.
The back of the sandal was clinched to the
sole with two strips of copper, and another
piece may have held a toe loop. The embossed ankle strap is not long enough to
encircle the ankle and thus must have had
ties at the front. The perfunctory, and vari-
able, workmanship and impractical construction found on these sandals in the
collection suggests that their purpose was
ceremonial. Perhaps they were worn by sacrificial victims. One sandal was presented
by the Peabody Museum to Mexico in 1959,
and more were excavated by Mexico in
1967 (Piña Chan 1980, fig. 109).

Late Postclassic (A.D. 1450–1539)
S. K. Lothrop 1952, p. 80, fig. 66a, table 22

148. Two metal sandal soles

Sheet copper, gilt; black coating; burned
Hammered, cut; perforated
Peabody Museum 10-71-20/C7649, Analysis
no. 19, L. 15.0 cm.; 984-2-20/25616,
L. 6.1 cm.

It is reported that chiefs of the Grijalva
River region in Tabasco gave Cortés "two
gold soles for sandals" (Bray 1977, p. 376).
They were probably like these, and the size
of this large one. There is the possibility
that sacrificed babies and small children
wore the tiny gilt sandals into the Cenote,
but they might also have been worn by
idols, or even offered by merchants, for
whom the footprint was an important identifying emblem.

   Different methods for affixing the sole of
the sandal to the foot are evident here, and
a third can be seen on the sandal that retains its heel guard (no. 147).

Late Postclassic (A.D. 1450–1539)
S. K. Lothrop 1952, p. 80, fig. 67b; Piña
Chan 1980, fig. 109

149. Two hemispherical bowls

Sheet copper, gilt
Hammered, cut
Peabody Museum 10-71-20/C7657,
D. 6.7 cm.; 10-71-20/C7657A, Analysis
no. 1309, D. 8.8 cm.

The Conquistadores reported that Moctezuma had a complete gold table service, but the six "gold" bowls found in the Cenote are the only extant examples, since any that were found by the Spaniards were melted down. The Cenote bowls are actually made of a heavy sheet copper covered with gold foil. Two of the six bowls were presented to Mexico in 1959.

Late Postclassic (A.D. 1450–1539)
S. K. Lothrop 1952, pp. 80–82, fig. 68a, e, table 22; Willard 1926, facing p. 144

150. Claw-shaped bone

Tapir humerus
Carved, polished; incised; "talons" broken off
Peabody Museum 07-7-20/C4949,
L. 15.2 cm., W. 6.5 cm.

This distal end of a tapir humerus was carved to resemble a five-clawed bird talon (?) or paw; it may have been held in the hand or affixed to the top of a staff, since it is hollow. The shaft is somewhat crudely decorated with three transverse divisions. These are most deeply incised near the "claw," with alternate cross-hatched and plain triangles. The central band has faintly scratched step frets, and the third has alternating triangles with some horizontal incisions.

Tapirs are large, long-snouted, water-loving mammals. In the sixteenth century they were considered dangerous, and their hunters very brave; the remains of a tapir were treasured for generations (Tozzer, ed. 1941, p. 203).

The transformation of suggestive natural shapes into carved objects was a Postclassic trait practised on bone at Mayapán and on wood found in the Cenote (no. 173). Such transformations suggest the common use of homonyms and of punning in the Maya language.

Middle–Late Postclassic (A.D. 1350–1539)
Moholy-Nagy and Ladd n.d.

151. Tripod grater bowl

Fired red/gray-slipped clay
Hand built, incised; worn; broken; partially
restored
Peabody Museum 07-7-20/C4669,
D. 17.2 cm.

The pleasing contrast between red and gray
on this Mayapán Red grater bowl was unin-
tentional. Red, produced by oxygen in the
firing, was the desired color, whereas a lack
of oxygen, or a reducing atmosphere, acci-
dentally created the gray. The rough grater
was smoothed, the interior slip was worn
away, and the tripod feet were ground down
through the use of this bowl before it was
thrown into the Cenote.

Middle Postclassic (A.D. 1300–1450)
Ball and Ladd n.d.; Brainerd 1958, fig. 96i;
R. E. Smith 1971, fig. 47a

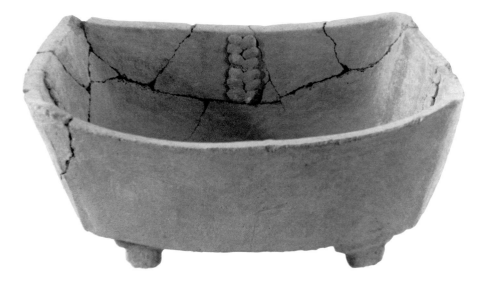

152. Rectangular tetrapod vessel

Fired partially buff/gray-slipped clay; post-
fire blue, red, yellow pigments; copal resin
Hand built, appliqué; worn; partially
restored
Peabody Museum 07-7-20/C4715,
L. 23.2 cm., H. 9.1 cm.

Four stepped legs, the rectangular shape,
and four appliquéd braids within the diagonally painted interior of this vessel all
combine to make it unique at Chichén Itzá,
although the individual traits are known
from others collected on the surface at the
site (R. E. Smith 1971, fig. 29y–cc).
   The quadriparite design may have had directional significance, with the narrow red
and yellow ends possibly connoting north
and south, and the longer blue sides east
and west. A copal offering that was in the
vessel has been lost.

Middle–Late Postclassic (A.D. 1400–1539)
Ball and Ladd n.d.; Brainerd 1958, fig. 96

153. Deer effigy vessel with copal and rubber offering

Fired unslipped clay; post-fire red, black, white pigments; copal resin; rubber; blue pigment; burned; Cenote muck; preservative
Hand built; broken
Peabody Museum 07-7-20/C4541,
H. 11.0 cm., Rim D. 16.5 cm.

This effigy vessel represents a deer, with characteristically large ears and cloven hoof. Post-fire-painted red, black, and blue vertical stripes once decorated the wall of the vessel, and the deer's head was painted with the same colors. Two similar effigy vessels, but representing a rabbit and a squirrel (?), were found by the Mexican expedition (Torres Montes 1967). These were x-rayed and found to have stone beads at the center of the copal mass, with a small metal plaque in the rabbit offering as well. This deer may also have such inclusions.

The cylindrical object on top of the copal is probably the burned torso of a rubber figure which has lost its limbs.

Middle–Late Postclassic (A.D. 1300–1539)
Ball and Ladd n.d.; Brainerd 1958, fig. 96b

154. Tripod bowl with copal offering

Fired unslipped clay; post-fire blue pigment; copal resin; rubber; jade, shell; burned; Cenote muck; preservative
Hand built; broken
Peabody Museum 07-7-20/C4562,
D. 16.0 cm.

Like most of the Postclassic ceramics offered to the Cenote, this tripod bowl was painted "Maya blue" (see no. 157), then filled with a blue-painted copal mass studded with jade and shell beads. Finally, a blue-painted rubber form was inserted in the center and burned. Several different kinds of jade can be seen here among the beads and fragments. Jade and shell beads, like copper bells, were used as media of exchange.

Middle–Late Postclassic (A.D. 1300–1539)
Ball and Ladd n.d.

155. Tripod bowl with copal offering

Fired unslipped clay; post-fire brown/red pigment; burned; copal resin; jade; Cenote muck; preservative
Hand built; broken; partially restored
Peabody Museum 07-7-20/C4561,
D. 12.5 cm.

Twenty copal pellets and five jade ornaments once topped this copal offering which seems to overwhelm its small graceful tripod bowl. The bowl has elongated hollow feet and a decorative band at the base that recalls earlier Puuc Slate Ware tripod plates. There was no blue paint on the offering, but a brown/red pigment was used on the sides of the vessel.

Middle Postclassic (A.D. 1300–1450)
Ball and Ladd n.d.

156. Square copal offering

Copal resin; jade; blue-green, red pigments; rubber; Cenote muck; preservative
Modeled
Peabody Museum 07-7-20/C4655,
H. 9.0 cm., W. 8.8 cm.

Copal is still used in religious ceremony all over Mesoamerica. It is an incense that, in Yucatán, is made from the *Protium copal* tree. In Yucatec Maya it is called *pom*—a word meaning "that which is to be burned" (Barrera Marín, Barrera Vásquez, and López Franco 1976, pp. 124, 414). Copal was, and is, the essential ritual offering to the gods, their nourishment, and, through the dark, perfumed smoke, the means of reaching to them in the sky (García Ruiz 1981).

This offering originally filled a square container; one hundred pellets of copal, some once painted red, studded the top, and a biconically drilled jade bead was pushed into its center. Blue-green pigment, probably symbolic of sacrifice (Tozzer, ed. 1941, p. 117) was smeared all over the copal mass before it was put into the container; then a stripe of rubber was painted (?) on top and the latter burned, perhaps during the act of offering.

At the beginning of this century the Lacandon Indians of Chiapas made gifts of modeled copal to their gods (Tozzer 1907, pp. 126, 127). These conical offerings were considered male if decorated with small nodules on the top, and they were exhorted to come to life during the offertory ceremony to help serve the gods.

Middle–Late Postclassic (A.D. 1300–1520)

157. Round copal offering

Copal resin; blue-green pigment; Cenote muck; preservative
Modeled
Peabody Museum 07-7-20/C4645,
H. 7.0 cm., D. 6.5 cm.

"I am the one who raised (you) up to life. Awake! Be alive!" Thus did the Lacandon Indians address the modeled lumps of copal which they offered to the gods, at the beginning of this century (Tozzer 1907, p. 179).

Twenty-five blue-painted pellets stud this ball of copal. The Bishop de Landa speaks of the use of a "blue bitumin" for painting bodies and objects (Tozzer, ed. 1941, p. 159). The blue colorant was probably indigo, but the vehicle identified on blue-painted ceramics has been derived from local clay (Littman 1982); a stickier bituminous binder may not have survived. The proper color of this "Maya blue" can be seen best on nos. 154, 192, and 194, where it has not been coated with a preservative.

Balls of copal, with a round cross-hatched area on the top, can be seen heaped in a tripod bowl at the feet of the old man wearing a turtle carapace in the Lower Temple of the Jaguars at Chichén Itzá (Maudslay 1889–1902, vol. 3, pl. 51). The cross-hatching on the depicted balls may be arrayed nodules like these, or it may indicate that the balls had a coating of rubber, like many from the Cenote, since cross-hatching connotes black, the color of burned rubber. In either case this image suggests that balls of copal were in ritual use at Chichén Itzá in Terminal Classic times. However, there is no evidence that balls of copal were thrown into the Cenote before the Middle Postclassic. When copal found in the Cenote has any associations, they are always to the later phase of ritual.

Middle–Late Postclassic (A.D. 1300–1539)
Seler 1915, vol. 5, figs. 1,2

158. Copal head effigy

Copal resin, impurities; blue pigment; Cenote muck; preservative
Modeled
Peabody Museum 07-7-20/C4594,
D. 13.5 cm.

Rounded to conform to its offering bowl, which was separated from it in the Cenote, this globular effigy head has large applied features. The loose lips are affixed below a nose with flaring nostrils and round, outlined eyes. A copal bar on the forehead was added after some of the blue pigment and has no clear decorative significance. As is often true, the color of the copal varies, and it has vegetal and other accidental (?) inclusions. This offering was probably made in a fairly deep tripod bowl.

Middle–Late Postclassic (A.D. 1300–1539)

159. Copal effigy figure

Copal resin; blue pigment; rubber; Cenote muck; preservative
Modeled; broken
Peabody Museum 07-7-20/C4654,
H. 13.5 cm.

This blue-painted copal figure once squatted with arms on knees and with a bundle on its back that was connected to its forehead by a tumpline. The bundle and part of the tumpline are still there, as are the earflares which frame a face that has lost most of its features. Like some of the copper objects from the Cenote (nos. 137–139), it seems possible that this was the offering of a traveling merchant—a profession that was regularly portrayed carrying a load; in fact the name of the merchant's tutelary deity, Ek Chuah, means Black (or Astral) Porter.

Of the hundreds of copal offerings found by Edward H. Thompson and the Mexican expeditions, virtually all of those that were still with their ceramic vessels were mounded in Mayapán Red tripod bowls, and the shape of this one suggests that it was no exception. There is no reason to believe copal was thrown into the Cenote before Middle Postclassic times.

Middle–Late Postclassic (A.D. 1300–1539)

160. Copal effigy figure in Mayapán Red tripod bowl

Fired red-slipped clay; blue pigment; copal resin; blue pigment; preservative
Bowl: Hand built; broken.
Effigy: modeled; broken; partially restored
Peabody Museum 07-7-20/C4579,
Est. H. 7.0 cm., Est. D. 16.5 cm.

This broken, headless frog-like copal form is actually a bow-legged male figure wearing a loincloth and holding a large ball in its right hand. The simple costume suggests this is not a ball player, so the "ball" may be a colossal copal offering; masses of copal of this size, relative to a human figure, were found in the Cenote.

Perhaps this figure might be considered a co-celebrant who was exhorted to come to life during the offering ritual, in a practice like that of the Lacandon Indians early in this century (see nos. 156, 157).

The depression in the chest probably held a small stone celt, a "life-giving" attribute analogous to the green-stone "hearts" of Aztec idols.

Middle–Late Postclassic (A.D. 1300–1539)

161. Tripod bowl with copal and rubber offering

Fired buff-slipped clay; post-fire blue pigment; copal resin; rubber; burned
Hand built; broken
Peabody Museum 07-7-20/C4544,
D. 16.5 cm.

"Maya blue" pigment, symbolic of sacrifice, was splotched on the inner and outer walls of this tripod bowl before blue-painted copal filled the bottom, and fourteen or more blue-painted rubber (Castilla elastica) balls were placed on top and burned. Usable rubber came in sheets and strands so that it had to be wound to form a ball, as here (and probably for ball game balls); whereas on figurines it served as a skin or thin covering (see no. 177). The glyphic designator for "rubber" refers to this property (Lounsbury 1973, pp. 112–116). Copal and rubber were still burned together in rituals performed by the Lacandon Indians early in this century (Tozzer 1907, p. 102). Both substances are, metaphorically, the blood of trees, and both give off a dark, aromatic smoke, but the rubber may be easier to light, hence its presence, burned, on top of so many of the copal offerings.

Middle–Late Postclassic (A.D. 1350–1539)
Ball and Ladd n.d.

162. Head pendant

Jadeite, gray-green blotched with blue-green
Large biconical horizontal perforation; cracked
Peabody Museum 10-71-20/C6592,
H. 5.7 cm., W. 3.8 cm., Th. 2.9 cm.

Edward H. Thompson found eight "bib and helmet" heads in the Cenote (three of these were presented to Mexico in 1976), and two more were found by the Mexican expedition of 1961. These heads usually have "helmets" worn low on the forehead and simple flanges in place of ears, with a bib-like extension below.

Recently two Late Preclassic caches excavated in northern Belize included, in one case four, in the other five, of these heads (Freidel 1979; Hammond 1974). The heads have three or four different styles of helmet—the largest with a squared medial crest, like this one. In each context this type is the largest head. The Cenote bib-helmet heads may once have been part of such caches.

The most interesting aspect of these heads is that they were apparently made in Late Preclassic times, perhaps as long as a millennium before they were thrown into the Cenote. Their soft modeling in combination with incised detail and pits drilled in the corners of the mouth recall the conventions of the much earlier Olmec jadeworking. An important trait they also all share is an unusually large biconically drilled horizontal bore.

Few of these heads have been excavated in their primary, Late Preclassic contexts, and the largest number come from the Cenote. One of these was imbedded in copal in a Late Postclassic tripod bowl (see no. 171). Another was excavated from a cache at the Postclassic site of Mayapán (D. Thompson 1955, fig. 2g), while another is known from a Late Classic burial at Tancah, Quintana Roo, on the east coast of the Yucatán Peninsula (Miller 1982, pp. 23, 24). These are secondary depositions which suggest that earlier caches may have been encountered in the course of later construction, or possibly sought by people looking for jade when it had become rare.

Late Preclassic (300 B.C.–A.D. 200)
Proskouriakoff 1974, pp. 96, 97, color pl. 3b, pl. 53a: 1

163. Figure pendant

Jadeite (?), gray-green
Large biconical horizontal bore
Peabody Museum 10-56-20/C5976,
H. 3.9 cm., W. 2.3 cm., Th. 1.0 cm.

The helmet and the large horizontal bore placed high on the head identify this small bow-legged figure as of Late Preclassic date. As on the bib-helmet head (no. 162) the nose is a triangle with the mouth serving as its base, and the pupils of the eyes are drilled—traits that suggest a Preclassic date. In other ways this figure resembles the cached Classic jade and shell forms that J. Eric S. Thompson called "Charlie Chaplins" (1939, fig. 97), although the southern lowland "Charlie Chaplins" have no specifically Preclassic traits. A figure like them that does, however, have Preclassic characteristics comes from the Postclassic "High Priest's Grave" at Chichén Itzá (E. H. Thompson 1938, fig. 19). Thus the two Preclassic examples at Chichén Itzá both come from Postclassic contexts and, like the bib-helmet heads, represent the ritual re-use of very ancient jades. These may have been predecessors of the "Charlie Chaplins" of the Classic Period.

Late Preclassic (A.D. 1–250)
Proskouriakoff 1974, p. 96, color pl. 3a, pl. 52c: 9

164. Monkey head pendant

Jadeite (?), glassy blue-gray on brown
Large biconical horizontal bore
Peabody Museum 10-71-20/C6598,
H. 3.4 cm., W. 2.5 cm., Th. 1.1 cm.

Like one of the bib-helmet heads in each of
two Late Preclassic caches excavated in
Belize (Hammond 1974, fig. 7a; Freidel
1979, fig. 9e), this one lacks the characteristic helmet (see nos. 162, 163) but
otherwise conforms to the type, especially
in its large, high, biconical bore. Also like
some of the heads in the Belize caches, its
features were blocked out with grooves.
This one is made distinctly simian by the
addition of a shallow horizontal trough below which the nose and mouth project.
This trough with its two round drilled eyes
is highly polished, without any incising,
suggesting the working of "axe gods" in
Costa Rica (Snarskis 1981, nos. 26, 163).
Closer to the Maya lowlands, small polished-
groove head pendants were excavated in an
Early Classic context at Zaculeu in the
Guatemalan highlands (Woodbury and Trik
1953, fig. 281a–d).
    Like many of the very early jade pieces
from the Cenote, this one was probably
imbedded in copal and offered in Late
Postclassic times.

Late Preclassic–Early Classic (A.D. 1–400)
Proskouriakoff 1974, pp. 96, 97, color pl. 3c,
pl. 53a : 7

165. Figure pendant

Jadeite (?), dull gray-green
Perforation at top
Peabody Museum 10-71-20/C6634,
H. 4.5 cm., W. 1.3 cm., Th. 0.7 cm.

Unique in its simple miniature celt form,
with an apical ring for suspension, this little
figure has no known Mesoamerican an-
alogs. The head, with closed eyes and
diagonal grooves descending from nostrils
to chin, suggests a possible affinity with
the style of the Late Preclassic boulder
sculpture of the Pacific slope of Guatemala
(Parsons 1981, figs. 29–42). Otherwise it
recalls the larger "axe gods" of Costa Rica,
which have this tapered shape with notches
at the neck, and may have incised hands
splayed across the chest in conjunction
with areas of cross-hatched detail (Snarskis
1981, no. 33); but axe gods have neither
legs nor loincloth aprons. The date and
provenience of this little pendant are among
the most conjectural of those for the precious stones from the Cenote.

Late Preclassic–Terminal Classic (?) (A.D.
1–900)
Proskouriakoff 1974, p. 94, pl. 51c

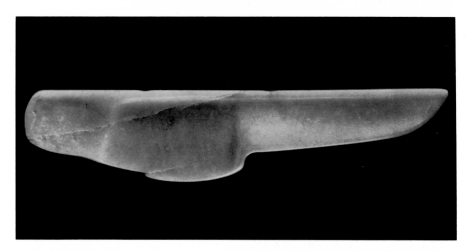

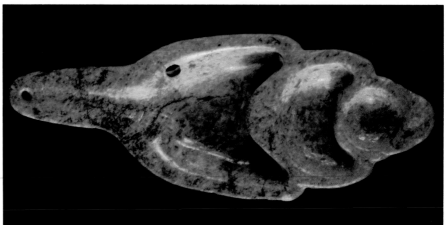

166. Concave trapezoidal pendant

Jadeite, translucent bluish, white flecked, with brilliant green vein
Diagonal biconical perforation
Peabody Museum 10-71-20/C6562,
H. 2.9 cm., W. 3.4 cm., Th. 0.4 cm.

The Olmec workmanship of this beautifully polished and smoothly shaped pendant is evident in the subtle concavity of the face, bordered by a faint incision, and in the use of the "jewel green" streaked blue jade worked primarily in Olmec times in Meso-america, and occasionally reworked later in Costa Rica (E. Easby 1981, p. 138).

Middle Preclassic (700–300 B.C.)
Proskouriakoff 1974, p. 36, color pl. 3h,
pl. 38a : 5

167. "Spoon" pendant *(top)*

Jadeite, gray-green
Two diagonal biconical perforations
Peabody Museum 10-71-20/C6561,
L. 10.5 cm., W. 2.2 cm.

The smooth transition between raised border and sunken surfaces on this "spoon" identifies it as of Olmec workmanship, as does the waxy jade. Technically the form resembles "clamshell" pendants excavated at La Venta and in Costa Rica (Drucker 1952, pl. 53; Snarskis 1979), but although several of the "spoons" are known, this is the only one of this size of known archaeological provenience (Pohorilenko 1981). Like the bib-helmet heads (nos. 162, 163) this object was probably removed from a Preclassic context by Postclassic peoples, and offered during the final phase of Cenote ritual.

Middle Preclassic (700–300 B.C.)
Proskouriakoff 1974, p. 36, color pl. 3j,
pl. 38a : 7

168. Shell effigy pendant *(bottom)*

Jadeite, gray, light green speckled
Two diagonal biconical perforations, tiny perforation
Peabody Museum 10-70-20/C6122,
L. 4.9 cm., W. 1.8 cm., Th. 0.8 cm.

The transverse section of a conch shell commonly identifies the Mexican deity Quetzalcoatl in Postclassic times, but this slender, longitudinally sectioned univalve does not follow that iconographic convention. Its delicately modeled form, with smooth depressions, raised borders, and diagonal biconical perforations suggests Olmec workmanship, like that of the "spoon" (no. 167). However, Tatiana Proskouriakoff observes that this shell belongs to a tradition of naturalistic sculpture like those of the Maya or the Aztec, and that since there were no identifiable Aztec objects found in the Cenote, it may be Maya.

Middle Preclassic–Terminal Classic
(700 B.C.–A.D. 900)
Proskouriakoff 1974, p. 93, pl. 51a

169. Effigy (?) pendant

Jadeite, blue-green translucent
Large biconical horizontal bore
Peabody Museum 10-71-20/C6583,
H. 3.5 cm., W. 2.8 cm., Th. 0.9 cm.

This blue-green stone is characteristic of
Olmec work, although it is also found in
Costa Rica, where such softly rounded
shapes and high polish are common on "axe
gods." The highly conventionalized pendant
is convex on the back, with a perforated
horizontal ridge at the top of the concave
front; it may have been reworked from an
"axe god," like several found in the Atlantic
watershed of Costa Rica (Snarskis 1981,
nos. 150–153). It is postulated that this
piece, like the other Preclassic jades in the
Cenote, was offered in Postclassic times,
although if reworked during the Early
Classic Period it might have been imported
to Chichén Itzá with the cast *tumbaga*
figurines from Costa Rica. It is, however,
undamaged like the late jade offerings, and
unlike the shattered Terminal Classic ones.

Middle Preclassic–Early Classic (700
B.C.–A.D. 500)
Proskouriakoff 1974, p. 36, pl. 37f:1

170. Hunchback pendant

Dark green stone
Two diagonal perforations
Peabody Museum 10-71-20/C6633,
H. 2.6 cm., W. 3.9 cm., Th. 0.8 cm.

The two suspension holes for this pendant
were drilled along its back so that it hung
face down. It is carved in a soft, low relief
characteristic of Early Classic jadeworking,
and is closely related to three groups of
such figures from the southeastern frontier
of Mesoamerica. The most securely dated
are two hunchbacks found in an Early Classic cache at Quiriguá, Guatemala; four
more, two hunchbacks and two acrobats,
were excavated from a cache at Copán,
Honduras (Ashmore 1980, figs. 10, 11). Recently at least seven hunchbacks were
encountered in a cache at Salitrón Viejo in
central Honduras (Lara Pinto 1982, fig. 4);
and jades from a seventh-century tomb at
Altun Ha, Belize, are also closely related to
these figures (Pendergast 1982, fig. 56a, c).
All of the hunchbacks crouch, wearing
only loincloth belts, with arms bent at the
elbows to bring their hands beneath the
chin, often, as here, cradling an earflare in
the crook of the elbow. Eyes and mouths are
outlined by grooves, and there is a headband or cap on top of the head. The figures
all have over-sized heads in addition to
their hunchbacks, and they may be an
early manifestation of the Late Classic
preoccupation with dwarves, as seen in
three figurine pendants from the Cenote
(nos. 67–69).

Early Classic (A.D. 250–550)
Proskouriakoff 1974, pp. 93, 94, color pl. 3f,
pl. 51b:4

171. Pebble head

Jadeite, light green
Two large diagonal biconical perforations
Peabody Museum 10-56-20/C5930,
H. 5.9 cm., W. 2.9 cm., Th. 1.8 cm.

It is not clear how this pebble carving was
worn, since it was drilled diagonally to the
back at either end. The natural shape of the
stone was used, and enhanced by incising,
so as to suggest a head in profile, with a
three-part ear ornament (fig. 15). This head
is closely related to jades excavated from a
cache at Copán, as is no. 170, and stylistically is particularly like a crude pebble
figure in that group (Digby 1964, pl. 23d).

This undamaged jade was inbedded in
copal in a Late Postclassic tripod bowl and
thrown into the Cenote in Late Postclassic
times.

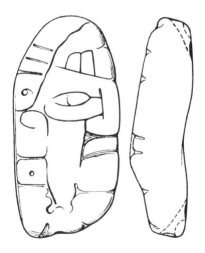

Figure 15. Jade pebble head.
From T. Proskouriakoff 1974, pl. 51b:7.

Early Classic (A.D. 250–550)
Proskouriakoff 1974, p. 94, pl. 51b:7

172. Pebble head bead

Jadeite (?), bright, speckled gray-green
Large vertical biconical bore
Peabody Museum 10-71-20/C6600,
H. 3.7 cm., W. 2.2 cm., Th. 1.5 cm.

This pebble was carved in soft, rounded re-lief to exploit a thin layer of bright green stone. The thick features are delineated by grooves in a style reminiscent of the hunch-backs as a group (see no. 170), and like them it has a rolled band at the forehead with a cap above.

A long Early Classic figural bead exca-vated at Kaminaljuyú, in the Guatemalan highlands, is like this and the hunchback, in that it would have been worn with the face directed down, and wears a similar cap above features carved in the same style (Kidder, Jennings, and Shook 1946, fig. 148l). Another pebble head, with these same traits, was found in a cache with a cast *tumbaga* (gold-copper alloy) "claw" at Altun Ha, Belize. This cache has been dated close to A.D. 500, the earliest known appearance of gold in Mesoamerica (Pen-dergast 1979, fig. 55b, pp. 150–153).

Two more pebble heads, stylistically re-lated to this one, were found in the Cenote by the Mexican expedition of 1961 (Little-hales 1961, pp. 548, 553).

Early Classic Period (A.D. 250–550)
Proskouriakoff 1974, p. 84, pl. 44d

173. Phallus effigy

Wood; black coating; paraffin impregnated
Carved; cut; split, warped; partially restored
Peabody Museum 10-71-20/C6759,
Est. L. 20.2 cm.

This realistic phallus resembles another ex-cavated from the Cenote by the Mexican expedition of 1967, now in the Mérida Museum. Both have a black coating that probably served as a preservative, in addi-tion to producing a striking appearance. This phallus, unlike the other, has one testicle carved as a bird. This kind of trans-formation is probably a typically Maya play on words and forms; part of the explanation may be that one word for "testicle," *he*, is also the word for "egg" (Barrera Vásquez 1980). The creation of such naturalistic wooden phalluses was probably a Middle to Late Postclassic practice, although some kind of a phallic cult had existed at Chichén Itzá since Early Postclassic times, and per-haps before (see no. 9).

There is a long, rounded cavity on the shaft which was part of the original carving.

Middle-Late Postclassic (A.D. 1300–1539)
Coggins and Ladd n.d.

174. Idol

Wood, black coating; copal, blue pigment;
burned
Carved; cracked
Peabody Museum 07-7-20/C4795,
H. 18.5 cm.

Sixteen rough-hewn wooden idols were
dredged from the Cenote by Edward H.
Thompson, and recently the Mexicans have
found fifty more. The Bishop de Landa reported that "they had idols of stone, but
very few, others of wood and carved but of
small size, but not as many as those of clay"
(Tozzer, ed. 1941, p. 110).

The wooden idols from the Cenote vary
somewhat in size, shape, and relative crude-
ness, but all stay close to the original shape
of the branch or board from which they
were hewn. They clearly represent a major
late Cenote ritual. Their surfaces were modeled with blue-painted rubber or stucco and
often copal so that they represented anthropomorphic deities (?) which would
have been differentiated by their attributes.
The angled notches in their bodies held
stick limbs (no. 177) that fell off when the
adhesive coating melted in the offering fire
or was lost in the water.

This idol was covered with a black skin
that was probably rubber, then painted with
"Maya blue" pigment. It was stuck into a
mass of copal, where it was burned slightly
before it was cast into the Cenote.

Middle–Late Postclassic (A.D. 1350–1539)
Coggins and Ladd n.d.

175. Idol

Wood; stucco, blue pigment; copal, black coating
Carved
Peabody Museum 07-7-20/C4798,
H. 20.8 cm.

"The wooden idols were so much esteemed that they were considered . . . as the most important part of inherited property . . . They held them in reverence on account of what they represented and because they made them with so many ceremonies, especially the wooden ones," the Bishop de Landa reported in the sixteenth century (Tozzer, ed. 1941, p. 111). Idols are described as being made of cedar, known in Yucatec Maya as *ku che*, or "god tree." However, one like these from the Cenote that was tested in Mexico proved to be pine (Torres and Vega 1970, p. 24).

"When the wood had arrived, they built a house of straw, fenced in, where they put the wood and a great urn in which to place the idols and keep them there under cover, while they were making them. They put incense to burn to four gods called Acantuns, which they located at the four cardinal points" (Tozzer, ed. 1941, p. 160). We do not know if any of these idols is made of cedar, but this type might actually have come in sets of four since many, like this one, are triangular in shape (Piña Chan 1968, photo 7; 1980, fig. 106) and thus might be one of four radial sections of a single log.

Middle–Late Postclassic (A.D. 1350–1
Coggins and Ladd n.d.

176. Idol

Wood; copal, blue pigment
Carved; broken; cracked
Peabody Museum 07-7-20/C4793,
H. 22.0 cm.

Hewn from the heart of a log, this idol was carved in the round. Before offering it was completely covered with copal and probably with blue pigment, but one can see grooved facial features carved lightly into the wood. Arms are indicated at the sides with hands resting on the belt, and a loincloth falls to the ground in front. Copal is also found on the bottom, suggesting that this figure was set into the incense when offered.

A late date for the wooden idols is based on their association with copal offerings and with a Chen Mul Modeled censer, as well as iconographic traits remaining on several in the collection. Many of the wooden idols cracked and split in drying out. Presumably they were never treated with paraffin because of their fragile surface coatings.

Middle–Late Postclassic (A.D. 1350–1539)
Coggins and Ladd n.d.

177. Idol hands: arm with hand and stick; hand with stick

Wood; rubber; copal; blue pigment; burned
Carved; broken; melted
Peabody Museum 07-7-20/C4763, Stick
L. 11.8 cm., Est. Hand W. 4.0 cm.;
07-7-20/C4783, L. 10.0 cm., Hand
W. 3.2 cm.

These fragile hands were partially modeled
in rubber. The blue-painted open hand
holds a short stick and wears a bracelet at
the wrist. Like most of the limbs belonging
to idols, this wooden arm is beveled at the
end, presumably to fit into one of the upper
notches of the idols (see nos. 174, 175). The
shriveled fingers and collapsed bracelet
show the effect of heat on rubber, probably
from the offering fire.

   The hand that holds the longer stick has
a black rubber skin covering fine-textured
yellow modeled copal. The stick may represent a weapon; it has been burned and
broken off. This hand is much larger in
scale than the other and must have come
from a big figure that was perhaps made
entirely of rubber-skinned copal.

Middle–Late Postclassic (A.D. 1350–1539)
Coggins and Ladd n.d.

178. Three-part textile fragment

Cotton; blackened in Cenote
Z-spun; woven; sewn; pierced (?),
disintegrated
Peabody Museum 984-2-20/25613,
L. 18.2 cm., W. 12.5 cm.

Three differently worked cotton textile
pieces are sewn together here. At the right
there is a fragment with Z-spun single
warps and wefts—one of the weaves most
frequently found in the Cenote. This is
sewn to a narrow band that is a rare example of warp float complete in width, with
intact selvages sewn to the other pieces;
this band may once have shown color differentiation. The third piece, which is more
tightly woven, has Z-spun warps and paired
wefts that, with bound warps, produce an
open-work design.

Blackening of the Cenote textiles is from
submersion, not burning, and this fragment
was partly protected from blackening at the
edges of a hole between the medial band
and the adjoining coarser weave.

The textiles in the Cenote are most likely
Middle to Late Postclassic in date, and elements in the Late Phase of Cenote ritual.
Conceivably they were related to the Late
Postclassic cult of Ix Chel, mother goddess
and patroness of weaving who was the
object of widespread veneration and the inspiration for pilgrimages to her shrine on
Cozumel, off the east coast of the peninsula. Cotton was an important Postclassic
Yucatecan crop, and woven cotton cloth a
prime export which was carried by the long
distance merchants whose god, Ek Chuah,
is represented on objects found in the
Cenote (nos. 137–139).

Middle–Late Postclassic (A.D. 1300–1539)
J. M. Lothrop n.d.

179. Three textile fragments

Cotton; blackened in Cenote
Z-spun; woven; embroidered; disintegrated
Peabody Museum 984-2-20/25612,
L. 11.5 cm., W. 18.1 cm.

Over six hundred textile fragments were
dredged from the Cenote by Edward H.
Thompson, and the more recent Mexican
excavations produced thousands—including pieces that are larger than any in the
Peabody Museum collection (García L.
1981). Sculpture and painting show the di-
versity and virtuosity of the Mesoamerican
textile tradition (Mahler 1965), but, unlike
the situation in drier Peru, the preservation
of such material in Mesoamerica is rare.
Mesoamerican textiles are preserved only in
dry caves, or at the opposite extreme in watery, oxygen-deprived environments like the
Cenote.

The base fabric of this embroidery is
plain woven Z-spun single-ply warps and
wefts. Embroidery yarns pass over and
around groups of warps to create the pattern. This motif of an eight-armed open
cross with a central diamond also occurs in
other techniques.

Middle–Late Postclassic (A.D. 1300–1539)
J. M. Lothrop n.d.

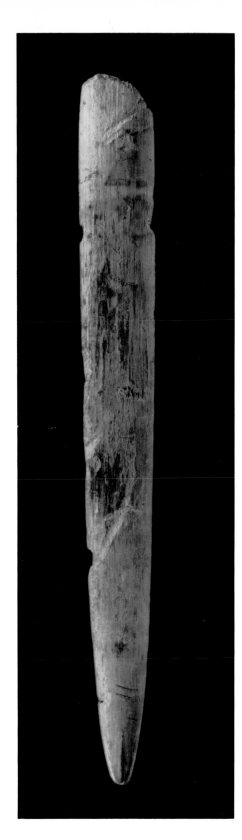

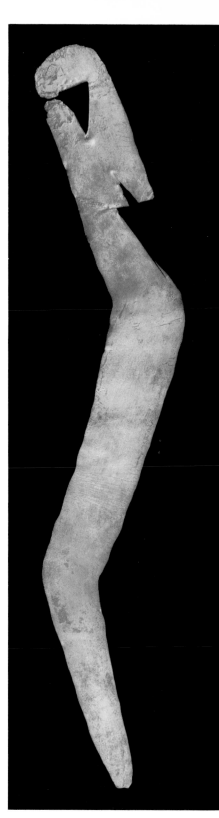

180. Weaving batten (?) (left)

Wood; dark coating; red stain; paraffin impregnated
Carved; notched; cut, gouged, broken
Peabody Museum 10-71-20/C6746,
L. 21.9 cm., Th. 0.8 cm.

The flat, tapered, and pointed shape of this wooden blade suggest that it is a batten, or beater, used in weaving to push down the weft. However, since some material which has left a red stain was tied near the broken, wide end, above the matched notches, there is the possibility that it was used as a shuttle, to carry the weft yarn. Superficial parallel cuts on both sides may have been made as part of the offering ritual.

Postclassic (A.D. 1300–1539)
Coggins and Ladd n.d.

181. Weaving tool (?) (right)

Sheet copper
Hammered, cut
Peabody Museum 10-71-20/C7653,
L. 21.5 cm.

Although this copper object resembles a lightning bolt and thus presents the possibility of a symbolic interpretation, it is more likely a weaving tool—a bobbin or a bodkin. It has an "eye" with a slit opening at the upper corner, and a jagged indentation below to secure the yarn or fiber as it was worked through a textile. The copper is crudely cut. There are no signs of wear on the edges or surface.

A second one of these was excavated by the Mexican expedition in 1967.

Late Postclassic (A.D. 1450–1539)
S. K. Lothrop 1952, p. 82, fig. 69b

182. Weaving tool (?) *(left)*

Sheet copper; gilt
Hammered, cut, embossed; worn
Peabody Museum 10-71-20/C7652,
L. 19.5 cm.

This object is surely functional, like no. 181.
It was probably used as a pick to lift threads
in the process of weaving. On page 79c of
the Madrid Codex, tools of this shape are
held by two goddesses who work at looms
attached to trees (Villacorta C. and Villacorta R., eds. 1930).

The point is dulled and bent from use,
and the gold coating has worn off it, whereas
the handle, which has a depression on one
side for a better grip, was not gilt.

There is a textile impression on the blade
from the woven fragment that Edward H.
Thompson found with it, sandwiched between two gilt discs.

Late Postclassic (A.D. 1450–1539)
S. K. Lothrop 1952, p. 82, fig. 69a

183. Serpentine object *(right)*

Wood; black coating; paraffin impregnated
Carved, scratched
Sheet copper; gilt
Cut, embossed; torn
Peabody Museum 10-71-20/C6696,
L. 20.2 cm.

There is a striking contrast between the
simplicity and elegance of this serpentine
wooden form and the crudely embossed
copper which overlaid it. An explanation
for this is found in three or more such objects that were excavated by the Mexicans
(Littlehales 1961, pp. 554–555). These
were cleaned of the black resinous adhesive, and the underlying wood was found
to be carved as a single serpent with a head
that loops around to grasp its own body in
its jaws. If there is a serpent's head on this
one, it is still largely covered with black
resin and with part of the copper sheathing.

With the Late Postclassic addition of the
embossed copper, this might have served as
a small scepter. Originally, however, as a
beautifully carved and unadorned object
with a serpentine shaft, it might have been
a hair ornament, or a bodkin, to thread yarn
through a weaving, as postulated for the
copper serpentine object (no. 181).

Middle–Late Postclassic (A.D. 1300–1539)
Coggins and Ladd n.d.; S. K. Lothrop 1952,
fig. 53b

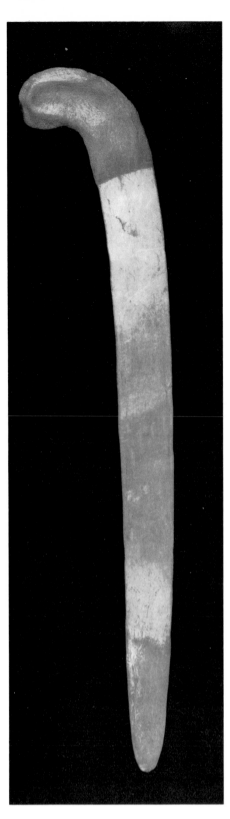
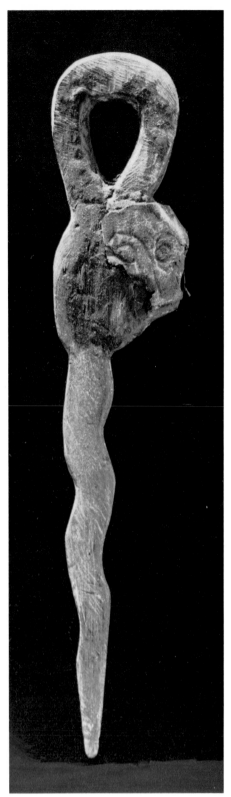

184. Spindle whorl

Wood; red pigment
Carved; central perforation; broken
Peabody Museum 07-7-20/C4944,
D. 4.5 cm., Hole D. 0.8 cm., Th. 1.6 cm.

The light weight of this truncated conical wooden spindle whorl seems to be symbolized by the graceful feather design that encircles it. What gossamer thread did it spin?

It was painted with red pigment before being offered to the Cenote.

Late Postclassic (A.D. 1450–1539)
Coggins and Ladd n.d.

185. Spindle whorl and spindle (?)

Wood; black coating; paraffin impregnated
Carved
Peabody Museum 10-71-20/C6729,
D. 2.7 cm., Hole D. 0.6 cm., Th. 1.2 cm.;
10-71-20/C6727, L. 8.8 cm.

Early museum records vary on whether this spindle whorl was impaled on this curved spindle (?) when it arrived; however, a similarly associated wooden pair was excavated by the Mexicans. The spindle (?) widens above its pointed end, then tapers to a flattened and spatulate shape at the other end. Both objects are so heavily covered with black resinous coating that they may have been sheathed with metal at one time, like no. 183.

Middle–Late Postclassic (A.D. 1300–1539)
Coggins and Ladd n.d.

186. Spindle whorl

Fired unslipped clay; burned
Molded, incised; cracked, chipped
Peabody Museum 10-71-20/C6727A,
D. 3.0 cm., Hole D. 0.8 cm., Th. 1.6 cm.

Few ceramic spindle whorls were found in the Cenote, although 106 came from the excavations of Chichén Itzá, where they were found in superficial deposits and rubbish (Kidder 1943). This shape, with an ovoid section, is commonest at the site, and there are numerous variations on its simple geometric design, which is confined to one surface. This quadripartite figure can be read as double-outlined arcs with short ticks at the edge of the whorl, or as a cross with ticks between the arms.

Virtually identical ceramic whorls were found at Chichén Itzá at the Monjas (Bolles 1977, p. 239) and in the nearby cave of Balankanche, as one of an offering of twenty-five spindle whorls (Andrews IV 1970, fig. 40f).

Spindle whorls served as weights, or fly wheels, to keep the wooden spindle turning as raw fiber was spun into yarn and then wound upon it.

Middle–Late Postclassic (A.D. 1200–1539)
Ball and Ladd n.d.

187. Three basket fragments

Plant materials
Coiled, split stitches; broken
Peabody Museum 10-71-20/C6785 (3), Wall
Piece H. 3.0 cm.; Flat Pieces
D. 8.0 cm., 7.3 cm.

Only eleven fragments of two coiled cylindrical baskets were found in the Cenote by Edward H. Thompson, although many baskets were probably thrown in. Impressions and bits of wickerwork baskets also remain on several large copal offerings.

These two baskets were cylindrical in form, with lids. They measured 8.0 and 7.3 cm. in diameter and at least 3.0 cm. high. Construction is close coiling with decorative splitting of the stitches on the work face, visible here on the base (?) piece with the smaller central hole. There is false braidwork at the edge of base and lid, with decorative color variation achieved through use of a different plant material.

Late Postclassic (A.D. 1450–1539)
Mefford n.d.

188. Hollow female figurine

Fired unslipped clay; post-fire white lime coating; red pigment
Modeled, molded; broken; partially restored
Peabody Museum 07-7-20/C4714, Head and Torso H. 28.5 cm., Waist W. 14.5 cm.

Most of the large hollow figurines typical of Middle to Late Postclassic Yucatán belong to a ceramic type called Chen Mul Modeled which was abundant at Mayapán and at sacred locations everywhere, including in the Cenote at Chichén Itzá (R. E. Smith 1971, pp. 210–212). This female figurine probably belongs to the type but differs in not being part of a censer and in having few identifiable divine attributes.

Her sharply defined features are characteristic of Chen Mul Modeled faces which were often molded, then reworked; within her open mouth, filed central incisors are just visible. She kneels, bare breasted, wearing a long skirt, a bead necklace, and large earflares with projecting elements. Her hair is parted in the middle with a simple rolled headdress. There was once an object on her lap.

The sole remaining limb, her left knee, is modeled over a clay tube made of a finer paste. All of the limbs may have been like this, and thus heavier than the rest of the torso, and easily broken off; most Chen Mul Modeled limbs are not made in this way (see no. 195). This coarse, low-fired clay was covered with a white lime coating, and traces of red paint remain over the white lime on the bottom of the leg.

If this figure is an idol, as most of the Chen Mul Modeled figures are thought to be (J. E. S. Thompson 1957), then she may represent the most important Maya goddess, Ix Chel, patroness of procreation and weaving. In the Madrid Codex (p. 102), Ix Chel is shown kneeling, bare breasted and wearing a long skirt like this, as she works on a textile (Villacorta C. and Villacorta R., eds. 1930).

Thousands of textile fragments were recovered from the Cenote by Edward H. Thompson and the Mexican expeditions (see nos. 178, 179); weaving tools were found there as well (nos. 180–186); and woven cotton cloth was one of the principal exports of Yucatán when the Spaniards arrived—it would not be surprising to find the effigy of Ix Chel, goddess of women and of weaving, in the Sacred Cenote at Chichén Itzá.

Middle–Late Postclassic (A.D. 1300–1500)
Ball and Ladd n.d.

189. Head with bird headdress

Fired gray-slipped clay; post-fire brown,
black, and white pigments
Modeled; broken
Peabody Museum 10-56-20/C5924,
H. 7.3 cm., W. 5.0 cm.

The large, distinctive nose of this individual
is echoed by the great curved beak of his
bird headdress. He wears earflares and an
ornament on his upper lip, and his face was
painted brown and black, with white on
the eyes.

There is a hollow spherical form inside
the head which suggests it was attached
directly to some object, perhaps the wall of an
effigy vessel (R. E. Smith 1971, fig. 32mm–
pp). Nothing quite like this head has been
published, but the gray-slipped coarse clay
resembles known Postclassic wares.

Middle–Late Postclassic (A.D. 1350–1539)
Ball and Ladd n.d.

190. Ceramic head pendant (?)

Fired unslipped clay; post-fire black, blue,
red pigments; burned
Modeled, perforated; broken
Peabody Museum 07-7-20/C4716,
H. 8.7 cm.

The upper and lower jaws of a crocodilian
headdress frame a modeled face at the center of this unusual object from the Cenote
which is perforated below the earflares and
on the back, possibly for suspension. Two
more perforations at the top are the eyes of
the headdress creature.

A flange on the right once matched the
one on the left, probably with a similar
blue-painted point; the collar is also blue.
Black was used to delineate the interior of
the upper jaw of the headdress animal and
to outline its eyes. Finally, probably in association with the offering ritual, the pendant
was burned and the inside of the head
painted red.

With its flanges and a circular projection
at the back, this object must have been designed to hang or to fit at the front of a
headdress, where it would have looked
downward. It does not resemble known
figurines from Yucatán or the East Coast. It
may have been imported, perhaps from the
southwest.

Middle–Late Postclassic (A.D. 1300–1539)
Ball and Ladd n.d.

191. Mask

Fired unslipped clay; post-fire white clay (?)
coating on face, red-brown pigment; black
substance
Molded, perforated, incised; broken
Peabody Museum 07-7-20/C4718,
H. 9.5 cm., W. 8.3 cm.

This is a mask that was once attached to
something, as can be seen by the encircling remains of the join—unlike the faces
of the common contemporary Chen Mul
Modeled heads (no. 193). The mask was
once entirely painted with a thick, dark red
pigment, and a black resinous substance
apparently attached a headband. There are
red and black painted areas inside the
mask, and the black covers the lips, in a
practice reminiscent of the Classic Period
Remojadas figurines of Veracruz. A row of
fine upper teeth is visible within the open
mouth and, unlike those of Chen Mul
Modeled faces, the eyes are outlined and
perforated.

Late Postclassic (A.D. 1450–1539)
Ball and Ladd n.d.

192. Post-fire painted sherd

Fired gray-slipped clay; post-fire white
stucco coating; black, blue pigments
Hand built; broken
Peabody Museum 07-7-20/C4757,
L. 8.8 cm., W. 5.3. cm., Th. 1.0 cm.

Most of a feathered headdress is painted
here in white and black against a blue background. If an entire figure was originally
included, this must have been part of a very
large jar. The vessel was slipped before firing; afterward the exterior was covered
with white stucco on which the design was
outlined in black. Finally a "Maya blue"
background was filled in (see no. 157). This
painting is technically, stylistically, and even
iconographically like the wall paintings of
Tulum, where figures wearing such headdresses are depicted in black and white and
blue on a blue ground (S. K. Lothrop 1924,
p. 52, fig. 25; Miller 1982, pl. 28). This technique is otherwise unknown at Chichén
Itzá and Mayapán.

Middle–Late Postclassic (A.D. 1350–1539)
Ball and Ladd n.d.

193. Head from effigy censer

Fired cinnamon-slipped clay; post-fire white
stucco; burned inside
Molded, modeled; broken
Peabody Museum 07-7-20/C4717,
H. 13.3 cm., W. 10.3 cm.

The head of this Old God was part of a body
attached to a large Chen Mul Modeled incense burner. These effigy censers were
one of the most important components of
Middle and especially Late Postclassic ritual. They are found on and near the surface
in the ruined ceremonial structures of many
northern Maya sites.

The figure was once covered with a white
calcareous coating painted with the identifying characteristics of this deity. The
mold-made face is that of an Old God, with
tusks, sagging cheeks, heavy upper eyelids,
an aquiline nose with a protuberance above,
and a cleft chin. Applied *adornos* have
fallen off the center of the headband bow
and the headdress, but one can see that
there were projecting flaps behind the ears
as on many of these censer figures (R. E.
Smith 1971, fig. 32). The incomplete headdress resembles that of a full figure censer
identified as Itzamna (J. E. S. Thompson
1957, pp. 604–606, 618–619, fig. 3d, e).

Middle–Late Postclassic (A.D. 1300–1500)
Ball and Ladd n.d.

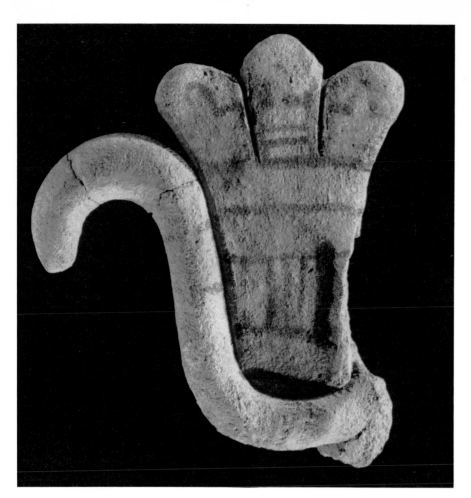

194. "Feathers" from effigy censer

Fired unslipped clay; post-fire white lime
wash; blue, orange, yellow, black pigments
Modeled; broken; partially restored
Peabody Museum 07-7-20/C4747,
    11.5 cm.

"Feathers" just like these, similarly painted
and outlined by a reverse-S clay element,
projected from the right side of Itzamna's
headdress on an effigy censer figure from
Mayapán (see no. 193).

   This fragment is valuable as an indication
of the bright colors that once animated the
thousands of Chen Mul Modeled effigy censers widely used to burn incense to the
gods of Postclassic Yucatán.

Middle–Late Postclassic (A.D. 1300–1500)
Ball and Ladd n.d.

195. Right arm from effigy censer

Fired unslipped clay; post-fire gray-buff
coating; white lime; red, black pigments
Modeled; broken; partially restored
Peabody Museum 07-7-20/C4729,
H. 9.1 cm.

A long, flexible thumb and fingers with
black-painted nails are typical of Chen Mul
Modeled effigy censers, and, like most of
them, this figure once held an offering in its
right hand. Since it is hollow, this object
resembles an inverted cup, but it may represent a conical copal offering with nodules,
like much of the copal found in the Cenote.
This hollow arm had a red-painted bead
bracelet at the wrist, and red paint, bordered with black, covered the elbow as on
arms recovered from the mixed deposit in
the "High Priest's Grave" at Chichén Itzá
(E. H. Thompson 1938, fig. 4).

Middle–Late Postclassic (A.D. 1300–1500)
Ball and Ladd n.d.

196. Two axes

Copper
Cast
Peabody Museum 07-7-20/C4970,
L. 5.6 cm.; 10-70-20/C6035, L. 12.5 cm.

Described by Samuel K. Lothrop as "of
Oaxacan type," these axes are among the
few tools from the Cenote, although the
large one was gilt and shows no sign of
wear. The small axe does show wear on its
sharp edge, and there is evidence of hafting
having covered the butt.

Postclassic (A.D. 1200–1539)
S. K. Lothrop 1952, p. 83; Willard 1926,
facing p. 193

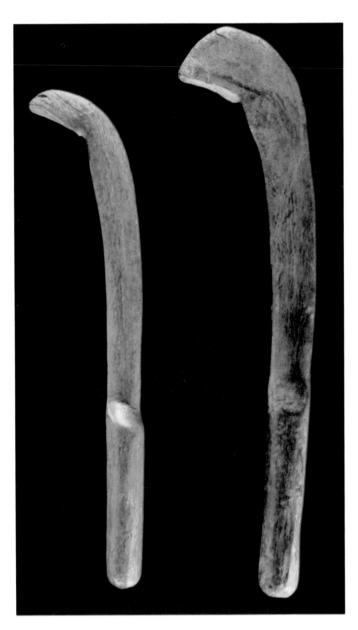

197. Two sickle-like tools

Wood; black coating; paraffin impregnated
Carved; scratched, worn; broken
Peabody Museum 10-71-20/C6730,
L. 34.2 cm., Handle D. 2.6 cm.;
10-71-20/C6734, L. 30.0 cm., Handle
D. 2.3 cm.

Five of these objects, missing only the
tip of the hook, were found by Edward H.
Thompson. He described the first ones as
pruning knives; the next he called bill
hooks; finally he decided they were primitive atlatls. These possibilities all reflect the
fact that they are clearly functional objects
that have seen use. The blades all have a
flattened area that is polished from use just
below the break, and all have scratches
along the blade, with perhaps more on the
back—assuming the tool was held in the
right hand with the handle offset so that the
thumb gripped the angled surface, which
was on top.

These objects closely resemble the modern Yucatec *coa*, a wood-handled, steel-
bladed tool used for weeding, but *coa* is a
Nahuatl (Mexican) word that in this context actually refers to the snake-like curve
of the blade. The Yucatec Maya word for
such a tool is *lohche'*, and the derivative
verb means "to weed" (Barrera Marín,
Barrera Vásquez, and López Franco 1976,
p. 33).

It is likely that the tips were broken off in
use, although the breaking could have been
ceremonial. These may be among the most
modern objects from the Cenote.

Late Postclassic–Colonial (A.D. 1500–)
Coggins and Ladd n.d.; Piña Chan 1980,
fig. 106

198. Three animal effigy vessels from the Monjas, Chichén Itzá

Fired unslipped clay; post-fire white lime coating; dark red, black pigments
Modeled; broken; partially restored
Peabody Museum 99-40-20/C2705 ("dog"), H. 10.2 cm.; 99-40-20/C2706 ("opossum"), H. 9.5 cm.; 99-40-20/C2707 (monkey), H. 10.4 cm.

These three effigy vessels were found by Edward H. Thompson cached together beneath the stairway leading to the third story of the Monjas (Nunnery). Three different anthropomorphically seated mammals are represented in these small effigies, which were filled with ashes when found. They were all painted with a white calcareous coating before identifying detail was added in black and red. On the long-snouted creature, this consisted of black lines that suggest fur, outline the eyes, and form bands on the face. Although it lacks a tail, this may be an opossum.

The second, shorter-snouted animal is dog-like, with prominent canines and black dots outlining its muzzle. It is painted dark red all over except for the ventral area, where there is a large hole.

The third animal is clearly a monkey with a long curling tail. Like the second, it is painted red everywhere except for the muzzle and the ventral area, which here is framed by black lines and dots, with testicles and penis painted below.

The gaping holes in the abdomen of the red-painted "dog" and monkey may refer to the heart sacrifice of small animals, particularly dogs, whose hearts were burned as described by the Bishop de Landa (Tozzer, ed. 1941, p. 114, n. 528); the heart sacrifice of a dog is depicted in the Mixtec Codex Nuttall (Nuttall, ed. 1975, p. 69). Recent analysis of ritually disposed faunal remains has also suggested that monkeys, dogs, and opossums were part of year-renewal rites (Pohl 1983, p. 65).

Stylistically, these effigies are related to small Chen Mul Modeled figures known from Mayapán (R. E. Smith 1971, figs. 64, 65). They probably date from Middle to Late Postclassic times, when Chichén Itzá was primarily a religious shrine. During this phase, offerings were made in its abandoned temples, as these were found in the Monjas, as well as to the Cenote.

Middle–Late Postclassic (A.D. 1350–1539)
Ball and Ladd n.d.; Brainerd 1958, fig. 90p, q, r

199. Human skull incense burner

Bone, teeth, meningeal lining; stucco (?);
red, pink pigments; burned rubber
Cranium cut; teeth missing, nose piece and
facial covering gone
Peabody Museum 07-7-20/C4884,
H. 16.0 cm.

The wooden eyes of this macabre censer
were still painted blue when it came from
the Cenote, much to the delight of the
blue-eyed Mr. Thompson, but now only
pink-tinted gums and nasal area and the
red-painted wooden lid retain any original
color. Traces on the surface suggest that the
face was covered with stucco (?), perhaps
tinted to resemble skin; it was not covered
with mosaic as was the skull with a similar
opening in the cranial vault found in the
Mixtec Tomb 7 at Monte Albán, Oaxaca
(Caso 1969, pl. 4).

This is the skull of a sub-adult male who
was recovering from the childhood anemia
so common among peoples dependent on a
diet of corn after weaning. Perhaps the
young man died in battle and his skull was
revered as that of a valiant ancestor, or
perhaps he was a glorious captive and sacrificial victim.

Rubber and copal were burned within the
cranium of this skull, sending clouds of
dense roiling smoke toward the heavens;
copal smoke resembles the dark clouds; in
fact copal was called "the brains of the sky"
(Roys 1933, pp. 90, 96).

Middle–Late Postclassic (A.D. 1250–1539)
Moholy-Nagy and Ladd n.d.; Tozzer, ed.
1941, p. 131, n. 613; Kidder, Jennings, and
Shook 1946, p. 154

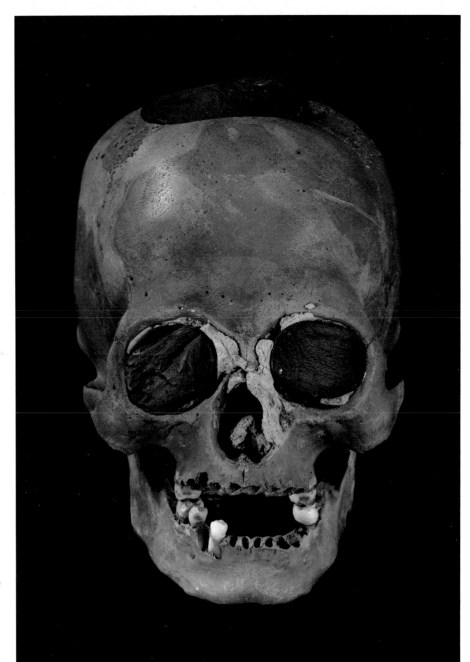

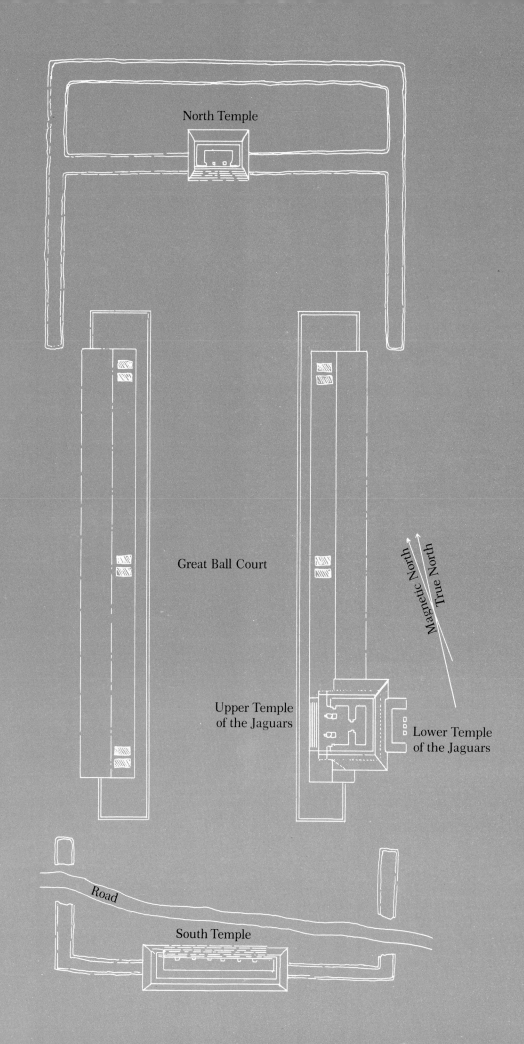

Murals in the Upper Temple of the Jaguars, Chichén Itzá

200. Introduction

Murals copied to scale by Adela C. Breton, 1904–1906;
copies painted in watercolor on paper at one-fourth scale
East wall, Peabody Museum 45-5-20/15066 (see fig. 17)
North wall, Peabody Museum 45-5-20/15061 (see fig. 18)
West wall, Peabody Museum 45-5-20/15062 (see fig. 19)
South wall, Peabody Museum 45-5-20/15063 (see fig. 20)

The Upper Temple of the Jaguars is located at the south end of the east range of the Great Ball Court, or at its southeast corner (fig. 16), and appears, stylistically, to have been the last structure built in that assemblage of buildings. Six narrative scenes were painted on the walls of the inner (eastern) room of this west-facing temple, with a double portrait on the east wall facing the doorway (figs. 17–20). Themes of military conquest animate these paintings, which illustrate five victories over non-Mexican peoples carried out by warriors under the command of the Central Mexicans known as Toltec, who are identified by their weapons, regalia, and association with tutelary serpents. Much of the detail of the paintings has been lost, but Adela Breton's meticulous copies, traced from the disintegrating and mutilated walls in 1904–1906, preserve an extraordinary wealth of historical and ethnographic information. Enough was preserved so that we can postulate the structure of the narrative sequence and divine its cultural purpose.

These paintings in the Upper Temple of the Jaguars, which cover earlier ones (Breton 1906, p. 166), were probably painted around A.D. 850 for the Toltec warrior elite whose portraits are carved on the jambs, whose heraldry decorates the façade, and whose exploits are documented on the walls of the temple (Maudslay 1889–1902, vol. 3, pls. 26–41). It is postulated that the purpose of the building was to glorify the conquerors, to show how their conquests fit into celestial cycles, and perhaps to demonstrate how these victories signified a reinterpretation, almost a reversal, of the cosmic order.

It is further proposed that the paintings, and the historic events they document, are arranged according to the daily cycle of the Sun and the related cycle of the planet Venus. Thus the events occur: (1) before dawn, at the heliacal rising of Venus, on the southeast; (2) at sunrise, in the middle of the east wall; (3) in the morning, on the northeast; (4) at noon, and possibly at the superior conjunction of Venus, on the north wall; (5) in the afternoon, on the northwest; (6) at sunset, with Venus as Evening Star, over the west doorway; (7) after sunset, on the southwest; (8) in the middle of the night, with Venus at inferior conjunction, on the south wall.

What seems implicit in this solar/Venus cycle is the victory of Venus over the Sun, of night and the stars over day, and of the Venus-warrior Toltec over the Maya and other Sun-associated peoples. This cyclic narrative sequence recording the defeat of the Sun people is analogous to the cycle of human life, culminating in death, or night; yet its moral is the victory over this inevitable outcome by the star warriors, who, like Venus, fought, or shone, both by day and by night. The correlation of a decisive battle with an important point in the Venus cycle is also made in the sequence of Late Classic Maya paintings in Structure 1 at Bonampak, Chiapas, and in monumental inscriptions at a number of other southern lowland Maya sites (Lounsbury 1982).

Figure 16.
Plan of the Great Ball Court.
After Maudslay 1889–1902, vol. 3, pl. 26.

Figure 17.
Painting, east wall, Upper Temple of the Jaguars.
Copy by Adela C. Breton at ¼ scale.

The positions of these eight paintings within the rectangular inner room of the Upper Temple of the Jaguars corresponds to the positions of the eight temples and shrines that are arranged around the Great Ball Court itself (fig. 16). These are the Upper Temple of the Jaguars in the first, or southeast, position at the Great Plaza entrance to the ball court; then, proceeding counterclockwise, the two shrines that are also located on top of the east playing wall, at positions 2 and 3; the North Temple at position 4; the three shrines on the west wall at 5, 6, and 7; and the South Temple, completing the cycle, at position 8.

Stephens 1843, 2:211–213, pl. 37; Le Plongeon 1886, facing pp. 78, 80; 1896, p. 83, pls. 37–40, 44–51, 69, 70; Holmes 1895, pp. 132, 133, figs. 38, 39; Maudslay 1889–1902, 3:30–31, pls. 30–41; Breton 1906; Spinden 1913, figs. 12, 21, 129, 136, pl. 29:2; Seler 1915, 5:324–356, figs. 118, 119, 121, 198–228; Fernández 1925, figs. 8, 9; Willard 1926, facing pp. 216, 221, 228; 1941, facing p. 170, pp. 182, 184; Morley 1946, figs. 28e, 42, 54; Tozzer 1957, pp. 119, 128, 176–180, figs. 105, 106, 164, 269, 270, 286, 392, 394, 396, 398, 526, 557, 682; Covarrubias 1957, fig. 126; Marquina 1964, fig. 433; Edwards 1966, pp. 52–54, figs. 28–30; Kubler 1967, pp. 55, 56, fig. 9; 1975, pp. 213, 214, fig. 73; 1982, figs. 22, 24, 25; Kelemen 1969, pp. 318, 323–325, pl. 263b,c; Gendrop 1971, pp. 82–83, figs. 192–195; Miller 1977, 1978; Cohodas 1978a, pp. 62–70, figs. 39–50; Ruz Lhuillier 1979, color plates, pp. 214–215, 222; Piña Chan 1980, fig. 91

201. Southeast; before dawn (fig. 17)

Upper panel: H. 70.5 cm., W. 70.8 cm.
Basal panel: H. 12.0 cm.
(Measurements for all panels omit borders, which are 1.0–1.5 cm. wide.)

Here in the quiet before dawn, when the Morning Star has risen on the upper left, the inhabitants of a town in hilly rain forest are busy in their masonry houses while soldiers talk and perhaps prepare for departure. There is no remaining evidence of the frenetic activity found in other painted scenes in this temple; instead there is almost an air of expectation, as Arthur G. Miller, who first published all of the Breton copies, has noted (1977, p. 214). Birds fly among the trees of the forest, where a feline is climbing, a canine bays at the sky, serpents coil menacingly, and on the upper right there is a rabbit. If canoes are shown in the center of this scene, then the place must be near water. The numerous warriors with round shields, spears, and atlatls may be supervised by a Toltec on the upper left

who wears the typical square-cut hat with two white feathers and carries an atlatl and spears. To his left is the star-skirted warrior who appears to symbolize Venus, in its heliacal rising, as the Morning Star. At the lowest level of the scene soldiers are standing, and as in other scenes there is a round yellow hut, here on the lower left with a spire or peak. These huts are probably portable shelters, perhaps made of thatch, used for bivouacs by the officers of the traveling army.

The basal panel beneath this and the other narrative scenes included two Bacabs (two of four mythological old men who support the sky, and often at Chichén Itzá the realms of mytho-historical human activity). These two flank a smaller figure, and all three, entwined with waterlilies, inhabit the watery realms of the underworld (see fig. 19). Near the bottom of the large scene, below and behind the black-painted figure with a standard, there is a graffito that depicts a figure holding an object in its right hand, heading south. Such graffiti are common in Classic Period Maya buildings (Trik and Kampen 1983), and this one is surely pre-Conquest.

In this visual historical account, on the south end of the east wall, there is apparently what the Toltec saw as an epic beginning—perhaps the inception of the conquests that culminated in the domination of Chichén Itzá, northern Maya capital. Venus at heliacal rising, when it was considered most dangerous, presides over the events, and it is likely there was once a Sun Disc below, analogous to the one in the corresponding "after sunset" painting in the opposite, southwest panel (fig. 19).

202. East; sunrise (fig. 17)

Upper panel: H. 71.8 cm., W. 49.1 cm.
Basal panel: H. 10.7 cm.

At the center of the east wall there is a double portrait that is largely destroyed. This was associated with the rising Sun, and indeed the dominant warrior on the right is refulgent with gold and solar rays. Encircled by the descending body of a Toltec green feathered serpent, he wears a gold disc on his chest and another in his blue and red headdress, where three white feathers, projecting from collared jade tubes, also identify him as Toltec. He carries darts or spears in his left hand, and dart-like objects, alternating with the golden serpentine rays, emanate from his body. Such emanations also come from the body of a figure centered on the west wall of the Lower Temple of the Jaguars, immediately below (fig. 6); both also have square-cut hair, wear two gold discs, and, most significant, both have gold feathered serpent eyepieces, like those found in the Cenote (no. 32). If these are not the same person, then the figure in the earlier Lower Temple may have played an analogous role in the history of the Toltec conquest. Arthur Miller in his analysis of these paintings has called this man Captain Serpent (1977, p. 209). He might also be called Quetzalcoatl in view of his association with a green feathered serpent (*quetzalcoatl*), and of the legend that associates a Toltec Quetzalcoatl with Chichén Itzá. However, in the battle scenes more than one Toltec officer has a tutelary green feathered serpent, and "Quetzalcoatl" may have been a military title.

The second figure in the double portrait is depicted as lower than Captain Serpent, although he is armed with the same weapons. He wears a green quetzal feather crest on his head with long feathers pendant behind, and his hair, like Captain Serpent's, is square cut and blond; however, at the back it hangs at least to his waist and is strung with jade beads. He wears a jade earflare with projecting bar, exactly like Captain Serpent's, and his rectilinear jade necklace is of Toltec style (see nos. 14, 18), but the bar through his nose is Maya and so is the profile jade god mask at the front of his headdress (see nos. 34, 35).

Miller calls this person Captain Sun Disc and equates him with the Mayoid figure in the Sun Discs of these paintings and on the wooden lintel (fig. 19). All have the projecting jade god mask and nose bar, and carry Toltec weapons, but otherwise this figure resembles the Sun Disc person only in confronting Captain Serpent. Miller suggests that Captain Sun Disc is the man depicted on Stelae 10 and 11 (A.D. 849) at Seibal in Petén, Guatemala (1977, pp. 220–223), and that he had been defeated by Captain Serpent. There are numerous indications that Chichén Itzá was in contact with the region of the Usumacinta River drainage in Terminal Classic times (many of the jades from the Cenote probably came from there), and the ruler portrayed on Bonampak Stela 1 has similarly beaded hair (Mathews 1980, fig. 3). However, this Chichén Itzá portrait does not portray a defeated, or even a humbled, captain. Rather he appears to be an honored Mayoid ally who shares (even if slightly subordinately) in the symbolism of the rising Toltec Sun.

Immediately beneath the double portrait, eight yellow vertical bars may possibly represent the supports of a table throne upon which the two figures sit; or they may be part of the rising Sun imagery.

In the basal frieze beneath the double portrait, where Bacabs are shown below the narrative scenes, there is a single supine figure. This wears a long-skirted dress studded with *chalchihuitls*—the perforated jade discs that connote preciousness, earthwater, and female. (The perforations in the discs, not visible here, are shown in a carved depiction of this figure in the North Temple of the Ball Court [Marquina 1964, photo 439]). Two diverging feathered serpents once emerged from the umbilicus of this figure who is, in fact, Mother Earth. She is the surface of the Earth, which in this eastern portrayal is just below the rising Sun, personified by the two glorious warriors; whereas on the west wall, she is located above the Sun Disc, which has just set (fig. 19).

203. Northeast; morning (fig. 17)

Upper panel: H. 70.3 cm., W. 73.5 cm.
Basal panel: H. 12.0 cm.

Only the upper half of this scene has survived. It depicts abrupt red hills where a battle is in progress. Located at the north end of the east wall, it corresponds to morning in the narrative cycle. The missing Sun Disc may have been located in the lower half, whereas it is probably the warrior Venus which emerges from the open jaws of a serpent on the upper left; Venus may be depicted in this way on a contemporary (A.D. 863) painted capstone from the Temple of the Owls at Chichén Itzá (Tozzer 1957, fig. 384; Jones 1975, p. 94).

Arthur Miller began his sequence of paintings here, and suggested that this battle took place in southern Oaxaca because of the red hills and cactus, neither of which is found in Yucatán (1977, pp. 211–213). There is evidence of a Oaxacan connection at Chichén Itzá, in the architectural style of the Castillo (Kubler 1961, p. 55) and in objects thrown into the Cenote and included in this exhibition, so it seems

Figure 19. Painting and carved wood, west wall,
Upper Temple of the Jaguars.
Copy by Adela C. Breton at ¼ scale.

covered with a long loose fringe sleeve into which a hafted stone point is tucked. This kind of sleeve, with tucked weapon, bag, fending stick, and spears, is exactly like the left arm accoutrements of the warriors on the great Atlantean columns at Tula (Acosta 1961), as is the standard back disc. These large circular protective discs are worn at the waist by Toltec soldiers; they take the place of shields, at least in official portraiture, supplemented only by the defensive/offensive fending sticks. The discs wrap around the waist and are tied on in front, suggesting that they were made of a flexible material. This man, Rodent, wears the standard, rectilinear, mosaic-covered pillbox hat, with two large white feathers and with a descending "butterfly" on top. When, more frequently, worn as a pectoral, these winged ornaments are inverted. His unusual collar, which seems to be made of five flint blades strung on a rope, rests on top of a massive, multistrand jade bead necklace. Like most Toltec, he wears nose beads and fur or feather bracelets on his

right arm, with one below each knee, and like all Toltec he has an atlatl with fur (?) pieces attached to the finger holes and to the distal end.

The head of a colorful, fanged denizen of the waters of the underworld is shown in both the upper and lower panels framing the jamb figures, which thus partake of the imagery of the dying Sun, visible in the doorway between them.

The warrior on the south jamb is named Snake. His regalia differs in a few distinctive details which, like his relative position, suggest he is of somewhat lower rank than Rodent. He wears a long bar through his ear lobe instead of a carved circular earflare, his collars are composed of square-cut jade beads, and he has the flounced protective sleeve so commonly worn in the reliefs at Chichén Itzá (fig. 5). Apparently he does not have a fending stick.

Lintels: In the carved wooden lintel above the doorway, Captain Serpent and Captain Sun Disc are represented in peaceful confrontation, both with their atlatls

held across their chests. On the right, north, and in the dominant position, Captain Serpent is identified by his protective feathered serpent and wears the two large white feathers, nose beads, and flounced sleeve of a Toltec warrior. Captain Sun Disc, on the south, is more heavily bedecked with jade and feathers, including a variant jade god mask at the front of his projecting headband. Seated on a jaguar throne (Maudslay 1889–1902, vol. 3, pl. ...), he speaks or breathes an elaborate serpent upper jaw phrase, as in the Sun Disc portrait in the Lower Temple of the Jaguars (fig.).

At this point, over the western door, the Sun Disc passes below the horizon, as symbolized by the skeletal mask with water-lilies at the center of the lintel, and probably also by the offering vessel filled with balls of copal (?). Just to the right, or north, of the Sun Disc, the glyph for Venus can be seen, trailing behind, as Evening Star. This imagery of the setting Sun is framed by the body of a bicephalic serpent whose heads are at the north and south ends of the lintel.

Immediately above this carved wooden lintel there is a much larger, plain, purely structural one. Above this the "Mother Earth" motif, which was in the basal position on the east, is now located above the setting Sun, and the serpentine umbilical cords emerge directly above the skeletal, surface-of-the-earth mask. Above this painted lintel scene, again directly above the central, umbilical axis, a victim is arched over a sacrificial stone. Such sacrificial scenes may once have been above the centers of all four walls.

207. Southwest; after sunset (fig. 19)

Upper panel: H. 71.3 cm., W. 70.0 cm.
Basal panel: H. 11.1 cm.

On the south end of the west wall, the Sun Disc is shown set upon a standard near the bottom of a scene of intense activity, perhaps a victory celebration. The Sun has, in fact, been captured at one level of interpretation, and at another a town at the top has clearly been taken—sad women with bundles on their backs leave their houses, sent away by soldiers with round shields. But the clearest sign of dominance over the Sun is the arrival, at the upper right, of what may be the two legendary conquerors of Chichén Itzá, surrounded by red auras. These are Captain Serpent, or Quetzalcoatl, and behind and above him Mixcoatl (Cloud Serpent), his father (?), who is protected by his mosaic-covered Cloud Serpent, as also represented in the Lower Temple of the Jaguars (fig. 5; Seler 1915, p. 340; Kelley 1983a, p. 168). Mixcoatl wears the classic Toltec fringed sleeve and head gear, and both have diving birds at the front of their headdresses. Mixcoatl's right arm—held out before him—has a green rod, or bone (?), in place of a hand, and there are green spots around his chin that may indicate tattooing. Quetzalcoatl carries a round shield emblazoned with green crescents like the shield that decorates the façade of this building and one that is carried by a bearded Toltec on one of the gold discs (no. 14). Gold crescents that might have come from such a shield were also found in the Cenote (no. 15). Many of the soldiers, who seem to be executing the varied maneuvers of a war dance, carry shields with a single large crescent in the middle; these are the same as shields from the façade of the east building of the Monjas (Bolles 1977, p. 232). Others have draped shields. On the left, a third important warrior with a red aura and a protective feathered serpent advances on the scene. He carries a round shield with green spots, has blue crossed bands on his chest, and wears a blue beret, like three other people on the left side.

In general in this scene the important Toltec are on the right (north) side of the Sun Disc. In the camp at the bottom, seated officers receive humbled petitioners with their hands across their chests. When they are at ease, Toltec officers keep their fending sticks, which, in any case, ordinary soldiers do not have. The most important captain in camp, with a red aura, a feathered serpent, and a blue beret, sits to the left of the base of the Sun Disc standard, possibly with a rubber ball at his feet.

At the upper right corner of the scene a bit of the lower edge of what resembles a Sun Disc is visible. If this is a second Sun Disc, then this model for the interpretation of the murals may be inaccurate. If, however, this upper disc is a star disc, then Venus may be depicted, victorious, as it dominated the sky after the descent of the Sun. A similarly framed portrayal of Venus is found in the painted capstone of the Temple of the Owls at Chichén Itzá (Tozzer 1957, fig. 384).

208. South; night (fig. 20)

Upper panel: H. 70.8 cm., W. 57.5 cm.
Basal panel: H. 11.5 cm.

The last narrative scene, on the south wall,
takes place at night and in the underworld.
South connoted "down," as north did "up,"
and at night the Sun was believed to pass
into the underworld below. Venus also appeared to pass into the underworld during
its week-long period of inferior conjunction—just before the heliacal rising which
occurs in the following or first scene of the
cycle.

This final field of battle is near a lake
town located on hilly terrain that necessi-
tated the use of siege towers and a scaling
ladder. Round-shield Toltec warriors prevail,
and they are supported by a group on the
upper left with prominent red regalia. Their
important captain, within a red aura, is protected by a red serpent—the only one in the
entire cycle of paintings. He is probably
named Red Serpent.

Massacre of the town's population is over-
seen by three celestial serpent warriors
that do not wear Toltec uniforms. They are
more like the airborne warrior on Stela 4 at
Ucanal (A.D. 850; Graham 1980, 2:3) than
the usual Toltec celestial warriors on the
north wall, or on the gold discs (figs. 5, 7).

On the right in the camp below, Toltec
officers sit on campaign stools in front of
their huts, with a single star in the center of
their night sky (Tozzer 1957, fig. 278). Prisoners bow before a seated feathered-serpent
captain who gestures toward a sacrificial
stone (?) on the ground before him. The
stone is located on the central axis, beneath
the star and a heart sacrifice scene that was
immediately above the painting.

This last astronomically significant battle,
on the south wall, may actually have taken
place well to the south of Chichén Itzá, and
at night during the inferior conjunction of
Venus. The star-skirted Venus warrior, riding a feathered serpent, leads the Sun Disc,
and looks upward, to the east, where the
Sun will soon rise.

Figure 20. Painting, south wall,
Upper Temple of the Jaguars.
Copy by Adela C. Breton at ¼ scale.

A.D. 1539	PHASES OF CENOTE RITUAL	NORTHERN LOWLAND MAYA PERIODS	SOUTHERN LOWLAND MAYA PERIODS	MAYA LONG COUNT (GMT)
				11.16.0.0.0
				13 Ahau
		Colonial		
1461			Late Postclassic	11.2.0.0.0
	Late Phase			8 Ahau
		(End of Mayapán)		
		Decadent		
		(Founding of Mayapán)		
1283			Middle Postclassic	11.3.0.0.0
				13 Ahau
1145				10.16.0.0.0
				1 Ahau
	Early Phase II	Modified Florescent	Early Postclassic	
899				10.3.10.0.0
				13 Ahau
830	Early Phase I		Terminal Classic	10.0.0.0.0
		Pure Florescent		7 Ahau
770				9.17.0.0.0
				13 Ahau
692			Late Classic	9.13.0.0.0
				8 Ahau
		Early Period II		
554	?			9.6.0.0.0
				9 Ahau
		Early Period I	Early Classic	
435				9.0.0.0.0
				8 Ahau

Figure 21. Chronological chart.

Bibliography

Abel-Vidor, Suzanne, et al. 1981. *Between Continents/Between Seas: Pre-Columbian Art of Costa Rica*. New York: Abrams.

Acosta, Jorge R. 1957. Resumen de los informes de las exploraciones arqueológicas en Tula, Hidalgo, durante las IX y X temporadas, 1953–54. In *Anales del Instituto Nacional de Antropología e Historia* 9:119–169. Mexico City.

———. 1961. La indumentaria de las cariátides de Tula. In *Homenaje a Pablo Martínez del Río*, pp. 221–228. Mexico City: Instituto Nacional de Antropología e Historia.

Andrews, E. Wyllys, IV. 1970 *Balankanche, Throne of the Jaguar Priest*. Middle American Research Institute, Tulane University, Publication 32. New Orleans.

Andrews, E. Wyllys, IV, and E. Wyllys Andrews V. 1980. *Excavations at Dzibilchaltun, Yucatan, Mexico*. Middle American Research Institute, Tulane University, Publication 48. New Orleans.

Andrews, E. Wyllys V. 1977. Some Comments on Puuc Architecture of the Northern Yucatan Peninsula. In *The Puuc: New Perspectives*, edited by Lawrence Mills, pp. 1–17. Pella, Iowa: Central College.

———. 1978. The Northern Maya Lowlands Sequence. Endnote to Eastern Mesoamerica, by Gareth W. Lowe. In *Chronologies in New World Archaeology*, edited by R. E. Taylor and Clement W. Meighan, pp. 377–381. New York: Academic Press.

Ashmore, Wendy. 1980. Discovering Early Classic Quirigua. *Expedition* (University of Pennsylvania Museum) 23(1):35–44.

Aveni, A. F., ed. 1982. *Archaeoastronomy in the New World*. Cambridge: Cambridge University Press.

Aveni, A. F., et al. 1975. The Caracol Tower at Chichén Itzá: An Ancient Astronomical Observatory? *Science* 188(4192) 977–985.

Ball, Joseph W. 1977. Ceramics, Culture History and the Puuc Tradition: Some Alternative Possibilities. In *The Puuc: New Perspectives*, edited by Lawrence Mills, pp. 18–35. Pella, Iowa: Central College.

Ball, Joseph W., and John Ladd. n.d. Ceramics from the Sacred Cenote. In Coggins, ed. n.d.

Balser, Carlos. 1966. Los objetos de oro de los estilos extranjeros de Costa Rica. In *Actas, 36th International Congress of Americanists, Seville, 1964*, vol. 1, pp. 391–398.

Barrera, Marín, Alfredo, Alfredo Barrera Vásquez, and Rosa María López Franco. 1976. *Nomenclatura etnobotánica maya: Una interpretación taxonómica*. Colección Científica 36 (Etnología). Mexico City: Instituto Nacional de Antropología e Historia.

Barrera Vásquez, Alfredo. 1980. *Diccionario maya Cordemex*. Mérida: Ediciones Cordemex.

Barthel, Thomas. 1955. Versuch über die Inschriften von Chich'en Viejo. *Baessler-Archivo*, n.f. 3:5–33. Berlin.

———. 1964. Comentarios a las inscripciones clásicas tardías de Chich'en Itza. *Estudios de Cultura Maya* 4:223–244.

Baudez, Claude F., and Pierre Becquelin. 1973. *Archéologie de Los Naranjos, Honduras*. Collection Etudes Mésoaméricaines, no. 2. Mexico City: Mission Archéologique et Ethnologique Française au Mexique.

Becquelin, Pierre, and Claude F. Baudez. 1979, 1982. *Tonina, une cité maya du Chiapas*. Collection Etudes Mésoaméricaines, no. 6, vols. 1–2. Mexico City: Mission Archéologique et Ethnologique Française au Mexique.

Benson, Elizabeth P., ed. 1973. *Mesoamerican Writing Systems: A Conference Held at Dumbarton Oaks, 1971*. Washington, D.C.: Dumbarton Oaks.

Bolles, John S. 1977. *Las Monjas: A Major Pre-Mexican Architectural Complex at Chichén Itzá*. Norman: University of Oklahoma Press.

Brainerd, George W. 1958. *The Archaeological Ceramics of Yucatan*. University of California Anthropological Records, no. 19. Berkeley and Los Angeles.

Bray, Warwick. 1977. Maya Metalwork and Its External Connections. In Hammond, ed. 1977, pp. 365–403.

———. 1981. Gold Work. In Abel-Vidor et al. 1981, pp. 153–175.

Breton, Adela C. 1906. The Wall Paintings at Chichen Itza. In *Proceedings, 15th International Congress of Americanists, Quebec, 1901*, vol. 2, pp. 165–169.

Bullard, William R., ed. 1970. *Monographs and Papers in Maya Archaeology.* Papers of the Peabody Museum, Harvard University, vol. 61. Cambridge, Mass.

Callaghan, James, and Tomás Gallereta Negrón. 1976. Informe del rescate arqueológico del Hotel VillasArqueológicas, Chichen Itza, Yucatan, Octubre-Noviembre, 1976. Ms. at Centro Regional del Sureste, Instituto Nacional de Antropología e Historia, Mérida.

Caso, Alfonso. 1965. Lapidary Work, Goldwork, and Copperwork from Oaxaca. In Wauchope and Willey, eds. 1965, vol. 3, pp. 896–930.

———. 1969. *El tesoro de Monte Alban.* Memorias del Instituto Nacional de Arqueología e Historia, no. 3. Mexico City.

Castillo, Noemi. 1968. *Algunas técnicas decorativas de la cerámica arqueológica de México.* Investigaciones del Instituto Nacional de Antropología e Historia, no. 16. Mexico City.

Charnay, Désiré. 1887. *The Ancient Cities of the New World.* New York: Harper and Brothers.

Chase, Diane Z., and Arlen F. Chase. 1982. Yucatecan Influence in Terminal Classic Belize. *American Antiquity* 47(3): 596–609.

Cirerol Sansores, M. 1940. *El Castillo, Mysterious Mayan Pyramidal Temple of Chichen Itza.* Mérida: Talleres Gráficos del Sudeste.

Coe, Michael D., and David C. Grove, organizers; Elizabeth P. Benson, ed. 1981. *The Olmec and Their Neighbors: Essays in Memory of Matthew W. Stirling.* Washington, D.C.: Dumbarton Oaks.

Coe, William R. 1959. *Piedras Negras Archaeology: Artifacts, Caches and Burials.* Museum Monographs, no. 4. Philadelphia: University of Pennsylvania.

———. 1967. *Tikal: A Handbook of the Ancient Maya Ruins.* Philadelphia: University Museum, University of Pennsylvania.

Coggins, Clemency. 1974. Kunst der Maya. In Willey, ed. 1974, pp. 230–244.

———. 1979. A New Order and the Role of the Calendar: Some Characteristics of the Middle Classic Period at Tikal. In Hammond and Willey, eds. 1979, pp. 38–50.

———. ed. n.d. Artifacts from the Cenote of Sacrifice, Chichen Itza: Textiles, Wood, Ceramics, Stone, Bone, Shell, Copal, and Other Vegetal Materials. Memoirs of the Peabody Museum, Harvard University, vol. 10, no. 3. Cambridge, Mass.

Coggins, Clemency, and John Ladd. n.d. Wood artifacts from the Sacred Cenote. In Coggins, ed. n.d.

Cohodas, Marvin. 1978a. *The Great Ball Court at Chichen Itza, Yucatan, Mexico.* New York: Garland Publishing.

———. 1978b. Diverse Architectural Styles and the Ball Game Cult: The Late Middle Classic Period in Yucatan. In *Middle Classic Mesoamerica: A.D. 400–700,* edited by Esther Pasztory, pp. 85–107. New York: Columbia University Press.

Cole, Leon J. 1910. The Caverns and People of Northern Yucatan. *Bulletin of the American Geographical Society* 42: 321–336.

Cole, Leon J., Glover M. Allen, and Thomas Barbour. 1906. *Vertebrata from Yucatan. Bulletin of the Museum of Comparative Zoology, Harvard University,* vol. 50, no. 5.

Colección de Documentos Inéditos. 1885–1900. Relativos al descubrimiento, conquista y organización de las antiguas posesiones españoles de ultramar, 2d ser., vols. 11, 13. Madrid.

Covarrubias, Miguel. 1957. *Indian Art of Mexico and Central America.* New York: Alfred A. Knopf.

Craine, Eugene R., and Reginald C. Reindorp, eds. 1979. *The Codex Perez and the Book of Chilam Balam of Mani.* Norman: University of Oklahoma Press.

Davoust, Michel. 1977. *Les Chefs mayas de Chichen Itza.* Angers, France.

De Grinberg, D. M. K., and F. Franco. 1979. Estudio químico y metalúrgico de los objetos de metal de Tonina, Chiapas. In Becquelin and Baudez 1979, pp. 1143–1164.

Digby, Adrian. 1964. *Maya Jades.* London: British Museum.

Drucker, Philip. 1952. *La Venta, Tabasco: A Study of Olmec Ceramics and Art.* Smithsonian Institution, Bureau of American Ethnology, Bulletin no. 153. Washington, D.C.

Easby, Elizabeth K. 1964. The Squier Jades from Toniná, Chiapas. In Lothrop et al. 1964, pp. 60–80.

———. 1981. Jade. In Abel-Vidor et al. 1981, pp. 135–151.

Easby, Elizabeth K., and Dudley T. Easby, Jr. 1953. *Apuntes sobre la técnica de taller jade en Mesoamérica. Anales del Instituto de Arte Americano e Investigaciones Estéticas,* no. 6. Buenos Aires.

Easby, Elizabeth K., and John F. Scott. 1970. *Before Cortés: Sculpture of Middle America.* New York: Metropolitan Museum of Art.

Eaton, Jack D. 1978. Archeaological Survey of the Yucatán-Campeche Coast. In *Middle American Research Institute, Tulane University, Publication 46,* pp. 1–67. New Orleans.

Ediger, Donald. 1971. *The Well of Sacrifice: An Account of the Expedition to Recover the Lost Mayan Treasures of Chichén Itzá.* Garden City, N.Y.: Doubleday and Co.

Edmonson, Munro S., trans. 1982. *The Ancient Future of the Itza: The Book of Chilam Balam of Tizimin.* Austin: University of Texas Press.

Edwards, Emily. 1966. *Painted Walls of Mexico: From Historic Times until Today.* Austin: University of Texas Press.

Ekholm, Gordon F. 1961. Some Collar-Shaped Shell Pendants from Meso-américa. In *Homenaje a Pablo Martínez del Río*, pp. 287–293. Mexico City: Instituto Nacional de Antropología e Historia.

———. 1962. U-shaped "Ornaments" Identified as Finger Loops from Atlatls. *American Antiquity* 28(2):181–185.

Emmerich, André. 1965. *Sweat of the Sun and Tears of the Moon.* Seattle: University of Washington Press.

Falchetti de Sáenz, Ana María. 1979. Colgantes "Darien." *Boletín del Museo del Oro, Banco de la República* 2:1–55. Bogotá.

Fernández, Miguel Angel. 1925. El Templo de los Tigres. *Ethnos*, Epoca 3, 1:35–42. Mexico City.

Follett, Prescott H. F. 1932. War and Weapons of the Maya. In *Middle American Research Series, Tulane University*, no. 4, pp. 375–410. New Orleans.

Freidel, David A. 1979. Culture Areas and Interaction Spheres: Contrasting Approaches to the Emergence of Civilization in the Maya Lowlands. *American Antiquity* 44(1):36–54.

———. 1981. Continuity and Disjunction: Late Postclassic Settlement Patterns in Northern Yucatan. In *Lowland Maya Settlement Patterns*, edited by Wendy Ashmore. Albuquerque: University of New Mexico Press.

Furst, Peter T. 1964. Gold before Columbus. *Quarterly of the Los Angeles County Museum* 2(4):4–9.

Gann, Thomas. 1900. Mounds in Northern Honduras. In *Smithsonian Institution, Bureau of American Ethnology, 19th Annual Report*, Part 2, pp. 655–692. Washington, D.C.

García L., Gabriela. 1981. Conservación del material procedente del Cenote Sagrado de Chichén Itzá. In *Memoria del Congreso Interno, 1979*, pp. 255–259. Mexico City: Centro Regional del Sureste, Instituto Nacional de Antropología e Historia.

García-Ruiz, Jesús F. 1981. La Cervelle du ciel: Ethnologie du copal. *Technique et Culture: Bulletin de l'Equipe de Recherche 191* (Ivry Cedex, France: Centre National de la Recherche Scientifique, Maison des Sciences de l'Homme) 5:84–148.

Gay, Carlo T. 1967. *Mezcala Stone Sculpture: The Human Figure.* Museum of Primitive Art Studies, no. 5. New York.

Gendrop, Paul. 1971. *Murales prehispánicos. Artes de México*, no. 144.

Graham, Ian. 1980. *Ixkun, Ucanal, Ixtutz, Naranjo. Corpus of Maya Hieroglyphic Inscriptions*, vol. 2, part 3. Cambridge, Mass.: Peabody Museum, Harvard University.

Graham, Ian, and Eric Von Euw. 1977. *Yaxchilan. Corpus of Maya Hieroglyphic Inscriptions*, vol. 3, part 1. Cambridge, Mass.: Peabody Museum, Harvard University.

Greene Robertson, Merle, ed. 1974. *Primera Mesa Redonda de Palenque, Part 1.* Pebble Beach, Calif.: Robert Louis Stevenson School.

———. 1980. *Third Palenque Round Table, 1978, Part 2.* Palenque Round Table Series, vol. 5. Austin: University of Texas Press.

Haberland, Wolfgang. 1953. The Golden Battle Discs of Chichen Itza. *Ethnos* 19:94–104.

Hammond, Norman. 1974. Preclassic to Postclassic in Northern Belize. *Antiquity* 48:177–189.

———. ed. 1977. *Social Process in Maya Prehistory: Studies in Honour of Sir Eric Thompson.* New York: Academic Press.

Hammond, Norman, and Gordon R. Willey, eds. 1979. *Maya Archaeology and Ethnohistory.* Austin: University of Texas Press.

Harrison, P. D., and B. L. Turner, eds. 1978. *Pre-Hispanic Maya Agriculture.* Albuquerque: University of New Mexico Press.

Hay, Clarence L., et al., eds. 1940. *The Maya and Their Neighbors.* New York: Appleton-Century.

Heizer, Robert F. 1942. Ancient Grooved Clubs and Wooden Rabbit Sticks. *American Antiquity* 8(1):41–56.

Holien, Thomas E. 1977. *Mesoamerican Pseudo-cloisonné and Other Decorative Investments.* Ph.D. dissertation, Department of Anthropology, Southern Illinois University. Ann Arbor: University Microfilms.

Holmes, William H. 1895. *Archaeological Studies among the Ancient Cities of Mexico.* Field Columbian Museum Anthropological Series, vol. 1, no. 1. Chicago.

Homenaje a Pablo Martínez del Río: En el XXV aniversario de la primera edición de "Los orígenes americanos." 1961. Mexico City: Instituto Nacional de Antropología e Historia.

Hooton, Earnest A. 1940. Skeletons from the Cenote of Sacrifice at Chichen Itzá. In Hay et al., eds. 1940, pp. 272–280.

Jones, Christopher. 1975. A Painted Capstone from the Maya Area. In *Studies in Ancient Mesoamerica II*, pp. 83–110. Contributions of the University of California Archaeological Research Facility, no. 27. Berkeley.

Kelemen, Pal. 1969. *Medieval American Art: Masterpieces of the New World before Columbus.* 3d rev. ed. New York: Dover.

Kelley, David H. 1962. Fonetismo en la escripta maya. *Estudios de Cultura Maya* 2:277–317.

———. 1968. Kakupacal and the Itzaes. *Estudios de Cultura Maya* 8:255–268.

———. 1976. *Deciphering the Maya Script.* Austin: University of Texas Press.

———. 1983a. The Maya Calendar Correlation Problem. In Leventhal and Kolata, eds. 1983, pp. 157–208.

———. 1983b. Notes on Puuc Inscriptions and History. In *The Puuc: New Perspectives*, edited by Lawrence Mills, pp. 1–18. Pella, Iowa: Central College.

Kidder, Alfred V. 1942. *Archaeological Specimens from Yucatan and Guatemala.* Carnegie Institution of Washington, *Notes on Middle American Archaeology and Ethnology*, no. 9. Washington, D.C.

———. 1943. *Spindle Whorls from Chichen Itza, Yucatan.* Carnegie Institution of Washington, *Notes on Middle American Archaeology and Ethnology*, no. 16. Washington, D.C.

———. 1947. *The Artifacts of Uaxactun, Guatemala.* Carnegie Institution of Washington Publication no. 576. Washington, D.C.

Kidder, Alfred V., Jesse D. Jennings, and Edwin M. Shook. 1946. *Excavations at Kaminaljuyu, Guatemala.* Carnegie Institution of Washington Publication no. 561.

King, Mary Elizabeth. 1979. The Prehistoric Textile Industry. In Rowe, Benson, and Schaffer, eds. 1979, pp. 265–278.

Kubler, George. 1961. Chichén Itzá y Tula. *Estudios de Cultura Maya* 1:47–79.

———. 1967. Pintura mural precolombiana. *Estudios de Cultura Maya* 6:45–65.

———. 1975. *The Art and Architecture of Ancient America: The Mexican, Maya, and Andean Peoples.* Harmondsworth and Baltimore: Penguin Books.

———. 1982. Serpent and Atlantean Columns: Symbols of Maya-Toltec Polity. *Journal of the Society of Architectural Historians* 41:93–115.

Kurjack, Edward B., and Sylvia Garza T. 1981. Pre-Columbian Community Form and Distribution in the Northern Maya Area. In *Lowland Maya Settlement Patterns*, edited by Wendy Ashmore. Albuquerque: University of New Mexico Press.

Lara Pinto, Gloria. 1982. El salvamento arqueológico en la región de El Cajón, Honduras. *Mexicon* 4(3):42–45.

Le Plongeon, Augustus. 1886. *Sacred Mysteries among the Mayas and the Quiches 1,500 Years Ago.* New York: Robert Macoy.

———. 1896. *Queen Moo and the Egyptian Sphinx.* New York.

Leventhal, Richard M., and Alan L. Kolata, eds. 1983. *Civilization in Ancient America: Essays in Honor of Gordon R. Willey.* Cambridge, Mass.: University of New Mexico Press and Peabody Museum, Harvard University.

Littlehales, Bates. 1961. Return to the Cenote: Into the Well of Sacrifice. *National Geographic* 120(4):548–561.

Littman, Edwin B. 1982. Maya Blue—Further Perspectives and the Possible Use of Indigo as the Colorant. *American Antiquity* 47(2):404–408.

Lothrop, Joy M. n.d. Textiles from the Sacred Cenote. In Coggins, ed. n.d.

Lothrop, Samuel K. 1924. *Tulum: An Archaeological Study of the East Coast of Yucatan.* Carnegie Institution of Washington Publication no. 335. Washington, D.C.

————. 1937. *Cocle: An Archaeological Study of Central Panama.* Memoirs of the Peabody Museum, Harvard University, vol. 7. Cambridge, Mass.

————. 1950. *Archaeology of Southern Veraguas.* Memoirs of the Peabody Museum, Harvard University, vol. 9, no. 3. Cambridge, Mass.

————. 1952. *Metals from the Cenote of Sacrifice, Chichen Itza, Yucatan.* Memoirs of the Peabody Museum, Harvard University, vol. 10, no. 2. Cambridge, Mass.

————. 1963. *Archaeology of the Diquis Delta, Costa Rica.* Papers of the Peabody Museum, Harvard University, vol. 51. Cambridge, Mass.

Lothrop, Samuel K., et al. 1964. *Essays in Pre-Columbian Art and Archaeology.* Cambridge, Mass.: Harvard University Press.

Lounsbury, Floyd G. 1973. On the Derivation and Reading of the 'Ben Ich' Prefix. In Benson, ed. 1973, pp. 99–143.

————. 1982. Astronomical Knowledge and Its Uses at Bonampak, Mexico. In Aveni, ed. 1982, pp. 143–168.

Mahler, Joy. 1965. Garments and Textiles of the Maya Lowlands. In Wauchope and Willey, eds. 1965, vol. 3, pp. 581–593.

Maler, Teobert. 1895. Yukatekische Forschungen. *Globus* 68:247–260, 277–292.

Marcus, Joyce. 1982. The Plant World of the Sixteenth and Seventeenth Century Lowland Maya. In *Maya Subsistence: Studies in Memory of Dennis E. Puleston,* edited by Kent V. Flannery, pp. 239–273. New York: Academic Press.

Marquina, Ignacio. 1964. *Arquitectura prehispánica.* 2d ed. Memorias del Instituto Nacional de Antropología e Historia, no. 1. Mexico City.

Matheny, Ray. 1978. Northern Maya Lowland Water-Control Systems. In Harrison and Turner, eds. 1978, pp. 185–210.

Mathews, Peter. 1980. Notes on the Dynastic Sequence of Bonampak, Part 1. In Greene Robertson, ed. 1980, pp. 60–73.

Mathews, Peter, and Linda Schele. 1974. Lords of Palenque—The Glyphic Evidence. In Greene Robertson, ed. 1974, pp. 63–76.

Maudslay, Alfred P. 1889–1902. *Archaeology: Biologia Centrali-Americana.* 5 vols. London: Dulau and Co.

Mefford, Jill J. n.d. Basketry and Woven Sandals. In Coggins, ed. n.d.

Merwin, R. E., and G. C. Vaillant. 1932. *The Ruins of Holmul, Guatemala.* Memoirs of the Peabody Museum, Harvard University, vol. 3, no. 2. Cambridge, Mass.

Miller, Arthur G. 1977. Captains of the Itzá: Unpublished Mural Evidence from Chichén Itzá. In Hammond, ed. 1977, pp. 197–225.

————. 1978. Capitanes del Itzá: Evidencia mural inédita de Chichén Itzá. *Estudios de Cultura Maya* 11:121–154.

————. 1982. *On the Edge of the Sea: Mural Painting at Tancah-Tulum, Quintana Roo, Mexico.* Washington, D.C.: Dumbarton Oaks.

Moholy-Nagy, Hattula, and John Ladd. n.d. Stone, Bone, Shell, and Palm Nut Materials from the Sacred Cenote. In Coggins, ed. n.d.

Morley, Sylvanus G. 1946. *The Ancient Maya.* Stanford: Stanford University Press.

Morris, Earl H., Jean Charlot, and Ann Axtell Morris. 1931. *The Temple of the Warriors at Chichen Itza, Yucatan.* 2 vols. Carnegie Institution of Washington Publication no. 406. Washington, D.C.

Nuttall, Zelia, ed. 1902. *Codex Nuttall: Facsimile of an Ancient Mexican Codex Belonging to Lord Zouche of Harynworth, England.* Introduction by Z. Nuttall. Cambridge, Mass.: Peabody Museum, Harvard University.

————, ed. 1975. Reprint of Nuttall, ed. 1902. New York: Dover.

Paddock, John. 1966. Oaxaca in Ancient Mesoamerica. In *Ancient Oaxaca,* ed. idem, pp. 83–242. Stanford: Stanford University Press.

Parsons, Lee A. 1969. *Bilbao, Guatemala: An Archaeological Study of the Pacific Coast Cotzumalhuapa Region,* vol. 2. Publications in Anthropology, no. 12. Milwaukee: Milwaukee Public Museum.

————. 1981. Post-Olmec Stone Sculpture: The Olmec-Izapan Transition on the Southern Pacific Coast and Highlands. In M. D. Coe, Grove, and Benson 1981, pp. 257–288.

Pendergast, David M. 1962. Metal Artifacts in Prehispanic Mesoamerica. *American Antiquity* 27(4):520–545.

————. 1979, 1982. *Excavations at Altun Ha, Belize, 1964–70.* 2 vols. Toronto: Royal Ontario Museum.

Pijoán, José. 1964. *Arte precolombiano, mexicano y maya. Summa Artis: Historia general del arte,* vol. 10. 4th ed. Madrid.

Piña Chan, Román. 1968. Exploración del Cenote de Chichén Itzá: 1967–68. *Boletín del Instituto Nacional de Antropología e Historia* 32:1–3. Mexico City.

————. 1970. *Informe preliminar de la reciente exploración del Cenote Sagrado de Chichén Itzá.* Investigaciones del Instituto Nacional de Antropología e Historia, no. 24. Mexico City.

————. 1980. *Chichén Itzá: La ciudad de los brujos del agua.* Mexico City: Fondo de Cultura Económica.

Pohl, Mary. 1983. Maya Ritual Faunas: Vertebrate Remains from Burials, Caches, Caves, and Cenotes in the Maya Lowlands. In Leventhal and Kolata, eds. 1983, pp. 55–103.

Pohorilenko, Anatole. 1981. The Olmec Style and Costa Rican Archaeology. In M. D. Coe, Grove, and Benson 1981, pp. 309–327.

Pollock, H. E. D., et al. 1962. *Mayapan, Yucatan, Mexico.* Carnegie Institution of Washington Publication no. 619. Washington, D.C.

Proskouriakoff, Tatiana. 1944. *An Inscription on a Jade Probably Carved at Piedras Negras.* Carnegie Institution of Washington, *Notes on Middle American Archaeology and Ethnology,* no. 47. Washington, D.C.

————. 1950. *A Study of Classic Maya Sculpture.* Carnegie Institution of Washington Publication no. 593. Washington, D.C.

————. 1960. Historical Implications of a Pattern of Dates at Piedras Negras, Guatemala. *American Antiquity* 25:454–475.

————. 1962a. Civic and Religious Structures of Mayapan. In Pollock et al. 1962, pp. 87–164.

————. 1962b. The Artifacts of Mayapan. In Pollock et al. 1962, pp. 321–442.

————. 1970. On Two Inscriptions from Chichen Itza. In Bullard, ed. 1970, pp. 459–467.

————. 1974. *Jades from the Cenote of Sacrifice, Chichen Itza.* Memoirs of the Peabody Museum, Harvard University, vol. 10, no. 1. Cambridge, Mass.

————. 1978. Maya Jade Plaque; Maya Jade Head. In *Masterpieces of the Peabody Museum,* pp. 62, 63. Cambridge, Mass.: Peabody Museum, Harvard University.

Rands, Robert L. 1965. Jades of the Maya Lowlands. In Wauchope and Willey, eds. 1965, vol. 3, pp. 561–580.

Recinos, Adrian, and Delia Goetz, trans. 1953. *Annals of the Cakchiquels.* Norman: University of Oklahoma Press.

Redfield, Robert, and Alfonso Villa Rojas. 1962. *Chan Kom: A Maya Village.* Chicago: University of Chicago Press.

Rivard, J. 1970. A Hierophany in Chichen Itza. *Katunob* 7(3):51–55.

Robertson, Merle Greene. *See* Greene Robertson, Merle.

Rowe, Ann Pollard, Elizabeth P. Benson, and Anne Louise Schaffer, eds. 1979. *The Junius B. Bird Pre-Columbian Textile Conference, 1973.* Washington, D.C.: Textile Museum and Dumbarton Oaks.

Roys, Ralph L., ed. 1933. *The Book of Chilam Balam of Chumayel.* Carnegie Institution of Washington Publication no. 438. Washington, D.C.

————, ed. 1967. *The Book of Chilam Balam of Chumayel.* Norman: University of Oklahoma Press.

Ruppert, Karl. 1935. *The Caracol at Chichen Itza, Yucatan, Mexico.* Carnegie Institution of Washington Publication no. 454. Washington, D.C.

————. 1943. *The Mercado, Chichen Itza, Yucatan, Mexico.* Carnegie Institution of Washington Publication no. 546, Contribution 43. Washington, D.C.

————. 1952. *Chichen Itza: Architectural Notes and Plans.* Carnegie Institution of Washington Publication no. 595. Washington, D.C.

Ruz Lhuillier, Alberto. 1954. Uxmal: Temporada de trabajos 1951–52. *Anales del Instituto Nacional de Antropología e Historia* 6(34):49–67. Mexico City.

———. 1973. *El Templo de las Inscripciones, Palenque*. Colección Científica: Arqueología, no. 7. Mexico City: Instituto Nacional de Antropología e Historia.

———. 1979. *Chichén Itzá en la historia y en el arte*. Mexico City: Editora del Sureste.

Sáenz, César A. 1952. El Adoratorio Central, Palacio del Gobernador, Uxmal. *Tlatoani* 1(5 / 6):45–60. Mexico City.

———. 1963. Exploraciones en la Piramide de las Serpientes Emplumadas, Xochicalco. *Revista Mexicana de Estudios Antropológicos* 19:7–25.

Salisbury, Stephen, Jr. 1877. The Mayas, the Source of Their History: Dr. Le Plongeon in Yucatan, His Account of Discoveries. Worcester, Mass.

Saville, Marshall H. 1922. *Turquois Mosaic Art in Ancient Mexico*. Museum of the American Indian–Heye Foundation Contributions, vol. 6. New York.

Schele, Linda. 1974. Observations on the Cross Motif at Palenque. In Greene Robertson, ed. 1974, pp. 41–61.

Seler, Eduard. 1902–1923. *Gesammelte Abhandlungen zur Amerikanischen Sprach–und Alterthumskunde*. 5 vols. Berlin.

———. 1915. Die Ruinen von Chichén Itzá in Yucatán. In Seler 1902–1923, vol. 5, pp. 197–388.

Sheets, Payson D., John Ladd, and David Bathgate. n.d. Chipped Stone Artifacts from the Sacred Cenote. In Coggins, ed. n.d.

Shepard, Anna O. 1948. *Plumbate: A Mesoamerican Tradeware*. Carnegie Institution of Washington Publication no. 573. Washington, D.C.

Smith, A. Ledyard, and Alfred V. Kidder. 1951. Excavations at Nebaj, Guatemala. Carnegie Institution of Washington Publication no. 594.

Smith, Robert E. 1971. *The Pottery of Mayapan, Including Studies of Ceramic Material from Uxmal, Kabah, and Chichen Itza*. Papers of the Peabody Museum, Harvard University, vol. 66. Cambridge, Mass.

Snarskis, Michael J. 1979. El jade de Talamanca de Tibas. *Vínculos* 5(2):89–107. San José, Costa Rica.

———. 1981. Catalogue. In Abel-Vidor et al. 1981, pp. 178–227.

Spear, Nathaniel, Jr. 1978. *A Treasury of Archaeological Bells*. New York: Hastings House.

Spinden, Herbert J. 1913. *A Study of Maya Art*. Memoirs of the Peabody Museum, Harvard University, vol. 6. Cambridge, Mass.

Stephens, John Lloyd. 1843. *Incidents of Travel in Yucatan*. New York: Harper and Brothers.

Stone, Doris, and Carlos Balser. 1965. Incised Slate Disks from the Atlantic Watershed of Costa Rica. *American Antiquity* 30(3):310–329.

Stromsvik, Gustav. 1941. Substela Caches and Stela Foundations at Copan and Quirigua. In *Contributions to American Anthropology and History*, no. 37, pp. 63–96. Carnegie Institution of Washington Publication no. 528.

Summa Anthropologica: En homenaje a Roberto J. Weitlaner. 1966. Mexico City: Instituto Nacional de Antropología e Historia.

Taschek, Jennifer T. n.d. *The Artifacts of Dzibilchaltun, Yucatan, Mexico: Shell, Polished Stone, Bone, Wood and Ceramics*. Middle American Research Institute, Tulane University, Publication 50. New Orleans.

Thompson, Donald. 1955. *An Altar and Platform at Mayapan*. Carnegie Institution of Washington Current Reports, no. 28.

Thompson, Edward H. 1879. Atlantis Not a Myth. *Popular Science Monthly* 15(6): 759–764. New York.

———. 1897a. *Excavations in the Cave of Loltun, Yucatan*. Memoirs of the Peabody Museum, Harvard University, vol. 1, no. 2. Cambridge, Mass.

———. 1897b. *The Chultunes of Labna, Yucatan*. Memoirs of the Peabody Museum, Harvard University, vol. 1, no. 3. Cambridge, Mass.

———. 1904. *Archaeological Research in Yucatan*. Memoirs of the Peabody Museum, Harvard University, vol. 3, no. 1. Cambridge, Mass.

———. 1932. *People of the Serpent: Life and Adventures among the Mayas*. Boston.

———. 1938. *The High Priest's Grave, Chichen Itza, Yucatan, Mexico*. Prepared for publication and with an introduction by J. Eric S. Thompson. Field Museum of Natural History, Anthropological Series, vol. 27, no. 1. Chicago.

Thompson, J. Eric S. 1937. *A New Method of Deciphering Yucatan Dates with Special Reference to Chichen Itza*. Carnegie Institution of Washington Publication no. 483. Washington, D.C.

———. 1939. *Excavations at San José, British Honduras*. Carnegie Institution of Washington Publication no. 506. Washington, D.C.

———. 1943. *Representations of Tlalchitonatiuh at Chichen Itza, Yucatan, and El Baul, Escuintla*. Carnegie Institution of Washington, *Notes on Middle American Archaeology and Ethnology*, no. 19. Washington, D.C.

———. 1957. *Deities Portrayed on Censers at Mayapan*. Carnegie Institution of Washington Current Reports, no. 40.

———. 1966. Merchant Gods of Middle America. In *Summa Anthropologica: En homenaje a Roberto J. Weitlaner*, pp. 159–172. Mexico City: Instituto Nacional de Antropología e Historia.

———. 1970a. The Bacabs: Their Portraits and Glyphs. In Bullard, ed. 1970, pp. 469–486.

———. 1970b. *Maya History and Religion*. Norman: University of Oklahoma Press.

————. 1972. *A Commentary on the Dresden Codex.* Memoirs of the American Philosophical Society, vol. 93. Philadelphia.

Torres Montes, Luis A. 1967. Estudio radiográfico de ofrendas de copal. *Boletín del Instituto Nacional de Antropología e Historia,* no. 28, pp. 38–40.

Torres Montes, Luis A., and Constanza Vega. 1970. *Tratamiento de madera humeda: Estudio comparativo de dos métodos.* Tecnología, no. 3. Mexico City: Departamento de Prehistoria, Instituto Nacional de Antropología e Historia.

Townsend, Richard. 1979. *State and Cosmos in the Art of Tenochtitlan.* Washington, D.C.: Dumbarton Oaks.

Tozzer, Alfred M. 1907. *A Comparative Study of the Mayas and the Lacandones.* Archaeological Institute of America. New York: Macmillan.

————. 1930. Maya and Toltec Figures at Chichen Itza. In *Acta, 23rd International Congress of Americanists, New York, 1928,* pp. 155–164.

————. 1957. *Chichen Itza and Its Cenote of Sacrifice.* Memoirs of the Peabody Museum, Harvard University, vols. 11–12. Cambridge, Mass.

————, ed. 1941. *Landa's Relación de las cosas de Yucatan.* Papers of the Peabody Museum, Harvard University, vol. 18. Cambridge, Mass.

Trik, Helen, and Michael E. Kampen. 1983. *The Graffiti of Tikal.* Tikal Report no. 31. University Museum Monograph no. 57. Philadelphia: University of Pennsylvania.

Valenzuela, Juan. 1945. Las exploraciones efectuadas en los Tuxtlas, Veracruz. *Anales del Museo Nacional de Arqueología, Historia, e Etnología* 3:83–107. Mexico City.

Villacorta C., J. A., and C. A. Villacorta R., eds. 1930. *Códices mayas: Dresdensis, Peresensis, Tro-Cortesianus.* Guatemala City: Tipografía Nacional.

Wardwell, Allen. 1968. *The Gold of Ancient America.* Greenwich, Conn.: New York Graphic Society.

Wauchope, Robert, and Gordon R. Willey, eds. 1965. *Handbook of Middle American Indians,* vols. 2–3, *Archaeology of Southern Mesoamerica.* Austin: University of Texas Press.

Willard, T. A. 1926. *The City of the Sacred Well.* New York: Century Co.

————. 1933. *The Lost Empire of the Itzaes and Mayas: An American Civilization, Contemporary with Christ, Which Rivaled the Culture of Egypt.* Glendale, Calif.: Arthur H. Clark Co.

————. 1941. *Kukulcan, the Bearded Conqueror: New Mayan Discoveries.* Hollywood, Calif.: Murray and Gee.

Willey, Gordon R., ed. 1974. *Das Alte Amerika.* Propylaean Kunstgeschichte, vol. 18. Berlin: Propylaean Verlag.

Willoughby, Charles C. 1908. The Preservation of Water-Soaked Archaeological Objects of Wood. *American Anthropologist* 10:348–349.

Woodbury, R. B., and A. S. Trik. 1953. *The Ruins of Zaculeu, Guatemala.* 2 vols. Richmond, Va.

Wren, Linnea H. 1982a. An Iconographic Analysis of the Sculptures and Murals from the Great Ball Court at Chichen Itza. Paper delivered at the 47th Annual Meeting of the Society for American Archaeology, Minneapolis.

————. 1982b. The North Temple of the Great Ball Court at Chichen Itza. Paper delivered at the 71st Annual Meeting of the College Art Association, Philadelphia.

————. n.d. The Sculpture and Painting of the Great Ball Court: Forms, Symbols, and Meaning. In preparation.

Catalogue Index

All numbers are catalogue entry numbers. Boldface indicates objects shown in illustrations.